THE HORSES OF THE SAHARA

The Emir Abd-el-Kader (1808–1883)
(From *Enciclopedia Universal Ilustrada, Europeo-Americana*; courtesy of the Hall of the Horsemen, The University of Texas at Austin.)

THE HORSES
OF THE SAHARA

By GENERAL E. DAUMAS

NINTH EDITION
REVISED AND AUGMENTED
WITH COMMENTARIES BY
The Emir Abd-el-Kader

Translated from the French by
SHEILA M. OHLENDORF

Preface by Stuart Cloete

UNIVERSITY OF TEXAS PRESS, AUSTIN

ISBN: 978-0-292-74071-6

Library of Congress Catalog Card No. 68–56130
Copyright © 1968 by Shelia M. Ohlendorf
All rights reserved

First paperback printing, 2012

For
General don Procopio Ortiz Reyes, E.E.,
Mexican Army, who taught me the
"art of riding versus the art of winning,"
with deepest gratitude

PREFACE

THIS IS A BOOK that will interest all horse lovers as it deals with the Eastern horses—Arabs, Barbs, and Turkomans—which are the foundation stock of all so-called "hot-bloods."

The late Lady Wentworth—the great Arabian authority—maintained that their pedigree went back for five thousand years. This may be excessive but the fact remains that Arabs were the first pedigreed animals of any kind and that the whole concept of pedigrees and breeding for performance originated with the Arabs.

Horses of the Sahara by General Melchior Joseph Eugene Daumas of the French colonial army was first published in 1850. At that time, and indeed until the end of the first World War, almost all transport except for the railroads was horse-drawn. At the turn of the century the automobile was a rarity, as horses are today. This fact is sometimes forgotten, but in those not so distant days the only way of getting from place to place—when the railroads had been left behind—was on horseback, in a horse-drawn vehicle, or on foot.

The General's description of the desert horses is of the greatest importance because his point of view was strictly utilitarian—that of a cavalry officer looking for remounts.

An additional reason for this book's value is that for all intents and purposes the pure-bred Arab is now extinct in the Near East, having been replaced by jeeps and other four-wheel drive vehicles. That the Arab in its original form has been preserved at all is due to the efforts of English, American, French, and possibly Polish and Russian enthusiasts. Their studs have all the hot-blood lines, and the popularity of the breed is greater every year, both for pure-bred animals and for cross-breeding with other horses and ponies to improve their quality.

The Arab is one of the few, perhaps the only, domestic animal which cannot be improved. It is already perfection and any attempted change is for the worse as becomes apparent when General Daumas' observations are taken into consideration. Its courage, endurance, intelligence, quality, and heart put the Arab in a class of its own.

STUART CLOETE

Hermanus, South Africa

ACKNOWLEDGMENTS

My FIRST THANKS are to those horses which—in any color, size, or shape—have made life so very interesting for me for over forty years.

In the translation of this book I am heavily indebted—for both great encouragement and assistance—to many people and institutions. Especially am I indebted to the following:

Mr. Stuart Cloete, fellow *aficionado* of the horse, who wrote the preface to this work.

Mrs. Garland Coker, who encouraged me to undertake the translation.

Mrs. Monica Heiman, without whose disinterested help I would not have been able to pursue a certain line of research.

La Bibliotheque Nationale, Paris, France, for invaluable assistance.

The U.S. Department of Agriculture, National Agricultural Library, Washington, D.C., for its aid.

The Library (and staff) of The University of Texas at Austin for immense help.

Mrs. Ruth D. Maseles, who enthusiastically assisted me in procuring certain statistics.

Monsieur André Monteilhet, Vice President of the Hippic Circle of France, horseman and scholar, who was willing to take the time to help a fellow horse-lover.

Mr. Walter Ohlendorf, my husband, who is not a horse-lover, but who patiently helped with the preparation of the manuscript.

Doctor Edward Larocque Tinker for the use of his splendid library and gracious permission to use photographs and prints from his collection at The University of Texas.

Sergeant and Mrs. Charles Webber for most appreciated, kindly interest in this project.

SHEILA M. OHLENDORF

CONTENTS

CHAPTER NINETEEN

CHAPTER TWENTY

ILLUSTRATIONS

The Emir Abd-el-Kader, *frontispiece*

TRANSLATOR'S INTRODUCTION

THIS BOOK—modest in length, but all-encompassing in knowledge of the horse, containing horse-lore as pertinent today as when it was first published, *circa* 1850—is the work of two remarkable men, who at first were enemies and then became friends.

The Emir Abd-el-Kader (1808–1883) of Algeria was a noted horseman and scholar. He led a Holy War (1832–1847) against the French and is said to have become a legendary figure, holding at bay half a dozen great French generals and several princes of the blood. Vanquished at last, he surrendered and was taken as a prisoner of war to France where he was treated with chivalresque generosity. He was frequently seen in Paris riding across the Place de la Concorde, haughty and aloof, surrounded by his Algerian bodyguards in their flowing white burnooses. After 1853 he was permitted to live in Damascus and in 1860 was awarded the Grand Cross of the Legion of Honor by the French government for assisting the Christian victims of a riot there.

General Melchior Joseph Eugene Daumas (1803–1871) was the son of a valiant soldier of the French Republic and the Empire. He took up the career of arms as an ordinary soldier and so distinguished himself that he was sent to study at Saumur.[1] Sixteen years of his military career were spent in Africa, where he learned Arabic and studied the Arabs. General Daumas was made commander of the Legion of Honor for bravery in battle, became a counselor of state and was named director of the Algerian Bureau in the Ministry of War in France.

General Daumas had won the respect of the Emir Abd-el-Kader

---

[1] *Saumur*: the home of the crack French cavalry school, founded in the eighteenth century—comparable to Weedon in England, and Fort Riley in the United States.

and from the respect and admiration the two men had for each other was born the collaboration in the General's work on the horses of the Algerian deserts.

General Daumas' book is one of the earliest exhaustive studies of the Arabian and Barb breeds made by a European who had access to the immense store of knowledge regarding horses possessed by the Arabs, creators of one of the world's finest breeds of saddle-horses. In the words of the author himself: "In truth, it requires a great deal of patience and tact for a Christian to obtain from the Mohammedans even the most insignificant of details . . ." But, he was persistent and was gently twitted about his zealous search for information by the Emir Abd-el-Kader, to whom he many times addressed himself seeking particulars about the horses they both loved.

The result of their collaboration is a book as fascinating to the historian as it is to horsemen everywhere.

THE HORSES OF THE SAHARA

1

PRELIMINARY CHAPTER

NUMIDIAN HORSEMEN were already famous in the days of the Romans. Arabic horsemen do not have to concede anything to their forebears. The horse continues to be the chief weapon of war of that bellicose race. A study of the Algerian horse, which still retains the characteristics of the Barb and Arabian breeds, is of interest not only to the art of horsemanship but also to our dominion in Algeria. The chief merit of a study such as this lies in the exactness of the information set forth, and to achieve this end I should make known its sources.

During the sixteen years of my life which I spent in Africa, I held positions which put me in frequent contact with the Arabs, with that alien people, so recently known, whom we should study in order to learn how to govern them. From 1837 to 1839 I was French consul at Mascara, close to the Emir Abd-el-Kader; later chargé of Arabic Affairs in the Department of Oran, which was under the command of General de Lamoricière, and lastly director general of Arabic Affairs in Algeria during the governorship of Marshal the Duke of Isly.

These circumstances led me into relationships with the native chieftains and the great families of the country. I learned the language and because of the knowledge I acquired I was able to write *The Algerian Sahara, The Great Desert,* and *The Great Kabyle,* works which have perhaps been of help to the French cause, clearing up important problems in connection with war, trade, and government. The study of the Arabian horse, which was the object of very careful investigations, would appear to be the complement to my previous works.

Also, this subject, replete with uncertainties and contradictory assertions, was then as now full of great interest. In the case of a war in Europe should we look to foreign countries or could Algeria come to our aid to furnish remounts for our light cavalry? That was the national question which I asked myself and that was why I gathered all the bases by means of minute research during my long stay in Algeria.

According to some, the Arabs are the world's foremost horsemen; according to others, they are nothing but torturers of horses. The former recognize among the Arabs the practice of all good methods used among us, and in other places. The latter hold them to be ignorant of horsemanship, hygiene, and knowledge of breeding horses. How much truth is there in all this? What is the real worth of Arabian horses? What is the nature of the services which can be hoped for [from them]? I wanted to learn, not from hearsay, but from personal observation; not from books, but from men. What you are going to read is, therefore, a summary, as much of what I observed personally, as it is of my conversations with Arabs in all walks of life, from the noble chieftain to the plebeian rider who, as he himself says in his picturesque way, does not have any career other than that of making a living by his spurs. It will be understood that I obtained information from those who possessed a great deal as well as from those who possessed very little; from those who bred horses and from those who only knew how to ride them. In short, from everyone. The information which I am going to set forth in these pages did not come from just one man alone. One will find it spread among all the horsemen of a great tribe. I do not deserve any credit other than that of having sought, collected, and put in order scarce documents very difficult to obtain. In truth, it requires a great deal of patience and tact for a Christian to obtain from the Mohammedans even the most insignificant of details, because a distrustful fanaticism makes them believe that such details are very important or dangerous for their religion.

Meanwhile, I make my reservations. I am not going to say: this is good, or this is bad. I simply say: good or bad, this is what the Arabs do.

GENERAL E. DAUMAS

Observations of the Emir Abd-el-Kader

"Mohammedan sages have written a great number of books dealing, in great detail, with the qualities of horses, their colors, everything which is reputed to be good or bad, their diseases and the way of treating them. One sage alone, Abou-Obeida, a contemporary of the son of Haroun-al-Raschid, wrote fifty volumes dealing with the horse.

"Abou-Obeida had a small contretemps which proved that it is not always the author of the thickest and most numerous volumes who gives the best advice and that the system of obtaining knowledge from the spoken word is not the worst.

" 'How many books have you written on the horse?' the Vizir of Mamoun, son of Haroun-al-Raschid, one day asked a famous Arabic poet.

" 'Just one,' answered the poet. Then the Vizir turned to Abou-Obeida and asked him the same question.

" 'Fifty,' answered the latter.

" 'Get up, then,' the Vizir said to him. 'Go over to that horse and tell me the names of the parts of his body, being sure to point out each one.'

" 'I am not a veterinarian,' said Abou-Obeida.

" 'And you?' the Vizir asked the poet. (The poet himself tells the tale.) 'I stood up and taking the horse by the forelock, I began to point out each part, placing my hand on each to indicate its position and quoting at the same time all relevant verses and all Arabic sayings and proverbs. When I had finished, the Vizir said: "Take the horse." I took him and every time I wanted to annoy Abou-Obeida, I mounted that horse to go and see him.' "

THE ORIGINS OF THE ARABIAN HORSE

> God has said: "As good for pursuit as for
> flight, you shall fly without wings. Riches
> shall be on your back and fortune shall
> come through your mediation."

PEOPLES AND THEIR GOVERNMENTS have always considered the horse
to be one of the most powerful elements of their strength and prosperity. In our own day no question of rural economy or military art is
more discussed than that of the betterment of the cavalry horse. Great
powers of the State, scientific societies, farmers, the Army, and all
Frenchmen have concerned themselves with the matter and yet, we
are still far from being in accord. On my own account I have never
ceased to study the invaluable animal, as much for reasons of devotion
as for those of state and patriotism. I have consulted the most competent authors, the most expert of men; and I must say that it is in
the opinions of the Arabs, above all, that I believe I have found the
most practical and just evaluation of the horse.

In order to make myself more clearly understood, I have frequently
addressed myself to the Emir Abd-el-Kader, that illustrious chieftain,
who, because of his high position in Moslem society, his science, and
his abilities as a horseman, is the man who could best clarify the
doubts I entertained. Here is the last letter he wrote to me in reply to
the questions I asked him as to the origins of the Arabian horse. It
seems to me noteworthy for the conclusions it contains as well as for

the view of zoology applied. It is, in any case, a sufficiently singular document so that I may be permitted to hope that it will be well received by those who are closely or even remotely interested in equestrian matters.

Letter of the Emir Abd-el-Kader

"May the one God be praised! He Who always remains the Same in the revolutions of this world.

"To our friend General Daumas:

"May health be yours, with the mercy and blessing of God [is the wish of] him who writes this letter, of his mother, of his children, of their mother, and of all his companions. I read your questions and here are my answers.

"You asked, or requested from me, information concerning the origin of the Arabian horses. But, are you then like the cracks in ground parched by the sun, which even a heavy rain cannot fill? Nevertheless, in order to quench your insatiable thirst for knowledge, on this occasion I am going to go back as far as the well-spring—the water there is always purer and more abundant.

"Know then that among us it is accepted that God created the horse from the wind, as He created Adam from clay. This should not be doubted. Many prophets (may health be with them) have proclaimed the following: 'When God wanted to create the horse, He said to the South Wind: "I want to make a creature out of you. Condense." And the wind condensed. Archangel Gabriel immediately appeared and took a handful of that stuff and presented it to God, Who made a brown bay or burnt chestnut (*koummite*—red mixed with black) upon saying: "I call you Horse (*frass*);[1] I make you Arabian and I give you the chestnut color of the ant; I have hung happiness from the forelock which hangs between your eyes; you shall be the lord (*sid*) of the other animals. Men shall follow you wherever you go; you shall be as good for pursuit as for flight; you shall fly without wings; riches shall be on your back and fortune shall come through your mediation." Then He put on the horse the mark of glory and happiness (*ghora*)—a white mark in the middle of the forehead.'

---

[1] *Frass*, "horse." The plural is *khéil*. This word comes, according to the sages, from the noun *ikhetïal*, which means "mettle." The Arabian horses have thus been named because of the mettle of their bearing.

"Now, do you want to know whether God created the horse before
He created man or whether He created man before the horse? Listen:
God created the horse before He created man and the proof is that
as man is the superior of the two, God had to provide him with everything necessary before creating him.

"The wisdom of God indicates that He made everything on earth
for Adam and his descendants; and here, furthermore, is proof. As
soon as God created Adam He called him by his name and said to
him: 'Choose between the horse and Borak.' (Borak was the animal
that served Mohammed as a mount on his journey through the skies,
who looked like a mule, but was neither male nor female.) Adam answered: 'The lovelier of the two is the horse,' and God answered him:
'Good. You have chosen your eternal glory and that of your sons; as
long as they live My blessing will be on them, for nothing that I have
created is as dear to Me as man and the horse.'

"In the same way, God created the stallion before the mare. My
proof is that the male is more noble than the female and is also more
vigorous and hardy. Although they both belong to the same species,
one has a more mettlesome nature than the other and divine Provi-
dence always made the stronger first.

"What the stallion desires most is combat and racing. He is also to
be preferred in war because he is swifter and hardier than the mare,
and because he participates in the sentiments of love or hate of his
rider.

"Not so with the mare. If a stallion and a mare are mortally
wounded, the stallion will continue as long as he can to carry his
rider, far from the battlefield; but the mare, on the contrary, will immediately fall on the spot without being able to hold out. There is no
doubt about it. It is a fact proved by the Arabs; I have seen such a
thing on various occasions in battle and I myself have undergone such
an experience.

"Taking this for granted, let us go on to another matter. Did
God create Arabian horses before He created those of other lands
(beradin) or did He create those of other countries before the Arabians?

"As a result of my first premise, it must be supposed that He
created Arabian horses first, because they are undoubtedly the noblest. Moreover, the berdoune is only a species of a genus and Almighty God never created any species before the genus.

"Now, where do the Arabian horses of today come from? Many historians relate that after Adam, the horse, like all animals such as the gazelle, the ostrich, the buffalo, and the ass, lived in a wild state. The first man, after Adam, to mount a horse was Ishmael, father of the Arabs, son of Abraham, the beloved of God, Who taught him to call horses and when he called they came. Then he took possession of the most beautiful and the fieriest and then trained them. But a great number of those horses, trained and used by Ishmael, lost in time their purity of blood. Only one line was preserved in all its nobility by Solomon, son of David, and it is that line called Zad-el-Rakeb (Gift to the Rider) to which all Arabians owe their origin. This is how that came about:

"It is said that certain Arabs from the Azed tribe went to Jerusalem the Noble to pay their respects to Solomon on the occasion of his marriage to the Queen of Sheba. Upon taking their leave, they spoke thus: 'Oh, Prophet of God! Our country is far away, our provisions are exhausted; thou art a great king. Give us the necessary provisions so that we may return to our homes.'

"Solomon gave orders that a magnificent stallion belonging to the line of Ishmael's horses be brought from his stables and he addressed the Arabs thus: 'Here is the provision which I give you for your journey. When you feel hungry, gather wood and light a fire. Place the best rider among you, armed with a good lance, on the horse's back and scarcely will you have gathered the wood and lit the fire, when the rider will be back with the spoils of an abundant chase. Go and may God cover you with His protection.'

"The Azed went on their way. At the first camping place, they did what Solomon had told them and no zebra or gazelle or ostrich managed to escape. Convinced then of the worth of the animal of which the son of David had made them a present, on reaching their homes they devoted him to stud, taking great pains with the matings, and thus they succeeded in producing that line to which, out of gratitude, they gave the name of Zad-el-Rakeb (Gift or Viaticum to the Rider.)

"That bloodline is the one whose great renown later spread throughout the entire world.[2] Consequently, it reproduced itself in the East and in the West following the Arabs who later penetrated to the limits of the East and West. A long time before Islamism, Hamir-Aben-

___

[2] It is distinguished by the length of the windpipe which permits it to run fabulous races.

Melouk and his descendants reigned in the West for one hundred years. It was he who founded Medina and Saklia. Chedad-Eben-Aâd conquered the countries, as far as the limits of Maghreb,[3] and there built cities and ports. Afrikes, who gave his name to Africa, conquered as far as Tangier while his son Chamar conquered eastwards to China, entering the town of Sad and destroying it. For that reason and from that time the place is called Chamar-Kenda, because *kenda* in Persian means 'he has destroyed' and the Arabs have corrupted it into Samarkand.

"From the beginning of Islamism, new invasions of the Moslems then extended the reputation of Arabian horses to Italy, to Spain, and even to France itself, where undoubtedly they left some of their blood. But what, above all else, populated Africa with Arabian horses was the invasion of Sidi-Okba and later the successive invasions of the fifth and sixth centuries of the Hegira. With Sidi-Okba the Arabs only camped in Africa, whereas in the fifth and sixth centuries they came as colonists to establish themselves with their wives and children and with their stallions and mares. It is these later invasions that established on the soil of Algeria the Arabic tribes, principally those of the Mehall, the Djendel, the Oulad Mahdi, the Douaouda, etc., etc., who have spread everywhere; and from them sprang the true nobility of the country. These invasions were what carried the Arabian horses as far as the Sudan and we can say that the Arabian breed in Algeria is as one with the breed in the East.

"Thus then, the history of Arabian horses can be divided into four great eras:

1) From Adam to Ishmael;
2) From Ishmael to Solomon;
3) From Solomon to Mohammed;
4) And from Mohammed to our day.

"It must be understood, however, that in the breed of the principal era, that of Solomon, perforce divided into various branches, certain differences must have established themselves, due to climate, more care or less care, or feeding, as has occurred with the human species. Colors of the coats have varied under the force of the same circum-

---

[3] *Maghreb*: the name given by the Arabs to the northern part of Africa (formerly Mauretania in English) which includes among others the modern countries of Egypt, Tunisia, and Algeria. [Translator's note]

stances. Experience has shown the Arabs that in rocky terrain horses are generally iron gray and that in places where the terrain is white, the majority are white; I have often proved to myself the truth of these observations.

"I have only one more point, at present, to exhaust with you.

"You ask me what characteristics the Arabs take into consideration to judge a horse as being well bred or what characteristics a drinker of the wind should have. Here is my answer: the pure-bred horse among us is characterized by the delicacy of his lips, the dilation of the nostrils, the leanness of the flesh covering the veins of the head, the elegance of the set of the neck, the silkiness of the mane, the coat, and the skin, the width of the breast,[4] the thickness of the joints and cleanness of the legs. According to the sayings of our forebears, we should judge the horse more by his character [moral attributes] than by his appearance. By outward indications one can judge the breeding. From character alone, you will have confirmation of the extreme care which is taken in breeding and of the vigilance which has been exercised to adamantly prohibit misalliances.

"Pure-bred horses are not ill natured. The horse is the most beautiful of all animals; but his moral attributes, according to us, under penalty of his being considered degenerate, must correspond to his physical appearance.

"Arabs will make every conceivable sacrifice to succeed in getting offspring from a stallion or mare when they are convinced that one or the other has given proof of extraordinary speed, notable sobriety, acute intelligence, or affection toward the hand that feeds it, as they

[4] *Breast and Chest*: I have taken the following definition from M. Horace Hayes' *Points of the Horse*:

The *breast* is the front portion of the chest which is bounded by a line connecting the points of both shoulders, and by the humerus (bone between the shoulder joint and the elbow) on each side. Among horsemen who are unacquainted with anatomy, the "breast" is frequently called the "chest." At the risk of employing a word contrary to colloquial custom, I would suggest that the term "chest" be applied exclusively to the cavity which occupies nearly the front third of the trunk, and in which the lungs and heart are situated. It is divided from the belly (abdomen) by the diaphragm.

I have chosen to use the term "breast" throughout this book in the sense in which Dr. Hayes defined it, because "breast" is much closer in meaning to the French "*poitrail*: the fore-part of a horse's body between the base of the neck and shoulders," than it is to the French "*poitrine*: the part of the trunk between the neck and abdomen which contains the lungs and heart." General Daumas drew a marked distinction between the two. [Translator's note]

are fully persuaded that the qualities of the parents will appear in the progeny.

"We grant then, that a horse is truly noble when, in addition to having beautiful conformation, he joins courage to fieriness and glows with pride in the midst of gunpowder and dangers. Such a horse will love his master and will not allow himself to be mounted by another person; he will not stale or leave droppings while carrying his rider; he will not eat the leftovers of other horses and he likes to paw any clean water he comes across.

"By means of sight, hearing, and smell, as well as by ability and intelligence, he will keep his rider safe from dangers inherent in the chase and in war. To sum up, he will share the feelings of sorrow or pleasure of his rider; he will help him in combat by fighting as well. He will, always and in everything, make common cause with his master. These are the indications which bear witness to the purity of a blood line. We have many anecdotes about the qualities of horses. From all of them it may be deduced that next to man the horse is the noblest creature, the most patient, the most useful. He feeds on little and judging him from the standpoint of strength, we find him to be superior to all other animals. The stoutest ox can pull a quintal [a weight of one hundred pounds,] but if this weight were placed on its back, it could move only with effort and could not run. The horse carries a well-built man, a banner, weapons, ammunition, and rations for both. Furthermore he gallops all day without drinking or eating; with him the Arab can guard what he has, attack the enemy, follow his tracks, flee, defend his family or his liberty. Suppose the Arab is wealthy, with all the goods that make life agreeable—nothing can protect him like his horse. Now do you understand the great love that Arabs have for the horse? It is equivalent to the services which he gives his master; his master owes to his horse his joys, his victories, and for that reason he prefers him even more than gold or precious stones.

"While paganism lasted, the Arabs loved the horse for selfish motives and only because he gave them glory and riches; but from the moment that the Prophet expressed himself in such glowing terms about the horse, that instinctive love turned into a religious duty. One of the first things the Prophet said concerning the horse is that which legend hands down from the time that various tribes of Yemen accepted his dogma and offered him, as a sign of submission,[5] five magnificent mares belonging to five different blood lines which Arabia possessed at the time. It is said that Mohammed emerged from his field tent to receive the noble animals which had been sent to him and, on stroking them with his hand, he expressed himself thus: 'May you be blessed, oh daughters of the wind!' Later, one sent by God (Rassoul Allah) said: 'Who tends and trains a horse for God's sake shall be counted among those who do charitable acts, night and day, in private or in public; he shall be rewarded. All his sins will be forgiven him and fear will never dishonor his heart.'

"And now I ask God to grant you a happiness that will never cease.

"Keep your friendship for me.

"The sages among the Arabs say: "Riches can be lost. Honors are but a shadow that vanishes; but true friends are a treasure that remains.'

"He who has written these lines, with a hand that Death will one day wither, is your friend, poor in the sight of God.

Sid-el-Hadj, Abd-el-Kader-ben-Mahi-ed-Din.

Damas (Damascus) end of Deul-Kada 1274 (end of August 1857).

"P.S. For better understanding in our correspondence, allow me to explain something to you. The name *frass* is not used only for the mare, as is the custom in Algeria; it can just as well indicate male or female. If one desires to refer to a mare one must say 'female *frass.*' If one desires to refer to a stallion one should say 'male *frass.*' This is the custom among the true Arabs. Ordinarily one calls a mare *hadjra* and a stallion *hossan.*"

Upon reading this curious document the reader will undoubtedly have noted the singular mixture of legendary facts, ideas about natural history, here true and there fabulous, in the style of Pliny and Aristotle, the whole dominated by religious beliefs.

It was thus that the Orientals wrote history, and with them the Arabs of the West, as both of them—until now being placed beyond the law of progress by voluntary or enforced seclusion, far from the intellectual movement which took place in Europe—are in arts and

---

[5] Could this not be the origin of the horses of submission (*gada*), which in Moslem countries the vanquished should offer to the conqueror?

sciences where their forefathers in Baghdad or Granada left them. Furthermore, it should be noted that the more learned an Arab is, the more the pages he writes are stamped with hyperbole, to such an extent that a reader accustomed to European clarity has to isolate himself from that unknown poetry and reflect upon it in order to arrive at the exact meaning of a document of possible historical or scientific value—in the sense which we give to these words.

Therefore, at first sight, the letter we have just read is no more than a fragment detached from an Oriental tale. It contains, however, undeniable truths, and in transformed or symbolized tradition, teachings which we might do wrong to disdain. In it the words deaden, but the spirit gives life. Let us seek, therefore, the spirit in the words. God created the horse from the wind, symbol of speed, which to the Arab is the principal attribute of his mount. The Greek poets also believed that the wind begot the horses of Thessaly, the swiftest in antiquity; and possibly those horses were imported into Greece from Syria or Arabia, accompanied by the fabulous genealogy which the poets of both countries simultaneously attributed to them.

In this respect real history is in agreement with legend. Arabian horses must have been then, as they are even now in their native country, the swiftest and therefore the best in the world. The Arabs— who neither understand nor practice military science in compact and closed formations as we do, but rather, in disorderly charges, and who do not consider retreat or dispersed flight as being inglorious—should, before all else, love the drinker of the wind and eulogize him. The drinker of the wind, according to them, is in combat the first to charge the enemy; after a victory the first in looting; and, in case of a defeat, the first [to find himself] far from danger. A poet puts it this way: "There are things which an intelligent king should never neglect and the first is a horse, which by reason of his swiftness, can save him from his enemy when the latter has not been able to vanquish him." The horse preferred by the Prophet Mohammed was named Ouskoub (The Torrent) from the word *sakab* (swiftly running water.)

The intervention of the Archangel Gabriel in the creation of the horse remanded that animal to the care of the true believers because the Archangel Gabriel is the incessant intermediary of God and the prophets, especially Mohammed. It was by means of the horse, and only with the horse, that the Moslems were able to make that immense emigration, that war of propaganda, to the East toward China, to the West to the ocean, which it was in the mind of Mohammed to impose on them.

It was essential that the horse become a sacred animal to the Arab, a providential instrument of war, created by God for a very special purpose and of a nobler essence than other animals. Not to allow the horse to be born according to natural law, but, on the contrary, to envelop his creation in a symbolism which escapes from natural law, deviating in the direction of the mysteries of legend, also to place him under the safeguard of a religious respect—these acts evinced, as the result has proved, a thorough knowlege of the spirit of the people over whom Mohammed wished to exert, and must have exerted, an influence.

The Koran, in speaking of horses, calls them El-Kheir, the supreme blessing, and from this simple expression the expounders of the Sourate (*sad*) have arrived at the conclusion that the Arabs should love the horse as themselves—to the extent of taking food from their children's mouths to feed him.

A volume could be written using phrases taken from the holy book or from the *hadites* of the Prophet (his conversations preserved by tradition) and of their comments which in the guise of precepts and maxims impose, as a religious duty, Moslems' love for the horse.

I shall quote a few:

"Blessings, triumph, and rich booty will be linked to the horse's forelock until the Day of Resurrection."

"Whoever looks after a horse for the sake of the Holy War increases the number of his good works."

"A horse's hunger and thirst, the water he drinks, the fodder he eats, every hair on that animal, the least step he takes, and even his urine and dung, all will be weighed in the balance on Judgment Day."

"The horse recites three daily prayers. In the mornings, he says: 'Oh God! Let my master love me!' At midday he adds: 'Do good unto my master so that he will do good unto me!' At night he prays: 'Allow my master to attain Paradise on my back!' "

Undoubtedly influenced by these words, El-Doumayry wrote in his history of animals, *Hayat-el-hayouan*: "The horse is the animal which, by reason of his intelligence, draws nearest to man." Apropos of this, I cannot help but note that when the Arabs expressed this opinion, they were well acquainted with the animals which, among us, are considered as being the most intelligent, such as the elephant, the dog, etc., etc.

Then where does this come from? Could it not be that the Arabs, because of their intimate association with the horse, have known how to develop in him faculties unknown to us, while we do not grant any more to the horse than the possession of the instinct of memory? To the Arabs the horse is a family friend; on the contrary, to us he is only a luxury or a tool for work, which we exchange at whim or for pecuniary interest—as witness our proverb: "One does not marry one's horse." The Arab does marry his horse.

Be that as it may, the maxims just quoted tend to identify man with the horse, and do not think that that is all. It is necessary, moreover, that the horse be the companion of the true believers to the exclusion of all infidels and this should be readily understood without our having to expatiate upon the political implications of this exclusion. God has said: "The horse shall be cherished by all My slaves; he shall be the despair of those who do not obey My laws and I will not place on his back any but men who know and adore Me." Needless to say, all the Moslem chieftains have used this as a precedent for prohibiting in the name of God, under penalty of sin and damnation, the sale of Arabian horses to Christians. These orders of divine origin were, I know, disregarded in some countries. It is true that Arabs love money, but it must be believed that in the majority of cases they have sold us mediocre animals and that the stallions and mares whose noble and marvellous attributes of speed or breeding have been proved will never be sold at any price to foreigners. If one member of a tribe were to agree to dispose of such an animal, the entire tribe would oppose such an action. This is the truth and it explains the discredit into which the Arabian horse in Europe seems to have fallen: only those animals that the Arabs have not wanted to keep have been seen there.

Let us now examine another aspect of the matter. The Emir Abd-el-Kader affirms that the horse was created *koummite*, red mixed with black, that is to say, brown bay or burnt chestnut. Separated from its cloudiness, this assertion has, at least, the merit of proving that such a color has always been considered among the Arabs as being indicative of superior qualities; this idea is firmly fixed in the heads of that very observant race. One encounters it often.

The Prophet has said: "If, after having gathered together all the horses of the Arabs, they were made to run together, it would be the *euchegueur meglouk* (the solid-color burnt chestnut) that would outdistance them all."

Moussa, the celebrated conqueror of Africa and Spain, has remarked: "Of all the horses of my armies, the ones which best endured the weariness and miseries of war were the solid bays."

The Prophet has added: "If you have a burnt [liver] chestnut, take him into battle. If you have nothing but a poor chestnut, take him anyway."

From all this it is clear that legendary traditions and experience agree in conferring a great superiority on dark, solid colors; and there would appear to be no esteem for light and washy colors. The color of the coat is then an indication of the horse's qualities. The long experience of Mohammed, the Prophet, and that of Moussa, the conqueror, agree and have been consciously confirmed by the experience of all Arabs, the world's best horsemen and the men most interested in the study of the horse, which constitutes their honor and their life; consequently it is worth the trouble of taking such experience into consideration.

What is indisputable is that the *koummite* (red mixed with black, chestnut, or bay), is among all, the one preferred by the Arabs. If I may be permitted to base myself on personal experience, I do not fear to say that if such a prejudice exists I share it with them. And what would appear to be a prejudice—could it not be a truth? Surely I may be permitted to say that all individuals of the same species are identical in color in the wild state and that they have all been given the same instinctive general qualities inherent in the species. Except in the case of domestication, neither their colors nor their attributes undergo changes or mixtures to the same extent as that of those individuals which, due to a retrogression better attested to than explicable, revert to the color of their progenitors. They can also be distinguished by more obvious natural attributes. (Canines give proof of this.) From this it follows that if a certain number of domesticated individuals had the same color and dominant characteristics one could reach the conclusion that these colors and characteristics were those of a species in a wild state. Now, as far as the Arabian horse is concerned, if it is true that those of a *koummite* color have been given a superior swiftness, could we not infer that that was the uniform color and an innate characteristic of their forebears? I humbly submit this observation to Science.

The Emir Abd-el-Kader tells us that it has been proved by the Arabs that horses change color according to the terrain in which they live. Is it not possible, then, that under the influence of an atmosphere more, or less, active; running or stagnant water; richer or poorer feed, according to what is produced by a soil more fertile or less fertile in certain elements; the coat of the horse would modify itself? Everyone knows that a coat changes color and texture according to the place where the animal lives, the state of its health, the water it drinks, the quality of its feed, and, above all, the care it gets. Perhaps in all this there might be a lesson in natural history which should not go unnoticed, because if the surroundings in which a horse lives influence his coat, inevitably in the long run they will exercise an influence on his structure and his attributes. The foregoing having been set forth, one should dwell upon one last point in the letter from the Emir Abd-el-Kader, which is that which divides the history of the Arabian horses into four eras as follows:

1) Adam to Ishmael;
2) Ishmael to Solomon;
3) Solomon to Mohammed;
4) and from Mohammed to the present day.

This history is that of all Arabs, insofar as they are identified with the horse, their necessary and indispensable companion. From Adam to Abraham, Arabs did not as yet exist. It was the period of pastoral peoples. There were no wars; at least, not bloody ones. No pillaging. The horse did not appear until the day of creation. He did not have any task other than that of leading the herds or being a peaceable servant for domestic tasks. However, in the second period, with Ishmael, his role changes. Ishmael is the bastard, the disinherited, he was abandoned in the desert; his life is that of struggle. He is engaged in open warfare with all men because, in brief, he must live well on that soil to which he has been relegated, without taking into account that that necessity of struggling to live gives, at the same time, an outlet to the resentment he feels toward his brothers, the inheritors—to his detriment—of the paternal acres.

One reads in the Bible that while Hagar was in exile in the desert, an angel appeared and said: "I will multiply your descendants and they shall be innumerable. You shall bear a son and call him Ishmael. He will be a fierce man. He shall lift his hand against all men and they shall lift their hands against him. He shall erect his tent in the midst of his brethren." Ishmael is the personification of the Arabic people. He calls to horses, chooses the best, and trains them for racing, the chase, and war. It is through them that he will live on booty from the rich caravans which venture into his lands and he will invade, from the country of thirst and hunger, the land of plenty. The horse made him the king of the desert and in exchange he made the noble animal his companion and friend. Between them there is a solidarity of interests. Nevertheless, the Arabs, some pushed toward the East by the great armies of the kings of Assyria, others toward the North by the people of God, the former absorbed and dispersed in these great struggles, the latter interned in their arid lands, and divided by internal strife, degenerated; and with them their horses also degenerated.

Legend has it that it was in Jerusalem the Noble, in the stables of King Solomon, where the only specimens of the breed were preserved. Travellers, perhaps the leaders of caravans, because they arrived in Jerusalem in great numbers, may have received as gifts horses of whose worth and quality they were completely ignorant. But under the influence of peace, trade once again discovered the forgotten road from Central Asia to the ports of Syria; and the Arabs, interested in making common cause, united themselves in alliances, one tribe after another. The horses then followed this phase of their destiny. Later a new degeneration came about due to the immigration to Arabia of foreigners—Jews and Christians—and to the differences among the Arabs themselves. Some of the noble and powerful tribes, the Korayche, for example, the strongest and most aristocratic among all the tribes, had preserved, in keeping with their innate dignity, the traditional love for horses. But, in order that the work of Mohammed could be carried to conclusion, this love of the few had of necessity to be felt by all, to be made popular, at the same time that it was imperative to join in national unity all the scattered elements of which the Arabic peoples were then composed.

We have seen how insistently the Prophet expresses himself in the Koran, in conversations, and in doctrines, about this need and how, at last, he made the care of the horse an obligation, a cult in Moslem life. Thus, from his time to ours, Arabian horses had to improve. Did he not say: "Who feeds and looks after a horse for the triumph of religion is making a magnificent loan to God?"[6]

I have but a few words more to add concerning the description which the Emir Abd-el-Kader gives of the pure-bred horse. The Emir takes physical and moral attributes as being inseparable. According to him, physical attributes alone do not constitute a perfect horse. It is necessary, because of his intelligence, because of his affection for the man who feeds him, cares for him, and rides him, that man and horse be as one.

To demand these attributes in a pure-bred horse is simply to place him, in the intellectual scale, immediately following man, in the same way that according to legend he followed [preceded?] him in the order of creation. We are far from taking his view, I know; but are we not too far?

---

[6] In a report made to our Society for Zoological Acclimation, the scholar Richard, referring to the letter from the Emir Abd-el-Kader which I sent to that institution, expressed himself thus:

Mohammed, as shrewd a politician as he was a skilful warrior, understood that the horse would play a very important role in wars and in order not to use a new inducement with which to succeed in obtaining the multiplication and perfection of the beautiful animal, he had the idea of mixing religion into the difficult art of breeding and training horses. Are not religious sentiments, whatever their origin, the strongest and most energetic motivations of the human heart? What great events have not been brought about in the lives of nations, as well as in those of individuals, under the influence of religious ideas? These ideas can give to the most modest lives, to the most timid souls great courage and great resignation. What proofs have we not been given by the martyrs, above all at the beginning of Christianity as in all the following epochs of that divine religion?

Mohammed on promising Paradise to those who would train a horse as he desired in the interests of his strength, power, and glory, found the best method of multiplying and perfecting the model for remounts for his cavalry. Among a people as God-fearing as the Arabs, it would not have been possible to find or use a more powerful means. If we had an exact history of the origin of the perfected Arabian horse, I am certain that it would be found that the betterment of the breed stems above all from the era of the Prophet and the opinion of the Emir Abd-el-Kader seems correct to me in this respect. With their religious ideas, the Arabs not only have succeeded in breeding the first and best war horse, but they have also succeeded in keeping the monopoly on its production. All other nations go to Moslem countries to buy stallions suitable for bettering their own breeds.

3

THE BARB HORSE

He lives between the sky and the sand.
Call him Arabian, Barb, Turk, Persian,
Nedji, it matters little for all these terms
are but baptismal names. The name of the
family is the Horse of the Orient. The
other family across the Mediterranean is
the European breed.

IT HAS FREQUENTLY BEEN SAID that the horse in our African possessions
—where we have tried to improve his qualities, unique in themselves,
to be sure—was very inferior to the Arabian horse. In spite of a conviction based on long experience and serious study [of the Barb], we
felt it a duty to seek and examine an opinion backed by authority.
We have wished to have as arbiter in this matter a man who, because
of his intelligence, his habits, his whole way of life, is extremely
knowledgeable about horses—the Emir Abd-el-Kader. We wrote that
horseman par excellence a letter in which we frankly set forth the
objections which our assertions will encounter. His reply is what we
are about to set forth. It will be seen from this curious document that
the Emir does not limit himself to confirming what we have asserted;
he develops by means of reflections or by facts all our opinions. According to him the Berber horse, far from being a degeneration of the
Arabian, is, on the contrary, superior. The Berbers occupied Palestine
long ago. It was there that they bred that animal which has become

the model for war horses. Taken to Africa by chance in their adventurous life, the tribe carefully looked after the guest in their tents, the instrument of their chases, the companion of their combats. The horses had preserved such outstanding qualities that an Asiatic sovereign, engaged in a perilous war, sent for Berber coursers. The reader will appreciate the worth of this historical dissertation, which, in whatever manner it may be judged, is still of indisputable interest.

What is certain is that the Barb owes to the sky under which he is foaled, to the training he receives, to the feed he is given, to the fatigues to which he is accustomed, a vigor which enables him to equal, if not surpass, the most vaunted horses of Persia and Syria. Based on the letter which we are going to set forth in print, we believe we can reiterate that today all the horses in Africa and Asia can be considered under a common name—opposed to the European horse— one horse, the Horse of the Orient, which, owing to the conquest of Algeria, we believe will be called upon, more and more, to render to our country greater and more appreciated services.

Here is the letter from the Emir Abd-el-Kader which reached me from Brousse [Anatolia]:

"Praise to the one God. Only His kingdom is eternal.

"May entire health and divine happiness be with the person of General Daumas, who ardently seeks the solution of great problems; may God guide and protect him.

"Next, you have sought our opinion with regard to the Barb horse, his attributes and origin. To please you I have again busied myself with these questions and today I can do no better than send you some quotations from the poems of the famous Aâmrou-el-Kaïs, who lived a short time before the advent of the Prophet. The quotations deal with the superiority of the Berber horses and, I believe, will furnish you with proofs against those who maintain that those admirable animals possess nothing but inferior qualities.

"The poet said, upon addressing himself to Caesar, Emperor of Constantinople, in a lengthy verse:

" 'And I make reply unto you, should I come to be restored as King, we shall take a gallop where you will see the horseman bent over his saddle to increase the speed of his mount;

" 'A gallop through a place crowded on all sides where no other eminences can be seen to guide the travellers, than the hump of an old nabatheen camel, laden with years and emitting plaintive grunts.

" 'We shall be, I tell you, borne by a horse accustomed to night marches, a horse of the Berber breed;

" 'With lean flanks like those of a wolf of Gada; a horse who presses his swift course, whose flanks, one will see, run with sweat.

" 'When, slackening the reins, one urges him on again by striking him with the reins on either side, he will precipitate his swift gallop, carrying his head on his flanks and champing the bit.

" 'And then when I say: "Let us rest,"—the rider will halt as if by magic and break into song, still in the saddle, on that vigorous horse, whose thigh muscles are long and whose tendons are dry and well separated.'

"Aâmrou-el-Kaïs was one of those ancient Arabic kings who made efforts, on fighting his enemies, to procure Berber horses; he doubted the outcome, should he not put his trust in the qualities of the Arabian horses.

"It is not possible, according to my way of thinking, to give a more invincible proof of the superiority of Barb horses; after such a testimony there is no longer any worthwhile argument to advance by anyone who should contest it.

"The Berbers are, according to El-Massoudi, descendants of the Béni-Ghassan and others; certain authors vow that they come from the Béni-Lekhm and the Djouzam. Their first homeland was Palestine from which they were hunted out by a king of Persia. They emigrated toward Egypt, but the sovereign of that country forbade them to stay. Then they crossed the Nile and spread over the lands to the west and across the river.

"Malek-ben-el-Merahel has said that the Berbers formed a very numerous people—made up of Hymiar, of Modher, of Copts, of Amalkas, and of Kanéan—who congregated in the province of Scham (Syria), and took the name of Berber. Their emigration to Maghreb, according to this historian, as well as according to El-Massoudi, El-Souheïli, and El-Zabari, was due [to the fact that] Ifrikech took them with him for the conquest of the African peninsula.

"Ibn-el-Kelbi adds that opinion is divided as to the real name of the chieftain under whose orders the Berbers emigrated from Syria toward Maghreb. According to this author, some believe that it was the Prophet David, others, that it was Youscha-ben-Enoun, others Ifrikech, others certain kings of the Zobor.

"El-Massoudi adds that they did not emigrate until after the death of Goliath, that they established themselves in the province of Barca-d'Yfrikia and in the Maghreb, after having conquered the Franks; that from there they invaded Sicily, Sardinia, the Balearic Islands, and Spain. Then it was agreed between them and the Franks that the latter would occupy the towns and they would establish themselves in the deserts which extend from Alexandria to the ocean, Tangiers and the country of Sousse.

"Ibn-Abd-el-Berr said that the colonization of the Berbers extended from the end of Egypt, that is to say, from the countries which are situated behind Barca [Cyrenaica] to the Arabian Sea and from the Straits of Gibraltar to the end of the desert which touches the Sudan. At that boundary one still finds a people, situated between the Habeuch (Abyssinians) and the Zendy (Zanzibar) known by the name of Berbers. The author of the Kamous [an encyclopedia] makes mention of them, but they are a very small population, whose insignificant and obscure history contains no important event.

"The essential point here is the quotation of the poet Aâmrou-el-Kaïs with respect to Berber horses. As far as the Berbers themselves are concerned, everything proves that they have been known from time immemorial, that they came from the East to establish themselves in Maghreb, where we can find them today.

"And may salvation be yours from the beginning to the end of this letter, from your friend, Abd-el-Kader-ben-Mahi-ed-Din. May God cover you with His protection!

                              Brousse, the first of safer, 1269 (1854)."

After the foregoing had been written, I received a confirmatory proof of my opinion on the excellence of Barbs and on their complete equality to other horses of Oriental origin. Here it is:

                                        "Paris, the . . . . , 185 . . .
"My dear General:

"I enclose the account of the horse races held in Alexandria, Egypt, on the 25th of July, 1836. I authorize you to publish it in your work as a useful argument in support of your theory as to the excellence of the Barb horse. I have told you how these races came about as a result of a conversation I had with Mehemet-Ali, in which the Viceroy of Egypt had twitted me about the arrival of a horse which my brother

Jules had sent to me from Tunis. Very truly yours, *etc.* [Signed] Ferdinand de Lesseps."

DISTANCE COVERED: 4 and ½ KILOMETRES IN A STRAIGHT LINE [One kilometre is nearly five-eights of a mile.]

First Race:

Nejdi horse, dapple-gray, 4½, owner Subi-Bey and ridden by him.

Nejdi horse, foaled in Cairo, bay, 9 years old, owner Jules Pastré and ridden by him.

Anézé horse, from Syria, iron-gray, 3½, owner M. Méreinier, ridden by J. Dufey.

Nejdi horse, foaled in Cairo, owner His Excellency Moharrem-Bey, son-in-law of Mehemet-Ali and ridden by Terata-Tutemy-i-Bachi of Pacha.

The horse ridden by Jules Pastré came in first.

Second Race:

Barb horse, from Tunis, bay, 4 years old, belonging to Ferdinand de Lesseps and ridden by him.

Nejdi horse, white, 6½, owner Étienne Rollaud, ridden by J. Dufey.

Nejdi horse, bay, 5 years old, owner Subi-Bey and ridden by him.

Nejdi horse, foaled in Cairo, 7 years old, owner His Excellency Moharrem-Bey, ridden by Cerkès-Osman-Sakallé.

The Barb ridden by M. de Lesseps came in first.

Third Race:

Nejdi horse, foaled in Cairo, gray, 6 years old, owner Hussein-Effendi and ridden by him.

Nejdi horse, dapple-gray, 5½, owner Dr. Gaetani-Bey, ridden by Ferdinand de Lesseps.

Nejdi horse, foaled in Cairo, iron-gray, 6 years old, owner W. Peel and ridden by him.

Horse from Samos, bay, 9 years old, owner Ibrahim-Effendi-Bimbachi and ridden by him.

The Egyptian horse ridden by Hussein-Effendi came in first.

Fourth Race:

Nejdi horse, foaled in Cairo, bay, 8 years old, owner M. Henricy, ridden by M. Escalou.

Egyptian horse from Atfé, bay, 8 years old, owner Samuel Miur Junior, ridden by M. Sanders.

Nejdi horse, foaled in Cairo, bay, 8 years old, owner Turki-Bachi and ridden by him.

Nejdi horse, gray, 4 years old, owner M. Roquerbe, ridden by M. Bartolomeo.

The Nejdi horse ridden by M. Bartolomeo came in first.

Recapitulation of the Winning Horses

First Race:
Horse from Cairo, owner M. Pastré and ridden by him.
Second Race:
Barb horse, owner Ferdinand de Lesseps and ridden by him.
Third Race:
Horse from Cairo, owner Hussein-Effendi and ridden by him.
Fourth Race:
Nejdi horse, owner M. Roquerbe and ridden by M. Bartolomeo.

According to the agreements made, the four winning horses then raced
each other, thus providing the fifth race. They came in in the following
order:

1. Barb horse from Tunis, owner Ferdinand de Lesseps and ridden by him.
2. Horse from Cairo, owner Jules Pastré and ridden by him.
3. Nejdi horse, owner M. Roquerbe, ridden by M. Bartolomeo.
4. Nejdi horse, owner Hussein-Effendi and ridden by him.
   I certify as to the exactitude of the foregoing account.

Signed: Ferdinand de Lesseps.

To wind up the subject of the Barb horse and give, among the
other qualities which he possesses, an exact idea of his power and
energy, I can do no better than to set down here what was the weight
carried in the greater part of our [military] expeditions by the horse
of an African chasseur.

Weight Carried by the Horse of an African Chasseur upon Departing on an Expedition.

[Note: one kilogram is equal to 2.2046 pounds.]

	Kilogram	Hectogram	Decagram
An armed and uniformed rider	82	0	0
Accoutrements with pistol	24	0	0
Bread for two days	1	5	0
Biscuit for three days	1	6	5
Coffee for five days	0	6	0
Sugar for five days	0	6	0
Lard for five days	1	0	0
Rice for five days	0	3	0
Salt	0	0	8

Rolled forage for five days	25	0	0
Barley for five days	20	0	0
Three clips of cartridges	1	3	0
Four horseshoes	1	6	0
	—	—	—
Total . . .	159	6	3

One hundred and fifty-nine kilograms, or be it nineteen more than the horse of a carabineer and twenty-six more than the horse of a cuirassier in France.

It is superfluous to say that that weight diminishes the farther the horse travels from his point of departure.

(Sent on the 21st of February of 1847 by Colonel Duringer, at the moment of the departure of a column.)

Now then, a horse which can, in a country which is generally very difficult and broken, walk, run, climb and descend, endure unheard of privations, and do his campaigning vigorously with such a weight on his back, is he or is he not a war horse?

THE HORSES OF THE SAHARA

Riding horses, coursing with Salukis,
And the tinkling of earrings
Would make you tear verses from your head.

THE HORSE is a vital necessity to a pastoral and nomadic people spread over a vast territory, whose number is not in proportion to the country which it inhabits. With his horse the Arab trades, makes journeys, looks after his numerous flocks, woos, fights, shines in battle, at weddings, and at the feasts of his marabouts; space is nothing to him. This is the reason why the Arabs of the Sahara dedicate themselves with a passion to horse breeding. They know the worth of a blood line; they keep watch over crosses; they improve the species. The anarchic times in which they have recently been living may have changed some of their customs, but they have not modified by one whit the breeding, perfecting, and training of their horses.

Love for the horse flows in Arabic blood; the noble animal is a comrade-in-arms and the friend of the chieftain; he is one of the family servitors; a study is made of his habits and needs; he is praised in verses, he is eulogized in conversation. Every day in the meetings outside the camp site, where the privilege of speaking belongs only to the eldest—who stands out among his listeners seated in a circle on the sand or on the grass—the young men add to their practical knowledge the advice and the traditions of the elders. Religion, war, the chase, love, and horses, inexhaustible topics, turn these talks in the open air into real schools, in which the warrior molds himself and where he develops his intelligence, compiling in his head a multitude of facts, precepts, proverbs, and phrases which will have a thousand applications during the course of his life, so full of perils which must be overcome. There [in the meetings] is where he acquires the horse lore which causes one such astonishment when it is met with, in even the least of the horsemen of a tribe living in the desert. He does not even know how to read or write, and yet each phrase of his talk is based on the authority of the sages, the Koran, or the very Prophet himself.

"Our Lord Mohammed has said"; "Sidi-Ahmed-ben-Youssef has added"; "Si-ben-Dyab has recounted . . ." And you may certainly believe him, that uneducated sage, because all his texts, all his anecdotes, which frequently are only found in books, he had from the *tholbas* [scribes or learned men] or from his chieftain who expresses himself thus, without realizing it, to maintain among his people love for the horse, useful precepts, sound doctrines, or the best rules of hygiene. All this is at times mixed with vulgar notions or ridiculous superstition; it is a shadow on the picture. But let us be indulgent, for it was not too long ago that in France almost the same absurdities were voiced as undeniable truths.

I was talking on a certain occasion to a marabout [Mohammedan holy man] of the tribe of Oulad-sidi-Cheikh about the horses of his country, and as I pretended to cast doubts on the opinions he had voiced, he said: "You, the Christians, cannot understand this matter," and got up abruptly.

"Horses are our riches, joys, life, and religion. Has not the Prophet said: 'The blessings of this world until Judgment Day shall hang from the forelocks between your horses' eyes?'"

"I have read the Koran," I answered, "but I have not found those words."

"You will not find them in the Koran, which is the Voice of God, but you will find them in the talks of our lord Mohammed (*Hadite sidna Mohammed*)."

"And you do believe?" I answered.

"Before I take my leave I am going to let you know what can happen to someone who believes," and my interlocutor gravely told me the following tale:

"A poor man, trusting in the words of the Prophet which I have just quoted, found one day a dead mare. He cut off her head and buried it at the door of the house he lived in and thought to himself: 'I shall become wealthy, should it please God.' But the days went by and no wealth appeared. However, the believer did not begin to doubt. The sultan of the country, who was on a pilgrimage to a holy place, happened to pass by the modest house of the poor Arab, which was situated at one end of a little plain bordered by big trees and made fertile by a gay little stream. The spot pleased the sultan and he made a halt with his brilliant escort and dismounted to rest in the shade. When he was ready to give the order to go on, a slave having been walking his horse in the meantime, that noble beast, impatient to devour space, began neighing; then he pawed and finally broke loose from his groom.

"All the groom's efforts to catch him were in vain and he began to despair, when the horse was observed to stop suddenly at the door of an old ruin which he sniffed and pawed. An Arab, until then immovable, neared the horse speaking to him without startling him, as if he knew him. He patted him, took him by the mane, for the bridle was in a thousand pieces and without any difficulty led him docilely to the astonished sultan.

" 'How did you do it,' his eminence asked, 'to thus subdue one of the fieriest steeds in Arabia?'

" 'Your Lordship will not be surprised,' replied the believer, 'When he learns that, as I have heard that until Judgment Day all the world's blessings shall depend from the forelocks between the eyes of our horses, I buried in the yard of my house the head of a dead mare that I found.' The rest was a blessing from God. The sultan immediately ordered that the indicated spot be dug up and when he had assured himself that what the Arab had said was true, he rewarded him who never doubted, for a moment, the words of the Prophet. The poor man received as a gift a beautiful horse, rich garments, and wealth which gave him shelter from want to the end of his days.

"Now you know what can happen to someone who believes," and without waiting for a reply, he saluted me with a glance, after the manner of the Arabs, and went away.

This legend is popular in the Sahara, and the words of the Prophet on which it is based are, there, an article of faith.

Whether the Prophet said them or not, does not take away from their author's intention. The Arabs love honors, power, and wealth;

and to tell them that all these things depend from the forelocks of
their horses is to make them love their horses very much and to make
them feel bound to the horse by personal interest. The ingenuity of
the Prophet went even further; he understood that the task of conquest which he had bequeathed to his people could not be accomplished except by daring horsemen and that it was necessary to
instill in them love for the horse at the same time as faith in Mo-
hammedanism.

These precepts, which all converge toward achieving the same
end, are expressed in many different ways: the marabout and the
thaleb have collected them in phrases and legends; the noble in
traditions; and finally, the man in the street in dicta and proverbs.

Later on, sayings, traditions, and legends took on a religious aspect
which has accredited them forever in the great Moslem family.

The Doulama proclaim that when God wished to create the mare,
He said to the wind: "I will make a being from you that will carry
My worshippers, that shall be loved by all My slaves, and that shall
be the despair of all those who do not follow My laws"; and He made
the mare, saying: "I make you peerless, all the blessings of this world
shall be placed between your eyes; you shall conquer My enemies;
everywhere, I will make you happy and preferred above all the other
animals; and tenderness will ever be in your master's heart. You shall
be as good for the charge as for retreat, you shall fly without wings,
and I will place on your back only those men who know Me, who
pray to Me, who give Me thanks; in effect, those who worship Me."
The most intimate thoughts of the Prophet are clearly shown here
in their entirety.

The Prophet wants to have his people, excluding all infidels, reserve
Arabian horses for themselves—those powerful weapons of war that
in the hands of Christians could have such disastrous results for the
Moslem religion.

This idea, which the lower classes in Arabia did not understand,
possibly because of the veil of symbolism with which it is covered, did
not go unnoticed by the chieftains. The Emir Abd-el-Kader, at the
height of his power, punished mercilessly with the death penalty
every true believer convicted of having sold a horse to the Christians.

In Morocco such export duties are put on horses that the permission
granted to take them out of the Empire becomes a hollow mockery.
In Tunisia no permission is given, except in the case of imperative

political need; the same thing occurs in Tripoli, in Egypt, in Constantinople—in short, in every Mohammedan state.[1]

Talk about horses to a *djieud*, that nobleman of the tent who still
boasts about the fact that his forebears fought ours in Palestine, and
he will tell you:

> "Riding horses, coursing with salukis,
> And the tinkling of earrings
> Would make you tear verses from your head."

And talk with one of those horsemen (*mekhazeni*)[2] whose bronzed
face, salt and pepper beard, and pronounced exostoses[3] show that he
has seen many adventures, and he will tell you:

> "For combat the horse,
> For the desert the camel,
> And for poverty the ox."

Or he will remind you that when the Prophet went on campaigns
it was a habit of his, in order to stimulate the Arabs into taking the
best possible care of their horses, to give two-thirds of the booty to
the man that had accompanied him on the best-cared-for horse.

The sensual *thaleb*, to the world a man of God, who lives in lazy
contemplation without any more concern than that of his toilette, or
without doing any work other than that of writing talismans and
making amulets for everything and everyone, will tell you with
downcast eyes:

> "Paradise on earth is found on the back
> Of a good horse;
> In the study of good books, or
> Between the breasts of a woman."

If you question one of these old Arabic patriarchs, famous for his
wisdom, his experience, and his hospitality, he will tell you:

"Sidi-Aomar, the Prophet's companion, has said: 'Love horses and
look after them; for they deserve your tenderness; treat them as you

---

[1] I am very certain that, in certain Mohammedan countries, on the list of obligatory presents, with regard to the name of a Christian, the donor has put: "a
nag for the Christian."

[2] *Cavaliers du Makhzen*: Arabic cavalrymen serving with French forces in
Algeria and Morocco, distinguished by their blue burnooses. [Translator's note]

[3] The pronounced exostoses of the tibias. The eye of the Arabic stirrup always
causes exostoses on the shins. By them, one can at first glance, distinguish the
rich from the poor, the horseman from the infantryman.

do your children; nourish them as you do friends of the family, and blanket them with care. For the love of God, do not be negligent for you will regret it in this life and the next.' "

If, by some lucky chance, you find in your path one of those strolling troubadours who spends his life wandering about from tribe to tribe, in order to while away the frequent idle hours of our pastoral warriors, accompanied by a flautist and accompanying himself on a tambourine, he will in a hoarse but not unmelodious voice sing to you:

"My horse is the champion of all steeds.
He is blue like a pigeon in the shadow
And his black mane and tail are undulant.
He endures hunger and thirst and can see a great distance.
He is a very great drinker of the Arabic air.
He is the terror of the enemy in combat.
At the moment of firing rifles
Mebrouk[4] is the great pride of the country.

"My uncle has pure-bred mares whose far-removed grandparents
Were numbered among our tribes from ancient times,
Modest and timid like the young girls of Guebla.[5]
One would say they were gazelles
Grazing in the valleys under their mothers' eyes.
To see them is to forget the authors of one's days!

"Decked with *djellale*[6] which make our flowers pale
They wear long cloaks ornamented for their pleasure;
A Negro from Kora[7] looks after them;
He gives them pure barley, waters them with milk,
And leads them to the bath.
God preserve them from the Evil eye.[8]

[4] *Mebrouk* means the Happy One.
[5] *Guebla*: south, Sahara, desert.
[6] *Djellale*: woolen blankets, more or less adorned with designs, according to the fortunes of the heads of the tents, very wide, very warm, which envelop the breasts and the croups of the horses.
[7] *Kora*: the slaves from Kora are very much sought after by the Moslems; they learn Arabic with great difficulty, are devoted to their tasks and very faithful to their masters.
[8] *The Evil eye*: here is what the Arabs understand by the Evil eye. Someone comes to say to you: "Oh, what a beautiful horse, what a lovely mare you have there!" Fear everything of him, because he has not spoken except out of envy;

"For his cherished mares my uncle asked of me Mebrouk in
     marriage.
And I have answered no;
Mebrouk is my support, I want to keep him faithful,
Full of health, swift and agile in his gallop.
Time turns back on itself and returns;
Today without a quarrel, tomorrow perhaps we shall see
The hour of confrontation come at giant strides.
For a goatskin full of blood, my uncle answered,
You have yellowed[9] my face in the presence of my children.
The earth is large; adieu.

"Mebrouk, why do you whinny thus, during the day, during the
     night?
You reveal my hiding place and warn my enemies.
You think too much of the daughters of our horses.
I shall have you wed, oh, my son!
But where to find my friends
Whose mares are so noble and whose camels are treasures?
News of them is buried;
Where are their vast tents which were so pleasing to the eye?
One found there a rug and braided mats.
There was one given the hospitality of God.
And the poor man filled his belly.
They are gone!
The scouts have seen the tips of the hills,
The warriors were the first to go,
The shepherds made the flocks follow,
And the hunters, on the heels of their fine salukis,
Have chased the gazelle.

"Have you heard the tribe of my brothers spoken of?
No? Ah well. Come with me to count their numerous horses,
They are of colors that will please you.

---

had he done it in good faith, he would not have failed to add: "May God protect
you," or "May God accord you His benediction!" The Evil eye, however, is not
possessed by everyone.

  [9] "You have yellowed my face." Red, light colors are, among the Arabs, a
sign of good luck; somber colors, particularly yellow, are an indication of misfortune.

See those horses white as the snow that falls in its season;
Those horses as black as the slave ravished in the Sudan;
Those green[10] horses like the rushes which grow on the banks of
    streams;

"Those horses red as blood, the first jet from a wound,
And those blue[11] horses like the pigeon when it flies under the
    sky.
Where are those rifles so true, as swift as the blinking of an eye?
That powder of Tunis and those bullets, made in the molds,[12]
Which go through the bone, rip the liver and
Cause death with mouth agape?

"When I cease to sing, my heart will still uphold me;
For it burns for my brothers with a fire that devours me inside.
Nowhere have I seen such warriors.
Oh, my God! Strike those who might envy them blind.
Do they not have vast tents well furnished with rugs, carpets,
Cushions, saddles, and rich weapons?
The traveller and the orphan, are they not always received
By these words of our fathers: 'Well come!'
Their women, fresh as the poppies,
Are they not borne on camels,
Those ships of the earth[13]
Who walk with the noble step of the ostrich?
Are they not covered with veils
Which trailing far behind them, made even our marabouts
    despair?
Are they not sprinkled with ornaments, with gems enriched with
    coral?

[10] *Green horses*: the Arabs consider as green the horse we term dun [wolf color], especially when he is close to the color of a not very ripe olive.

[11] *Blue horses*: the Arabs call a horse blue that is a dark grey like the starling.

[12] It is, generally speaking, a luxury for the Arabs and particularly for those of the desert to have bullets made in molds. The greater part of the time they make lead rods and then cut them in little pieces.

[13] The camel is an animal so useful to the Arabs of the desert that they rightly call it the ship of land. In effect, the camel is calm, he does not need grain for nourishment, he can suffer thirst admirably for many days, he can carry very heavy loads in the removals from one place to another demanded by nomadic life.

And the blue tattoo on their limbs, does it not give pleasure to
    see it?
Everything in them ravishes the spirit of those who believe in
    God;
You would say that they are the flowers of bean vines which the
    Eternal has created.

"You are deep in the South
And the days seem so long to me!
It has been almost a year that, nailed to this boring Tell,[14]
I have not seen more of you than the traces of your camps.
Oh, my dear pigeon,
Who wears trousers that reach to your feet,
Who wears a burnoose so well adjusted on your shoulders,
Whose wings are divers colors and who knows so well the
    country;
Oh you who sings so softly.
Go! Fly under the clouds, they will be as covers.
Go and find my friends. Give them this letter.
Tell them that it comes from a sincere heart.
Return quickly and tell me if they are happy or unhappy,
Those for whom I sigh.

"You will see Cherifa,[15]
She is a proud girl,
She is proud, she is noble, I have seen her by means of writing.
Her long hair falls gracefully over her wide white shoulders:
You would think it the black plumes of the ostrich
Which lives in the desert and sings near its clutch.

"Her eyebrows are arches come from the land of the blacks;
And her eyelashes you would swear to be the awn of an ear of
    wheat
Ripened by the sun toward the end of summer.[16]
Her eyes are the eyes of a gazelle

---

[14] The Arabs of the desert so love their independent and nomadic existence
that they regard as the dullest moment of their life that when they are forced to
go to the Tell, there to lay in stocks of grain.

[15] *Cherifa*: feminine of "Cherif," which means descendant of the Prophet.

[16] In their poems the Arabs frequently call the sun the "eye of the daylight."

When she is uneasy about her little ones
Or when it may be lightning preceding the thunder in the
  middle of the night.

"Her mouth is lovely,
  Her saliva sugar and honey,
  And her even teeth resemble the hailstones
  Which the winter in fury sows in our localities.
  Her neck is the standard planted by our warriors
  To brave the enemy and rally the fugitives;
  And her faultless body insults the marble
  Which one uses to build the columns of our mosques.
  White as the moon which comes to encircle the night,
  She shines like a star which no cloud can dim.
  Tell her that she has wounded her friend
  With two blows from a dagger, one in the eyes, the other in the
    heart.
  Love is not a light burden.

"I ask the Almighty to give us water;
  We are in the Springtime.
  And the rain has been long in coming for the people with flocks.
  I am hungry. I am fasting like a moon of Ramadan.

"They are in Askoura, God be praised!
  Bring my horse!
  And you, strike the tents!
  I am going to find my uncle;
  He will know how to pardon his brother's son;
  We shall be reconciled and by the Head of the Prophet
  I shall give a fete where the young men shall show off
  The stirrups that gleam and the richly embroidered saddles;
  Weapons will be fired[17] to the notes of the flute and tambourine.
  I shall have Mebrouk wed
  And his sons shall be called the sons of well-cared-for mares.
  Oh, tribes of the Sahara!
  You allege that you have camels[18]

[17] Among the Arabs no fete takes place without the firing of weapons.
[18] When a desert tribe is at peace, it sometimes sends its camels to pasture as much as ten or twelve *lieues* [some twenty-five miles] ahead of it and one can

But camels, as you know, seek only those who can defend them
And those who can defend them are my brothers,
Because in combat they know how to shatter the bones of the
rebels."

Thus it can be seen that among the Arabic people everything is
directed toward cultivating love for the horse; religion makes it a
duty, as the unquiet life, the ceaseless struggles, and the immense
distance to be covered in a country where there are absolutely no
means of rapid communication, make of the horse an absolute necessity. The Arab cannot survive without leading a life of two: his horse
and himself.

Observations of the Emir Abd-el-Kader

"Good horses are mostly found in the Sahara where the number of
poor horses is small. In effect, the populations of the Sahara and those
which are their neighbors do not destine their horses to anything other
than war or a dispute over speed; neither do they dedicate them to
ploughing nor to any other exercise but combat. It is for that reason
that with few exceptions, their horses are excellent.

"No individual in the Sahara possesses ten camels until he has a
horse with which to protect them against those who make attempts
upon them.

"In the Tell[19] the greater part of the Arabs destine their horses to
the plough and they use them equally for riding and divers purposes.
The Arabs [of the Tell] have no preference for a stallion because to
them the horse is nothing but a useful animal for doing everything of
which he is capable, not just for war.

"Terrain and pasturage do not improve a poor or even a mediocre
horse; but if a pure-bred horse is raised in the mountains and on rocky
ground, he will then be endowed with a greater patience and strength
than those horses bred on the plains.[20] For that reason the pure-bred

-----

conceive that if a coup has been attempted, it would be necessary to have excellent horses and hardy riders to recover them.

[19] *The Tell*: a region in northeastern Algeria and northern Tunisia. It is a very
fertile area and produces large grain crops. It attained great productivity under
French rule. [Translator's note]

[20] "The sure-footed way our mounts climbed the stony mountain side, with its

horse bred in the Sahara is preferable to the same horse bred in the Tell. The former, in effect, differing in this respect from the horse of the Tell, is subjected to weariness, hard gallops, thirst, and hunger, which enables him to be always ready for any work demanded of him.

"The Koran calls the horse the supreme blessing.

"The servant of the Prophet said: 'Together with women what the Prophet loves most is the horse.'

"Aissa-ben-Meryem (Jesus, Son of Mary), may health be His, met Eblis, the black demon, one day and said to him:

" 'Eblis, I want to ask you a question. Will you tell Me the truth?'

" 'Spirit of God,' replied Eblis, 'Ask what you will.'

" 'I ask you,' said Jesus, 'In the name of Him Who never lies, what is it that can reduce your body to a liquid state and cut your spine in two?'

" 'It is,' answered the demon, "the neigh of a horse in a city or a fortress; I have never been able to enter a house where there was a horse kept for God's sake.'

"One of the Prophet's companions, passionately fond of horses, asked him if in Paradise there would be horses. The Prophet answered: 'If God permits you to enter Paradise, you will have a horse made of rubies, provided with wings with which to fly at your behest.'

"A poet has said: 'Who are they that will mourn after my death? My sword, my Boudaïna lance, and my lean, long-legged chestnut, trailing his reins to the fountain, Death having carried off his rider.'

"From time immemorial among the Arabs the horse has been the object of the greatest solicitude; and the Prophet never loses an opportunity to develop, maintain, and increase this solicitude by means of a religious sentiment. Among the notes made of his talks, the following precepts may be found:

" 'Happiness in this world, rich booty, and eternal reward are attached to the horse's forelock.'

" 'An evil spirit cannot enter a tent where a pure-bred horse is kept.'

---

slope of forty-five degrees, proved their Arab ancestry though they looked the roughest kind of hacks. Nobility always leaves some trace and where French horses would have fallen twenty times, these Moroccan animals never once stumbled" (Alexandre Dumas, *Adventures in Algeria* [1846], translated by Alma Elizabeth Murch, p. 35). [Translator's note]

" 'The angels watch over only the following three of man's pleasures: the practice of war, the enjoyment of the husband with the wife, and horse-racing.'

" 'When someone cannot comply with all his religious duties let him keep a pure-bred horse for God's sake and all his sins will be absolved.'

" 'Who feeds a horse for the triumph of religion, makes a magnificent loan to God.'

" 'A horse scrupulously bred for the Holy War will save his master from the fire on the Day of Resurrection.'

" 'He who makes sacrifices and prepares a horse for the Holy War will be treated, in the other world, as if he had been a martyr.'

" 'He who looks after a horse for the love of God will be counted among the number of those who practice charity day and night, in private and in public; he will be rewarded and fear will never dishonor his heart.'

" 'Money spent on horses is, in the eyes of God, like giving alms.'

" 'He who looks after and trains a horse for the service of God will be rewarded like the man who fasts by day and spends the night in prayer.'

" 'Horses ask God to be loved by their masters.'

" 'God comes to the aid of those who take care of horses and repays the expenditures made on their account.'

" 'Each grain of barley given to a horse is inscribed by God in the ledger of good works.'

" 'The martyrs of the Holy War shall find in Paradise horses made of rubies, and they shall fly at their masters' whim'."[21]

[21] After having read all these precepts, all these religious adages made so powerful among the people by tradition and known to the wealthy as well as to the poor and to the ignorant as well as to the learned, one can understand how difficult it is to induce an Arab to sell a pure-bred horse to a Christian.

5

BLOOD LINES

God has said: "Man shall be the noblest of
beings and the horse the noblest among
animals."

THE TRIBES LIVING in the Sahara have always been able—better than
those of the Tell—to elude the oppressive, exploitatious whims of the
various conquerors of Africa. It is, therefore, evidently among them
that the Barb must have been able to preserve all those qualities of
elegance, speed, and sobriety which universal agreement attributes
to him. Hence, we will concern ourselves solely with those horses of
that country and, in order to avoid repeating what anyone might
have read in books, we shall let the numerous Arabs whom we ques-
tioned speak for themselves.

Here is the description given by those Arabs of the pure-bred: the
chareb-er-rehh—drinker of the wind. The pure-bred is well proportioned; his ears are slender and mobile; his bones are heavy; his jaws
are lean; his nostrils are as wide as a lion's mouth; his eyes beautiful,
black, and prominent.[1] His neck is long; his breast is thrust forward;
his withers are prominent; his loins are thick and short; his haunches
are powerful; his ribs in front are long and those behind short; his
belly is lean; his rump is rounded; his testicles are close together and

---

[1] Slender and mobile ears, as well as prominent and lively eyes, according to
the Arabs, always proclaim that the heart is functioning well and that the animal
is energetic.

well let down; his forearms are long like those of an ostrich and as
well muscled as those of a camel; the veins of the legs are barely perceptible; the hoof is of a black, solid color; the hairs of the mane and
tail are thick and fine; his flesh is firm; and the tail is very thick at the
root and tapered at the end.

When seen from in front he looks like a high mountain peak; seen
from behind he seems to incline forward as if he were going to pros-
trate himself; seen from the side he looks strong and has a well-
balanced stance.

To sum up, he should have:

Four wide things—forehead, breast, croup, and legs.
Four long things—neck, forearms, belly, and haunches.
Four short things—loins, pasterns, ears, and tail.

The Arabs say that all these qualities in a good horse prove that he
is pure-bred and certain to be swift, as his conformation is like that
of a saluki, a pigeon, and a *mahari* (racing camel).[2]

The mare should take from:

The wild boar—its courage and the length of its head.
The gazelle—its gracefulness, its eyes, and its mouth.
The antelope—its playfulness and its intelligence.
The ostrich—its neck and its speed.
The viper—its short length of tail.

A pure-bred (*hôor*)[3] can be recognized moreover by other indications. Thus he cannot be made to eat barley from any nose bag other

---

[2] See my book, *Le Grand Désert*, which contains (page 125 and following),
lengthy details on the *mahara* (singular *mahari*). We will confine ourselves
here to transcribing what we have said of the general conformation of the *mahari*:

The *mahari* is much more refined in its conformation than an ordinary camel
(*djemel*); it has the elegant ears of the gazelle, the supple neck of the ostrich, the
lean belly of the saluki; its head is lean and pleasingly set on the neck; its eyes
are black, beautiful, and prominent. Its long, closed lips conceal its teeth well.
Its hump is small, but that part of its chest which should rest on the ground when
it kneels down is strong and protuberant. The dock of its tail is short. Its legs
are clean in the lower part, but well muscled from the hocks and knees to the
trunk. The soles of its feet are not wide or thick. Lastly, its mane is sparse on
the neck and its hair, always tawny, is as fine as that of the jerboa. In the desert
the *mahari* is to the baggage camel what, among us, the race horse is to the draft
horse.

[3] *Hôor*, written in the plural *harare*: probably this word, brought back from the
Crusades by our ancestors, is the etymology of *haras* [stud, in French].

than his own; he loves trees, verdure, shade, and running water to the point of whinnying joyfully when he sees them. Very seldom will he drink without first ruffling the water; and, if circumstances are such that he cannot stir the water with a forefoot, sometimes he will kneel and ruffle it with his muzzle. He constantly twitches his lips, his eyes rove ceaselessly, he pricks and lowers his ears alternately, and he turns his neck to right or left as if he wished to speak or ask some question. If, in addition to all these attributes, the animal possesses sobriety, whoever owns him may consider himself as having two wings.

Such a horse will never consent to cover his dam, his sister, or his daughter.

A certain great man had a magnificent stallion, son of a mare famous throughout the desert, and he wanted to use the stallion to cover his dam; but he could not succeed. The stallion would momentarily approach, only to suddenly retreat, horrified. To overcome this repugnance, one day it occurred to his owner to blindfold him and present the mare to him so well covered up that she would be unrecognizable. Then the stallion did cover the mare; but immediately afterwards the son recognized his dam and, filled with despair, stampeded and threw himself over a cliff. This tale, popular among the Arabs, seems to us to prove that among them exists the belief that incestuous matings necessarily lead to a degeneration of the breed.

It has been noted that a fast horse has his head very closely joined to the transversal apophysis of the atlas which is very protuberant. "He has horns," say the Arabs.

The blood lines which are held in the highest regard in the western part of the Algerian Sahara are three: the Hâymour, the Bou-Ghareb (father of the garrot), and the Merizigue.[4] Their offspring are widely disseminated through a great number of tribes: among whom we shall cite the Hamyâne, the Ouled-sidi-Cheikh, the Leghrouâte-Kuesal, the Oulad-Yagoub, the Makena, the Aâmoure, the Oulad-sidi-Nasseur, and even the Harares.[5] Anyone, according to his taste or according

[4] The foundation sire of this line is probably the gray horse Mirezigg whose pedigree and history are given in the Appendix. It will be noted that his son Jerry, imported into England in 1750 was also a gray. [Translator's note]

[5] All these tribes—the Hamyâne, the Ouled-sisi-Cheikh, the Leghrouâte-Kuesal, the Oulad-Yagoub, the Makena, the Aâmoure, the Oulad-sidi-Nasseur, and the Harares—are ennumerated, with lengthy details on their customs, history,

to the career he follows, comes to offer his mare to the descendants of one of these three types.

The Hâymour generally produce bays; the Bou-Ghareb, whites; and the Merizigue, grays. The Hâymour are the most sought after. They have beautiful conformation and excellent wind, and, consequently, are very swift. They are considered to be the fastest horses in the Sahara. They attain an advanced age without a blemish; they bring good luck, and only the most noble and wealthy families own them.

Next comes the Bou-Ghareb line, which produces taller animals. The Bou-Ghareb can gallop for a very long time without tiring, but they are not as swift as the Hâymour; like them, they remain healthy until well up in years.

Finally come the Merizigue, of less height and bottom than the others. They are solid animals, with good legs, and are very calm. They are sought after above all by simple horsemen who have long journeys to make and great fatigues to bear.

The Hâymour line is superior to all others; and Arabic imagination has not omitted to attribute a marvellous origin to it. Here is the legend concerning the origin of this line:

A certain chieftain owned a magnificent mare which was wounded on an ostrich hunt; it was feared that she would be permanently lamed. Her master, seeing that she did not heal and tired of having to take her with him every time he moved camp, yet being unable to bring himself to have her destroyed, abandoned her on the grazing grounds. Upon his return from a lengthy journey he remembered his mare and became uneasy as to what might have become of her; she was in excellent condition and about to foal. He took her with him, gave her the best of care, and soon found himself the owner of a colt whose equal could not be found in the entire desert. No tribe had passed, for a very long time, through the place where the mare had been left. The Arabs wish to believe that she had been covered by a wild ass, Hamar el-ouâhhch, and they named the colt Hâymour, meaning that he was one of the products of that sire.

In the central part of the Algerian Sahara, the Arbâa strongly prize the descendants of Rakeby. They have height and bottom. They are disseminated among the Aghrazelias, the Oulad Chayb, the Oulad-

---

and geographical location in my book, *Algerian Sahara*, "Western Part, Route from Algiers to Insalah [El Touât]" (See that work from page 209 to page 260).

Mokhtar, as well as the Oulad-Krelif. The majority are grays or brown bays. They easily endure hunger and thirst, and can, for several days in succession, make journeys of from twenty-five to thirty leagues without coming to any harm. The best specimens are to be found today in the family of the Seuffrân. Rakeby must have been brought from Morocco by the forebears of Sidi-Hamed-Ould-Tedjiny, the famous marabout of Aaïn-Mady.[6]

The Oulad-Naïl make use of the offspring of a famous stallion named El Biod (The White One), which in bygone days was owned by one of the offshoots of the Oulad-si-Mahmed family. This blood line is renowned for its sobriety and speed.

A good horse in the desert should make for five or six successive days journeys of from twenty-five to thirty leagues. Two days' rest, good feed, and he could begin anew.

With a horse that, upon reaching his stable, shakes himself, stales, paws with his forefeet, and whinnies upon his feed being brought, and then putting his muzzle in the nose bag begins eating by snatching three or four mouthfuls of the grain he is given, one should never have to delay one's journey.

Journeys in the Sahara are not ordinarily such long hauls, but, on the other hand, it is not unusual to see horses travel fifty or sixty leagues in twenty-four hours.

A tribe, warned that an enemy plans a foray against it, will send out *chouâfin* (scouts)[7] to observe the enemy's movements. These scouts are mounted on mares—"daughters of a Jew," so adroit and wily are they. These horsemen carry with them only one measure of barley each, the mount's night's feed. They ride at different paces in such a way as to save their mounts' strength, and they go into hiding some thirty leagues from the point of departure to spy out the land. If what they observe makes them fear that their homes are in imminent danger, they will return very hurriedly in order to warn the tribe to flee at once. In a contrary case, they will return unhurriedly and will reach their camp before the hour of the evening prayer, after having covered sometimes almost fifty or sixty leagues in twenty-four hours. In case of a flight on the following day, the horses are able to

---

[6] I have dealt with the subject of that town and of its marabout, Tedjiny, the enemy of Abd-el-Kader, in my book *The Algerian Sahara*.

[7] Singular, *chouaf* (seer), from the verb *chaf* (he has seen).

take part. When the mount of a scout dies while on one of these re-connaissance missions conducted for the good of the common cause, it is replaced at the expense of the entire tribe. On the subject of the great distances covered by desert-bred horses, one quotes facts which would appear to be fabulous were it not that the heroes of them are still living and were there not witnesses to confirm the tales. Here is one, among a thousand, which was related to me by a man of the Arbâa tribe.

I shall let him speak:

"I had arrived in the Tell with my father and members of our tribe to buy grain. It was under the Pasha Aly. The Arbâa had had some terrible encounters with the Turks, and as their interest at the moment made them feign a complete submission in order to obtain the forgetfulness of what had happened, they agreed that they would win over with silver the entourage of the pasha, and they would send to the pasha himself, not a mediocre horse, as was usual, but a beast of the greatest distinction. It was a misfortune; but it was God's will and there was nothing else to do but be resigned. The choice fell on a mare, the gray of pebbles in a river, known throughout the Sahara. She belonged to my father. He was told to hold himself in readiness to leave the following day to take her to Algiers. After the evening prayer my father, who took great care not to make any comments, sought me out and said: 'Ben-Zyan, do you feel like yourself today? Are you going to leave your father in this strait; are you going to be the cause of reddening his face?'

" 'Only your will is in me, sire,' I answered. 'Speak and if your orders are not carried out it will be because I am dead.'

" 'Listen. Those sons of sin want to appropriate my mare in order to ingratiate themselves wtih the sultan. You know—my gray mare that has always brought good luck to our camp, to my children, to my camels; my gray mare, she who was foaled the same day that your youngest brother was born. Speak! Are you going to allow them to thus disgrace my white beard? The jubilation and happiness of our family are in your hands. Mordjana [Coral], (that was the mare's name) has eaten her barley; if you are truly my son, sup, take your arms, and, as soon as night falls, flee far into the desert with the treasure that we all love.'

"Without saying a word, I kissed my father's hand, ate my supper, and departed from Berouaguia, happy to be able to prove my filial affection and laughing to think of the discomfiture of our sheiks in the morning.

"I travelled far, afraid of being pursued, but Mordjana was well up on the bit, and it was more a question of holding her back than of urging her on. The night was about two-thirds over, and I began to get sleepy and halted. I dismounted, took the reins and wound them around my wrist. I placed my rifle under my head and went to sleep, lying comfortably under one of those dwarf palms which are common in our land. At the end of an hour I awoke and saw that Mordjana had eaten all the palm fronds. We went on. Dawn found us in Souagui; the mare had lathered and dried three times, and I applied the spur. She drank at Sidi-bou-Zid, in the Ouad-Ettouyl, and I made my evening prayers in Leghrouat,[8] after I had given her a little bit of hay in order to make her wait patiently for the large nose bag of barley which was coming to her."

Si-ben-Zyan told me on finishing his story:

"Those marches are not for your horses or for you Christians, who go from Algiers to Blida, thirteen leagues, the distance between my nose and my ear, but think that you have accomplished a great feat."

That man had travelled eighty leagues in twenty-four hours; his mare had eaten nothing but the fronds of the dwarf palm under which he had slept; she had drunk but once, halfway on the journey; and he swore to me by the Head of the Prophet that he could have gone on the following day to spend the night in Ghardaia (forty-five leagues farther on) had his life been in danger. Si-ben-Zyan belongs to a family of marabouts of the tribe of Oulad-Salahh, an offshoot of the large Arbâa tribe; he comes frequently to Algiers and recounts this story to whoever wants to hear it, and, if need be, calls on witnesses to bear him out.

Another Arab, named Mohamed-ben-Mokhtar, had come to buy grain in the Tell after the harvest. His camp was in Ouad-Seghrouan and the Arab referred to was engaged in trade with those of the Tell,[9]

---

[8] Berouaguia is six leagues south of Médéah; Souagui thirty-one leagues from Berouaguia; Sidi-bou-Zid, twenty-five leagues farther on; and lastly, Leghrouat twenty-four leagues beyond that or, one hundred and seven leagues south of Algiers.

[9] The Tell is the granary of the Sahara: the master of the Tell holds the people of the Sahara with the grasp of famine. They are so conscious of this that they

when the bey, Bou-Mezrag (Father of the Lance), fell upon him with
a numerous body of cavalry, to punish certain fancied wrongs—such
being the pretext the Turks invent to use as an excuse for their rapine.
No sound had been made. The pillaging was thorough, and the horsemen of the *makhzen* indulged in all the usual atrocities incident to
such an occurrence. Mohamed-ben-Mokhtar swiftly mounted his
dark-bay mare, a magnificent animal, envied and known by everyone
in the Sahara, and, comprehending the gravity of the situation, decided to sacrifice his entire fortune for the sake of his three children.
He set one, four years old, on the pommel of the saddle, another, six
or seven, behind him hanging on to the cantle, and was going to take
the third in the hood of his burnoose when his wife stopped him, saying: "I shall not give him to you for any reason, for they would never
dare to kill a child at the breast. Go, and I shall keep him with me;
God will protect us." Mohamed-ben-Mokhtar departed at a gallop,
firing as he went. But, hard-pressed, he travelled all that day and the
following night; and the next day he reached Leghrouat, a safe place.
Soon thereafter he learned that his wife had been saved by some
friends that he had in the Tell. Mohamed-ben-Mokhtar and his wife
are still living; and their two sons, saved on horseback, are now
counted among the best horsemen in the tribe. Is there a more dra-
matic incident, an incident more worthy of the artist's brush, than
this one of a family saved by a horse in the midst of looting and fierce
combat?

And why do I seek to prove these facts? All the veteran officers of
the Department of Oran can relate how in 1837 a general gave great
importance to the obtaining of knowledge of the lie of the land in
Tlemcen and even lent his own horse to an Arab to carry out this mission. The latter left Chateau-Neuf[10] at four o'clock in the morning and
returned the following day at the same hour, after having covered
seventy leagues over terrain that was much rougher and more broken
than the desert.

One of the best and most dangerous horsemen of that tribe of the
Arbâa is, still, El-Arby-ben-Ouaregla. "His bullet never falls to the

---

frankly acknowledge it in a phrase that has passed into a proverb: "We cannot be
either Moslems, Jews, or Christians; we are forcibly the friends of our belly."

[10] A fort built by the Spaniards, residence of the general commanding the
province.

ground." He belongs to an offshoot of the Hadjadj, where he is as well known for his personal reputation as for an adventure that befell him in infancy. He was still a babe in arms; his father, Mohamed-ben-Dokha, also surprised by his enemies, stuffed him into his wide *habaya*,[11] secured him with the cummerbund, and then, while the family and herds fled, mounted on a mare that "brought tears to the eye," he brought up the rearguard, fighting the whole day, saved his fortune, and killed seven men.

Here is how the Arabs of the Sahara sum up a horse's perfection. He must be able to carry a man, his weapons, a change of clothing, provisions for both of them, and a banner, even on a windy day, drag a corpse if need be, and gallop all day without thinking of eating or drinking.

According to the Arabic belief, the horse lives for twenty to twenty-five years and the mare for twenty-five to thirty years; and, concerning the use which may be made of them, a proverb explains as follows:

"Seven years for my brother; then seven years for me; and seven years for my enemy." It follows then that from seven to fourteen years old a horse is better able to withstand the hardships of war.

Several times I was curious enough to ask the Arabs if they knew the origin of those horses in which they took such pride. They answered this question by pointing toward the East with a finger: "They come from the land of the first man, where they were created one or two days before him," and they add, in support of this belief: "God has said: 'I have created for man everything that exists on the earth; I give everything to Adam and his descendants; man shall be the noblest of beings and the horse the noblest among animals.' When a chieftain takes office, the camp is made ready for him to live in, the rugs upon which he is to sit are put in place for him, the food with which he is to satisfy his tastes is prepared and, above all, the horsemen who are to accompany him to execute his orders are appointed. Therefore, the horse must have been created before the coming of Adam."

The Noble Horse

Where are those noble horses
Whose dam never mates but with a noble horse?

---

[11] A kind of woolen chemise which the Arabs frequently wear.

The stirrup is their life; inaction, their death.
Oh, Father of horsemen! The ignorant are found everywhere;
But they are as rare as true friends,
And, when they die, one sees the saddle weep.

In the arena of bravery
May God bless the noble horse!
His breast is of steel and his flanks are of iron;
He loves not anything but rapine, glory, and combats;
He nourishes his master and his family,
And when he gallops, he humiliates the lightning.
He goes by, look; voilá, you see him shot off;
Women, do not begrudge him the milk of our she-camels.

What has happened to the time when I was wont to ride a
    "swimmer,"
With black eyes, wide nostrils,
Clean legs, and faithful heart?
He was a bird of prey,
And now life is nothing to me,
As the bridle is no longer in my hand.
I was young, I sought danger,
I laughed at the ravens of ill omen,
Distance always seemed very near to me,
And my tent overflowed with booty.

In summer, when sleep has given its nourishment to my body,
When the eye of day has dissipated the shadows of the night,
And when the heat bites all, even the rock,
The song of the turtle-dove fills me with desires.
In the midst of the branches of the palm which the least wind
    stirs,
On the frond which complains and sighs,
Passion devours her.
By my head! She awakens in me the ardors of days gone by.

Someone has said to me: "Ah! You still desire those who
    blacken their eyelids?"
And I have replied: "No. In my eyes nothing today equals my
    pure-bred horse.
With him I am proud; I hunt and increase my wealth.

With him I fight; and I protect the poor and the orphan.
With him I punish insults and terrify my rivals;
He neighs as the lion roars in the mountain;
He is an eagle who soars through the skies."

But, begone, memories of that world!
The most powerful has never carried anything but a winding-
sheet.
I am known to the drinker of the wind, night, and combats;
I am known to the saber, the clash, the pen, and the paper;
I am sharper than the lance, and I endure hunger like the wolf.

It is all the same, today I desire solitude:
Solitude, that is good fortune, so time has taught me.
No one will ever again see me seek a horse, or women, or the
court of an emir.

Observations of the Emir Abd-el-Kader

"Horses, although they belong to one family, form two different
species. The first is the Arabian breed and the other the *beradin*—like
cattle, which are one family but [which]are divided into various
branches, the first being that of cattle which are the better known and
the second being that of the buffaloes, differing in their agility and
weight, as the Arabian horses differ from the *beradin*. The camel
family is also one, yet it has various branches: The Arabic breed and
the *bakhati*.[12]

"If a colt has for a sire an Arabian stallion and for a dam an Arabian
mare, he is undisputedly noble, *hôor*.

"If he has for a sire an Arabian stallion and a *beradi* mare for a dam,
he is called a *hadjin*.

"If he has for a dam an Arabian mare and a *beradi* stallion for a sire,
one calls him *meghrif*, and he is inferior to the *hadjin*. One can see
from this that the most important role always belongs to the sire.

"According to us, if it is impossible to make a pure breed of a breed
where the blood is mixed, we recognize, on the contrary, that one can
always return to its original nobility a pure breed which has been im-
poverished, be it for lack of feed, be it because of heavy tasks unsuited

[12] A breed of Khorazan which has two humps and which is larger than the
other.

to the nature of a horse, be it because of lack of care—if, in a word, the degeneration does not have as its cause a mixture of blood.

"When there is no public knowledge, it is by test, by speed in conjunction with bottom, that the Arabs judge horses, in which they recognize nobility, the purity of blood; but conformation also reveals their qualities.

"A pure-bred horse is one that has:

> "Three things long. Three things short. Three things broad. And three things pure.
> "The three long things are: ears, neck, and fore legs.
> "The three short things are: dock, hind legs, and back.
> "The three broad things are: the forehead, the breast, and the croup.
> "The three pure things [solid things] are: the skin, the eyes, and the hoofs.

"He should have high withers, lean flanks without flesh. 'Is it that you perform high-speed gallops on horses high in the withers and lean in the flanks?'

"The tail should be very heavy at the root in order to fill the space between the buttocks. 'The tail resembles the bride's veil.'

"The eye of the horse should incline, appearing to regard his nose, like the eye of a man that squints. 'Like the lovely coquette who glances sideways from behind her veil, his gaze turned toward the corner of the eye pierces through the forelock which, like a veil, covers his forehead.'

"The ears—they resemble those of an antelope startled in the midst of his herd.

"The nostrils—wide. 'Each of his nostrils resembles the lion's den, wind comes out when he is panting.'

"The fetlocks—small. 'The fetlocks of their hindlegs are small and the muscles of the two sides of the limb are prominent (The internal and external parts of the pastern).'

"The forelock—thick. 'In time of fear mount a fleet mare whose forehead is covered with a thick forelock.'

"The cavities of the nostrils completely black; if they are partly black and partly white, the horse is of mediocre worth.

"The hoof—rounded. 'The hoof is like the slave's goblet.'

"The frogs—hard and dry. 'The frogs concealed under the hoofs reveal themselves when he lifts his feet and resemble, by reason of their hardness, the pits of dates which evade, without breaking, the blow of a hammer.'

"The ergots—thick. 'They have ergots which resemble the black feathers concealed under the wings of the eagle; like them, they become black in the heat of combat.'

"The hoof—hard. 'They walk on hooves as hard as the moss-covered stones in stagnant water.'

" 'When my horse gallops toward a goal, he causes a sound to be heard like that of fluttering wings, and his neigh resembles the melancholy voice of the nightingale.'

" 'His neck is long and graceful like that of the male ostrich. His ear is split in two and his black eye full of fire.'

" 'By reason of his elegance, he resembles an image painted in a palace, he is as majestic as the palace itself.'

"If upon stretching his head and neck to drink from a stream which flows at ground level the horse stands straight on his four legs, without bending one of his forefeet, you may be sure that he has perfect conformation, that all parts of his body are in harmony, and that he is pure-bred.

"Among the horses belonging to the tribes of the Sahara, those of the Ahmian, those of the Arbâa, those of the Oulad-Naïl and their kin, are those which endure thirst and hunger longest and best. They are the ones most inured to fatigue, the fastest in galloping, and the most suited for maintaining a gallop of several days on end without stopping, *greatly differing in this from the horses of the Tell.*

"There have been, in ancient days, many stallions whose renown has reached us. Among them Koura[13] of the Beni-Timim tribe and Aouadj (hollow-back) of the Beni-Hilal. The following anecdote is told about the latter. Someone asked his owner what extraordinary thing he could relate about his horse. He told the following story:

" 'Riding Aouadj, I was wandering over the desert one day when I felt a great thirst; luckily I saw a flight of *ketâa*[14] on its way to a spring. I followed it and, even with reining my horse in as much as possible, I reached the watering place at the same time as the *ketâa*, without having stopped for a moment on the way.' This is a most ex-

---

[13] *Koura*: a popular ball game among the Arabs. [Translator's note]
[14] *Ketâa*: the desert partridge. [Translator's note]

traordinary example of speed, for the flight of *ketâa,* ordinarily very swift, is even swifter when they are on their way to water, driven by thirst. The owner of Aouadj added: 'Had I not rated my horse's speed, I would have out-distanced the *ketâa.*'

"Here is the origin of the name of that stallion: he was very young when his master was attacked by enemies and forced to flee. Thus, as the little creature could not keep up alone, he was put in a sack and loaded on the back of a beast of burden. As a consequence he got a curvature of the spine and was named Aouadj.

"Another celebrated stallion . . ." Here the Emir relates the origin of the Hâymour line and adds: "Whoever has seen horses of that breed does not doubt for an instant the truth of that story, for their resemblances to the zebra leap to the eye."

6

THE SUBJECT OF STALLIONS AND MARES

A gold jewel cannot be made
except from gold.

THE ARABS ASSERT that the most suitable age for breeding is four to twelve years in the case of mares and six to fourteen years in the case of stallions. As a matter of fact, only wealthy men observe this rule; but others, forced by necessity or by a misunderstood cupidity, depart from it with too much frequency. The Arabs prove to be difficult in the choice of a stallion to cover a mare. The latter should be well bred, fleet, tall, healthy, graceful, have an ample barrel and wide pelvis. It is not unusual to hear the Arabs say: "Choose and choose yet again the sire, for the product will always resemble the sire more than the dam. Always bear in mind that the mare is nothing more than a sack from which one will extract gold, if one puts in gold, and will extract only copper, if one puts in only copper."[1]

---

[1] "Choose and choose, yet again," etc.: Thinking that this Arabic principle would find many contradictors, I wanted to know the opinion of the man who is considered to be one of the most skilful horsemen of his race and I addressed myself to the Emir Abd-el-Kader himself, who told me:
The nobility of the sire is the more important. The Arabs very much prefer the offspring of a pure-bred stallion and common mare, to the product of a pure-bred mare and a common stallion. They consider that the dam transmits less to the product. She is, they say, a coffer which can be filled and emptied without transmuting what is put into it. Regardless of anything else, if a pure-bred is bred to a pure-bred, without a doubt, the product will be pure gold.

They do not see any drawback to the stallion's being of less height than the mare, provided that he is pure-bred and has perfect conformation.[2] They always place the qualities of bottom, speed, and sobriety ahead of that conventional beauty which never fails to seduce us. Thus, a fat, sleek, and rounded stallion, who owes his loveliness only to too much food, laziness, or inaction greatly arouses their suspicions. They say of him: "Let us not be in a hurry; let us see what he can do. Perhaps it is a question of his wearing a lion's skin over a cow's frame." On the other hand, the Arabs consider an ideal stallion to be one that has a long pedigree, whose flesh is firm, who has bare ribs, clean legs, and powerful respiration, when he has been endowed with a good temper and if he has proved that he has great powers of resistance to weariness, hardship, and the rigors of climate. As far as the mare is concerned, judgment has been pending for centuries. Today, as in former times, one takes pleasure in describing an Arab at the side of his mare. The gold to buy her gleams at his feet, but while that gold is being counted in order to pay it to him, the son of Ishmael casts a melancholy glance at the noble animal from which he cannot bear to part, springs on her back, and dashes off into the desert, where the eye cannot follow where he went. This is the accustomed picture and here is the truth, according to the Emir Abd-el-Kader: "It is true that the Arabs prefer mares to stallions, but only for the following three reasons. The first one is that they take into account what the mare can produce, which is one of the weightiest, for one has seen Arabs make up to fifteen or twenty thousand duros (seventy-five or one hundred thousand francs) from the product of one mare. One frequently hears them exclaim: 'The fountainhead of all wealth is a mare who foals a filly!' and this thought is borne out among them by the Prophet, he who was sent by God, who said: 'Prefer mares: their bellies are a treasure and their backs seats of honor.'

" 'The greatest of all blessings is an intelligent woman or a prolific mare.'

"These words are thus explained by them as follows: 'Her belly is a treasure because the mare with her product augments the wealth of

---

[2] "The Arabs of Nedj prefer to have their mares covered by an ugly, well-bred stallion to having them covered by a beautiful stallion of less pure lineage. They assert that the product of the former will continually improve, while the descendants of the latter cannot help but get worse and worse" ("Journey in Upper Asia," by Monsieur Pétiniaud, Inspector General of Studs; unpublished work).

her owner and the back of the animal is a seat of honor, for riding a mare is more agreeable and easier.' It is even supposed that because of the smoothness of her paces she can eventually cause her rider to become flabby and out of condition.

"The second reason is that mares do not whinny in combat. They are less sensitive than the stallion to hunger, thirst, or heat; and therefore they render more services to a people whose wealth consists principally of herds of camels and flocks of sheep. Everyone knows that sheep and camels do not really thrive except in the Sahara, where the terrain is so arid that many Arabs, not being able to drink water more often than every eight or ten days, content themselves with drinking milk. That is one result of the long distance which, because of grazing grounds, frequently separates the camps from the places where there are wells.

"The mare is like the snake. Her strength increases in times of heat and in torrid localities. The serpent that lives in a cold climate or in the water has little courage and venom, so that its bite is seldom fatal, whereas the serpent living in a warm climate is livelier and there also the strength of the venom increases. This is contrary to the stallion, who does not endure heat as well as the mare—whose energy, undoubtedly due to her constitution, redoubles the hotter it becomes.

"The third reason is the very little care that a mare requires; she can be fed on very little, and her owner can send her out to graze with the sheep and camels without having to keep constant watch over her. The stallion, however, must be better fed and his master cannot send him out to pasture wtihout a groom, for if he saw a mare he would follow her."

Those are the real reasons for the preference which the Arabs have for the mare, and this preference is not then based on the fact that the foal derives more from its dam than from its sire. It does not stem from the fact that it is better, in every place and on all occasions, to ride a mare sooner than a stallion; but is based on one side on material interests and on the other on the necessities imposed by the kind of life the Arabs lead.

It is necessary then to proclaim that the stallion is more noble than the mare and that the sire gives more to the foal than does the dam, which the Arabs explain by saying: "The foal takes after the sire." I agree that the best product is that from a pure-bred sire and dam; in that case it is gold allied to gold. I shall add that the stallion is stronger, braver, and swifter in a breakneck gallop; and he does not have the serious drawback of the mare who will stop dead, even in the midst of a fight, when her rider has the most imperative need to gallop. This happens when she is in season and she sees a stallion.

The foal, of course, comes from the sire and dam. But the experience of centuries has shown that the principal parts of its body—such as the bones, tendons, nerves, and veins—always come from the sire. There is no doubt at all, as even the least of the Arabs knows, that all inherent diseases of the bones, tendons, nerves, and veins, which were present in the sire at the time of mating, will be perpetuated in the product, after some time has passed. I shall cite principally the splints, blood spavins, curb, swellings, and el aâder, an unknown or disputed malady in Europe.

The dam can pass on to the foal her color, her looks, and some of her build. It is natural that the foal should have some of her who, for so long, carried him in her belly. But it is indisputable that it is the sire who gives him the strength of the bones, the vigor of the nerves, the solidity of the tendons, speed, and, on the whole, all principal attributes. Furthermore, he passes on his moral attributes; and, if he be truly noble, he will preserve the foal from all vice. The old Arabs say: "A noble horse has no malice." No matter to whom it may be, custom demands of all Arabs that they lend their stallions when requested to do so for stud.

This is to say that all stallions of good conformation are inevitably used for breeding. It turns out that if the stallions are of varying quality, this disadvantage is compensated for by the preservation of their vigor. In effect, stud service is spread among a great number. A stallion, never being given more than five or six mares to serve in a season, does not, therefore, know what exhaustion means. The master of a great tent very seldom permits his favorite stallion to cover more than two mares: to wit, one which has just foaled and one which is being bred for the first time. This, the Arabs believe, is the way to preserve the health of their stallions and not ruin them before their time. Thanks to this system the manes grow thick, the coats become sleek, and the stallions are livelier.

The owner of a beautiful mare is, therefore, less apprehensive about approaching the owner of a stallion with a great reputation for, as has been said, the owner of the stallion finds difficulty in evading such a request.

The common people say to their chieftain: "Lord, for the love of God, lend us your stallion for stud, because that can do no less than increase your *goum*.[3] We are masters-at-arms, feathers of your wings, and tomorrow my brother, my son, or I might die for you." However, the chieftain is adamant about receiving these protestations of devotion and refuses. The supplicant does not become downcast, however. He is not requesting a favor, he is almost asking for alms. He presents his saddle, reversed; misery is great for him; he does not even have the resources which make a warrior. That is not enough and the chieftain remains adamant. From making the claim of a comrade-in-arms, the supplicant descends to the humble supplication of the woman, of a slave. He enters the tent, takes the mortar in which the grain is ground, and then he sets himself to grinding a bit of flour, thus indicating limitless obedience to the wishes of the protector, feminine subservience to all his desires. How can one deny a woman, a poor slave who makes himself yours? The great man relents at last and, in exchange for that absolute self-denial, lends his stallion for stud.

Between equals this act of compliance is paid for, according to the custom of the tribe, with a large nose bag of barley, a sheep, or a large jug of milk. It would be a shameful thing to offer or accept money, for then they would be called pimps in a stallion's love affairs. The custom of lending a stallion for stud is not always without limits or conditions. The owner of a beautiful stallion can refuse when an inferior mare is presented or if he has already permitted the number of services he had mentally reserved. The owner of the stallion will then, however, explain his refusal by means of sincere words: "You are my friend, I could not ask for a better and I would give you my children; but I warn you that my stallion is as my own throat. Should you ruin him, who would save my camels and my family when danger threatened?"

I heard, one day when I was staying with a certain tribe, a conversation between two Arabs of more or less equal rank. I set it down here because it shows very clearly how much it displeases them to have to lend a stallion to cover an inferior mare.

"Why do you refuse me your stallion when you lend him to others in the tribe?"

"Because your mare has bad conformation and lacks breeding."

---

[3] *Goum*: a troop of horsemen of a tribe or a fraction of a tribe armed for war.

"I see that very well, but after all what harm would it do to your stallion?"

"What harm! Simply this: the mare would drop a bad foal and my stallion would lose his good name. It would be said everywhere that his get has neither blood nor quality."

"Those are excuses. Do we not all know that the foal is the exact image of his sire?"

"That is true, but he derives a great deal from his dam. Our forebears said: 'Do not sow grain except in good earth and, moreover, never put honey into a jug made of dog hide.'"

He continued: "When the beautiful is mated to the ugly the result is a peacock. When the ugly is mated to the ugly the result is a snail. But when the beautiful is mated to the beautiful, the result is pure gold. Friend, you can understand that. Therefore, I cannot agree to what you ask. Walk with good and may God protect you."

Turning to another aspect, never would an Arabic chieftain in the Sahara consent to giving his mare to an ass in order to obtain a mule. From the following tale, one can gather how abhorrent such a proceeding would be:

Abou-Zeïd of the Hilal tribe devoted himself to the breeding of pure-bred horses. God gave him a son whom he named Ben-Djaber and whom he taught to read and write. When the boy reached manhood, God caused him to fall in love with the beautiful Aycha (Life), daughter of El-Koryssi. The families were in mutual agreement and the marriage took place. As soon as the wedding feast was over, the father said to his son: "Oh, my son! Listen to my advice and follow my recommendations. Love horses, weapons, and the chase. With horses you can acquire wealth and well-being, and raise yourself in dignity; with weapons you can banish evil and guard yourself against the perversity of men. In the chase, you will learn the arts of war, improve your health, and dissipate ill humor."

Ben-Djaber bowed respectfully and promised to obey.

Later on, when the father observed that his son had a real passion for horses, he decided to put him to the test.

He sent for him anew and said:

"Oh, my son! Take your pure-bred mare Naâma (Ostrich) and have her covered by the ass belonging to So-and-So. It is an Egyptian ass. He will get a good mule or a lovely mare-mule and you know that the merchants call those animals 'the wealth-getters'."

"Yes, my lord," answered Ben-Djaber. "I shall obey your orders."

He left his father's presence astounded, thinking that either his father had entered upon his dotage or that perhaps he wanted to test him somehow.

"How can I allow that pearl among mares to be covered by an ass? That is impossible."

He became highly agitated and determined to resist. He took Naâma to a neighboring tribe where he had her bred to a stallion famous in the locality, named Ghrezal. A few days later Abou-Zeïd asked him if he had had Naâma covered by the ass and the son answered:

"Oh father mine! You are the knife and I am the flesh, yet I could not bring myself to do your bidding. It would have been to throw into degradation the purest thing in the world. Can the daughters of princes marry slaves? The slave is not the equal of a free man. To elevate a man of low degree, I would never break the line of a noble race."

"You have disobeyed me," answered the father. "Do you not know then that obedience to parental authority is one of the wide roads to Heaven?"

"That is true," answered Ben-Djaber. "But listen to me and do me justice. I had the gazelle among horses bred to the ostrich among mares. An animal of unrivalled beauty, precious as the diamond enclosed in a box made of rubies. I brought about the conjunction of the sun with the moon. What a marvellous being will be created in her bosom;[4] a pearl will be formed like the pearl created by the oyster. It will be a treasure protected by a talisman. Had I mated Naâma to the ass the result would have been a common and sterile animal which would have been a disgrace to us all and the degradation of a being as noble as she is generous."

His words gave Abou-Zeïd the liveliest of satisfaction.

"May God bless you, my beloved son. I only wanted to test you, and I see, with pride, that you are a link forged out of the purest gold."

Now I return to the difficulties which one experiences in obtaining a sire whose qualities are known. When an Arab has had his request refused, not just for that reason will he accept the first horse he finds.

---

[4] It is an Arab that speaks.

There are vices, blemishes, or hereditary diseases that are a constant cause for disqualification. He would not give his mare, for example, to a restive or vicious stallion. He would also be very careful not to present her to a broken-winded stallion or one that had a curb, a swelling, a curvature, a splint close to the vein, or to one with defective vision. These defects would reappear in the product. He would not want a stallion with spots around his eyes, in his nostrils, or on his testicles; or a bald-faced stallion with four white feet, no matter what the color of the rest of his coat; or a pied; or an isabelle with a flaxen mane and tail, which he terms Jew's yellow.

Too old a stallion would also be rejected. If an Arab does not trust his knowledge with respect to determining age, after having carefully examined the condition of the legs of the animal, he never fails to pinch the skin on the forehead, drawing it tightly toward him. If it springs back without leaving a trace of his fingers, he accepts the animal. If it is to the contrary, he will reject the animal as being too old or too soft.

The mare is given to the stallion in the first days of spring, so that the foal will have at least two seasons ahead of him to acquire the hardiness which will permit him to endure the rigors of winter.

It can be seen that the mare is in season when she urinates upon hearing the stallion neigh; when she secretes a white substance and immediately lowers and turns her head to hear if he is approaching.

Before giving the mare to the stallion it is a good idea to reduce her feed and on the eve of her being bred not to give her any feed at all. She will conceive better and faster in this manner. In case of its being necessary to get the mare ready, she should be sent out to graze with an ardent little teaser who, by playing with her, biting her, and exciting her, will warm her up and get her prepared.

The mare should be taken to the stallion on a Friday; that day being the Moslem Sunday. It brings good luck.

Whether it is because of modesty or whether it is in order not to distract the stallion, the mating takes place far from the camp. The mare is placed on an incline. The stallion wears a halter with a lunging rein. One man pulls the mare's tail to one side while the other directs the stallion's member.

The Arabs prefer a supervised mating to one that takes place in liberty, due to the accidents that may happen during the latter. Actually, it is not a rare occurrence that the stallion places his member between the mare's buttocks and is injured; it also happens that sometimes he introduces it into the rectum and causes the death of the mare. Moreover, the stallion wears himself out with mating at liberty.

The mating takes place in the morning, to avoid the heat, and never when the air is full of those big flies which the Arabs call *debabe*. They upset the animal, stinging until they draw blood. It is believed that they deposit eggs in the epidermis—eggs which would not appear to cause any trouble, but which will cause death with the first cold weather or when the snow begins to fall.

At the moment of presenting the stallion make him walk around the mare, permitting him to sense her. Then when he is ready remove him and only let him mount after you have seen him secrete a whitish, watery liquid; unless this is done, he will ejaculate on touching the mare. After mating has taken place, if possible, the stallion should be washed off and given a good nose bag of barley. The mare will be quietly walked about after she has been slapped three or four times with the flat of the hand under the flanks.

Some believe that an application of henna[5] on the loins or on the abdominal walls is an aid to conception.

An infertile stallion is one that has his member curved, or too short, so that it cannot reach the neck of the mare's uterus; or a stallion that produces liquid sperm, not very white and without consistency. The Arabs, to assure themselves on this point, warm up the stallion with a mare until they have convinced themselves.

It is known that the mare has conceived when, after mating, she turns her head to see her flanks. And there cannot be any doubt, if, after seven days, upon being presented to a stallion she hugs her tail and rejects his advances to the point of kicking, or if she no longer

---

[5] *Henna*: what the Arabs call henna is the *Lawsonia inermis* of the naturalists. It is a pretty shrub with beautiful, glossy green leaves which bears a great resemblance to the privet and grows to the height of three or four meters.

The leaves are a great article of commerce. They are harvested in the month of July, dried in the sun and then ground into a very fine powder. The natives, especially the women, make use of it to tint their nails, the tips of the fingers, the palms of the hands, the toes, and the hair. It is used to tint the manes, backs, and legs of horses, particularly if they have light coats.

In Arabic medicine henna is used for bruises, wounds, swellings, abcesses, *etc.*, to harden the parts or recent scars. It is also used on the mucous membranes, in the mouth against toothaches, *etc.*, and to avoid too great perspiration from some part of the body.

secretes that whitish liquid which she did upon the approach of a stallion or upon hearing him neigh.

The Arabs believe that excess weight is a barrier to conception and that is why they thin down their mares, as much by gradually and sensibly reducing their feed, as by exercise, before taking them to the stallion.

When a mare does not wish to conceive, they give her a hard, fast gallop and then present her to the stallion, lathered and winded, with her forefeet in a stream. If it is presumed that she might be sterile, it would then be necessary to give her to a tall jack. She would then foal a mule and become good for breeding.

Among some desert tribes renowned for their experience in equestrian matters, the following method is frequently used: two stallions are placed relatively far apart (but within seeing distance of each other)—at two kilometers, for example—thus arousing their jealousy and increasing their desire. This done, and the mare lathered as has previously been explained, she is presented to the first stallion. Once he has mounted her, she is then taken to the other stallion and then given a short canter, her rider at the same time yelling at the top of his lungs: "A foal, a foal, if God is willing." By yelling thus, the rider follows the words of the Prophet, who recommended that upon making a wish, one should speak words of good omen. Furthermore, this being an important point, the mare is prevented from urinating and thus expelling the semen that she has received.

The Arabs have, moreover, other means of combating sterility. A man smears his arm with butter, soap, or oil; introduces it into the mare's vulva; and, upon reaching the neck of the uterus, with great care opens it slightly by means of a date which he holds in his outstretched fingers, and ends up by introducing his whole hand. Then, as soon as he takes his arm away, the mare is presented to the stallion and the mare conceives because she was only "knotted." This operation requires great skill, and he who practices it should cut his nails very carefully. Is it not singular that the Arabs have made such a valuable discovery for our knowledge and science?

Three other procedures practiced in some localities have a great similarity among them, without being precisely identical. The first consists of entering the vulva, as we have said, and half opening the neck of the uterus leaving a lead bullet in place. The mare will conceive, but the bullet will be found in the foal.

According to others it is necessary to take the leaves of a plant called *lema,* squeeze them with the fingers in order to obtain the juice which drips onto a piece of unprocessed wool and the whole thing is then bound together with a piece of date and deposited in the uterus. This plant is found in the Sersou plateau.

Finally, some use tar or unprocessed wool and a white substance like curdled milk, found in the stomachs of young kids, gazelles, or lambs.

These methods, which are in use everywhere among the Arabs, as much in the Tell as in the Sahara, are of too constant and general application for their success not to have contributed to their dissemination.

Superstition makes the Arabs believe that the mare will not conceive except on the same day of the week on which her dam was foaled. This idea, without being universally prevalent, is sufficiently believed in to cause a great number of families to note the date in order to choose it later when the mare is to be bred.

When the mare has conceived, she is removed from the stallion with great care, for another stallion on tormenting her could spoil the foetus and perhaps even provoke an abortion. Care is also taken not to overwork the mare and she is not made to carry heavy loads during the first two months after conception. However, after the first two months are over one may again make use of her for war or for the chase, increasing her feed. During the last sixty days before foaling, she is left alone and wealthy families do not ride her again during that period.

Finally, when she nears her time, care is redoubled; she is blanketed at night; feed is carefully chosen, and never is barley given to other animals in her presence unless she is given some also. It would be a cause of abortion almost as infallible as thirst, should one allow her to suffer from the latter during gestation.

The mare that aborts becomes the object of the greatest care; she is blanketed night and day; fumigations are made with *chiehh;*[6] lastly, she is given a potion made of the finest wheat flour and cummin diluted in warm oil.

[6] *Chiehh*: a small shrub (*Artemisia judaïca*) which barely grows to a height of fifty centimeters and which covers immense stretches within the limits of the Tell and the Sahara. It is ordinarily called small absinthe, absinthe du Pont. [It is more than likely a variety of sage-brush.]

The Arabs believe that they have noted that when the mare is in foal with a colt, her rump gets considerably thinner.

The mare is very close to foaling when her teats swell and drip milk. "She has sprung the nails." Then her feed is gradually reduced so that she will lose a little weight, which helps the birth. Care is taken not to send her out to pasture very early. She is not sent out until the sun has dried the grass because experience has shown that the dew can cause great disturbances and even provoke an abortion. During the final days of gestation, the mare is kept well blanketed and care is taken to avoid accidents.

When the mare foals, the Arabic woman helps to receive the foal and takes every imaginable precaution on the spot so that the wind cannot chill dam or foal. If the new-born, upon arriving in the world, instead of shaking itself, seems on the contrary to be weak and drowsy, all rejoice, for it is an indication that the foal will have great qualities. God has sent him drunk; that is a good sign. His mouth is blown into to remove the foam; he is made to swallow one or two fresh eggs which help to keep him going until he can, or learns to, nurse. On the following day he is given a draught made of gum tragacanth, *tertar*, and red pepper, the whole mixed together and dissolved in hot butter—which is a good purge.

During the first eight days the foal's neck, ears, breast, and legs are rubbed, with a view to correcting such defects of conformation as can be noted by means of a massage as gentle as it is skilful. In certain tribes, in order to ensure a foal's having hard hoofs, the soles, coronets, and walls of the hoofs are rubbed with salt dissolved in a preparation of *bou-nafâa*.[7]

But let us return to the mare. As soon as she has foaled she is blanketed with care. The wealthy keep her in the tent and make her drink milk in which rancid butter called *dehane* has been melted. She is given a small portion of still-warm parched barley which alleviates her fatigue and replenishes her. Then a form of bandage, stuffed with wool, is put on her back, the belly is bound up, lapping it with four or five turns of a piece of cloth, wide enough not to cause discomfort. As a complement to this procedure, the mare is not allowed to drink for

---

[7] *Bou-nafâa*, father of usefulness, is an umbelliferous plant of the genus *Thapsia* [Meadow-parsnip and allied generea]. The Arabs make great use of it. They use it as a purgative, to fatten, as a remedy for sterility, and especially to cure certain blemishes or certain maladies of their horses.

two days after foaling, and then is given boiled water, a little at a time. The object is to try to get her organs, which were greatly distended during gestation, back to their normal state by means of dryness and constriction.

It is known, moreover, that the mare that foals when the grass is abundant and juicy does not have a great desire to drink. The padding and the bandages are left on for seven days and seven nights. These are called the Days of Waiting. As long as they last, care must be taken not to bother or frighten the mare.

After the foaling, which takes place in early spring, the greatest care is exercised in removing the placenta without breaking it, for if it were to break it could cause death. A watch is kept to prevent the mare from eating the placenta, which would do her great harm.

Many Arabs perforate the placenta in various places with a needle, especially if it is the first time that the mare has foaled. After this operation it is supposed that the mare will produce nothing but fillies. This belief proves, at least, the preference of the people in the Sahara for mares. Others believe that by hiding the placenta the same result can be obtained as by perforating it; and they hide it where it cannot be found or eaten by dogs or jackals.

The foal has seen the light of day; suddenly one of the helpers seizes it in his arms and walks about with it for a while, in the midst of the clamor and noise which everyone makes. In all the foregoing a good lesson for the future can be seen, for an animal accustomed to lots of noise from the moment it is born, will not be easily startled later. This lesson over, the lord of the camp places the right teat of the mare in the foal's mouth and proclaims: "In the Name of God. Great God, cause this new-born to be fortunate for us and to bring us abundance and health," and all those present say in unison: "Amen. May God bless you. This foal is one more son that He has sent you."[8]

To teach the foal to nurse, a fig or date soaked in lightly salted milk is put in its mouth and as soon as it has got the taste and begins

[8] "Among the Arabs of Upper Asia, but particularly in the Nedj, when a filly is foaled one cannot imagine the joy that animates the family: 'God has sent us a blessing. Our Lord Mohammed has entered our home.' Neither women nor children are permitted to hold back one drop of the milk which the camels, goats, and sheep might give. Everything is reserved for the fortunate filly, object of the love and most tender care of the inhabitants of the tent." ("Journey in Upper Asia," by M. Pétiniaud)

to suck, it is then placed under the mare. After a few tries it assumes the mare's teat to be the date or fig which it has just left. The foal is well blanketed against the chill of the night.

It is also necessary to accustom the foal to drink ewe's or camel's milk. Here is the method used: a goatskin which has held milk for several years is filled with air and gently presented to the foal. Pressing it lightly, one blows the air many times into the foal's nostrils. As a complement to this move, some dates are mashed in milk, which sweeten it. Then this mixture is placed under the foal's mouth and he is made to wet his lips with it. First he feels the mixture, then he savors it, and he does not take long to learn to drink, whether his dam gives him milk or not.

Great importance is attached to teaching a foal to drink milk, because then it can be left in the tent while its dam is used for other things, and also because later, due to lack of water, it will take milk as a drink and also as food when there is no barley.

If the mare takes a dislike to her little one the foal must be taken away from her and fed on camel's milk, which is better than that of either cows or goats, whose milk causes flabbiness and indigestion.

Some days or some months after the birth of the foal, some Arabs split one or both of its ears. There are many legends concerning this practice. Some say that it is solely practiced on foals born during the night because they must have better eyesight than those who arrive in the world during the day. Others say it is done to the foals born on a Friday, the day for the Moslems to congregate in the Mosque, because it is a good omen. Here is the truth:

The master of a tent has a son of tender age, whom he loves dearly and on splitting the ear of the foal he states that he is reserving the animal for his son. Should he die, no one would have the right to dispute the property thus marked for the child.

Others split the foal's ears when it has colics and such a bloodletting saves it.

Shortly after the birth of the foal some amulets or talismans made of small shells called *oudaâ*, and enriched by wealthy people, are hung around its neck. They are hung from collars of wool or camel's hair (*goulada*), which the women take pleasure in making themselves, always combining the colors with good taste. Bay or black horses are given white *gouladas*. All light-colored horses are given red *gouladas*. Such a collar is more than an ornament, for it can be used to restrain the foal if necessary, taking the place of our halter in a form more pleasing to the eye and less galling for the animal.

With respect to the talismans—they are simply little bags made of morocco leather, more or less ornamental, which contain words taken from holy books, by means of which it is hoped that the animal will be kept safe from wounds, diseases, and the Evil eye.

Sometimes, in time of war, a new-born foal is destroyed so that the dam may be used. A filly is never destroyed.[9] She is weaned. She is left in the tent to spare her from the sun, and frequently the women help to save her by giving her ewe's or camel's milk. If a filly is foaled during the course of a journey undertaken for purposes of trade or war, in order to spare her the fatigues of the journey care is taken of her to the point of placing her on the back of a camel, making a kind of nest as soft as possible for her; she can only nurse during halts and at night. I saw, during the expedition of Taguedempt in 1841, a horseman of the *makhzen* without any means of transport, carry in front of him on the saddle for the first four days after she had been foaled a filly which the said horseman's mare had foaled in bivouac. After that period of time, the filly followed her dam very well and did so throughout the entire campaign.

When the colts are not destroyed they are generally sold in the Tell at the time of the buying of stocks of grain, while the fillies are kept, as they might become a source of wealth through reproduction.

The owners of fine mares also at times destroy colts at birth for the sole purpose of not tiring the mare. When they take this step, they do not forget to have her milked by the women until she dries up. They then give the mare to the stallion seven days after she has foaled, plus one more time, twenty days later, if she has not conceived.

Only poor people who depend on the profits from breeding take their mares to be bred immediately after foaling. Wealthy people do not, for they have the idea that such a procedure would only result in

[9] "One never destroys a filly." Here one might be tempted perhaps to say to me: "But wait, you are contradicting yourself; for if the Arabs never destroy a filly it is evident that they attach a higher value to their mares than to their stallions." I repeat: In the desert, one prefers mares to stallions, *not* because one attributes to them the larger role in reproduction, but simply because they are calmer. They endure heat and thirst better, they can stale without stopping on gallops when life is at stake, they do not betray their riders by whinnies during risky enterprises, and, lastly, because their products increase the wealth of their owners.

weak and ill-formed animals. Ordinarily they give the mares a year or even two years of rest. Nevertheless, if a mare were to get in foal by chance and it was noted that the foal was not thriving, it would be necessary to wean it at once and continue to give it ewe's or camel's milk until it gained strength enough to survive. There have been cases of a filly of eighteen months or two years old, running loose in a pasture, getting in foal contrary to her owner's wishes. If she were to foal the Arabs would keep her two or three years without breeding her. The Arabs call the product thus foaled *guetita* (kitten) and they allege to have noticed that, although such a product is always weakly built, it has a remarkable turn of speed.

While the mare is still nursing a foal, if one has been obliged to gallop her very fast, she must be prevented from giving suck as soon as she reaches camp. Her milk under such conditions would cause in the foal a disease called *serba,* whose symptoms are inflammation of the anus and worms which come out of it. The Arabs cure this disease by giving the foal in its nose bag, in the place of barley, wheat which has been boiled, dried in the sun, and impregnated with butter. If the foal is healthy, the Arabs give it ground barley.

The greater the worth of the mare, the shorter the period of nursing, weaning usually taking place in the sixth to seventh month.

To wean the foal, first he is taken from his dam for one whole day, then two, and so on. So that the change will not be too brusque for him he will be given camel's milk sweetened with date honey, and to prevent him from going to seek his dam, his hind legs or forefeet will be tied with woolen cords, but in either case, always above the knees or hocks. That is the origin of the white marks which are frequently to be seen. If, at that age, he were to be hobbled by the pasterns, grave consequences would ensue. The foal would never be quiet; and since he would not know how to resign himself to the position in which he found himself, that which the Arabs call *louzze* (sidebone) would not be long in appearing.

Redoubled vigilance is kept over the foal which is being weaned. If he were to get loose and nurse, he would fall ill from sucking bitter and curdled milk and he would get *serba,* the disease we have already mentioned. During the day when the mare is making a journey, or is grazing, the weanling is equipped with a form of halter whose noseband is provided with porcupine quills, and then his dam herself refuses to let her little one nurse.

Once the foal is weaned it is necessary, in order to avoid an accu-mulation of milk, to milk the mare and reduce her feed. After wean-ing, the foal continues to be given ground barley in larger quantities, but gradually in order not to satiate him. A wooden measure called a *feutra* is used. This measure represents three cupped handfuls and is used by all tribes throughout the desert because its origin has a religious significance. The Prophet commanded all wealthy Moslems that after the feast celebrated after Ramadan, all the poor be given a *feutra* of food each: wheat, barley, dates, rice, etc., according to the products of the region in which they found themselves.

As soon as the foal is weaned the women take him over, saying: "He belongs to us; he is an orphan, and we are going to make his life as sweet as possible."

Observations of the Emir Abd-el-Kader

"The foal resembles the stallion; the mare is a coffer, closed with a padlock, and what you put in you will take out as it was.

"The best product is that born of sires and dams, both of which are pure-breds.

"The product of an Arabian sire and a foreign dam is less appreci-ated, but well below such a product comes the product of an ill-bred stallion and a pure-bred mare.

"Finally, the product of parents, both of which are of a foreign breed, does not have one good attribute.

"An Arab will leave his mare unbred for two or three years rather than permit her to be bred to a common stallion. To find a good stal-lion he does not hesitate when faced with the prospect of making a long journey.

"There are Arabs who close the vulva of the mare by means of a form of padlock to prevent her from being covered by surprise by some ill-bred animal. In case this accident has occurred the Arab immediately washes out the vagina with certain drugs, putting his hand into the uterus to destroy the stallion's semen.

"The Arab lends his stallion for stud without charge and he never charges a stud fee notwithstanding the fact that it is permitted by law to do so. Custom forbids this traffic which is entirely contrary to the generosity which characterizes the Arab and for which he is justly renowned. Although the Arab lends his stallion without charge, he does not necessarily lend him to the first person who requests the animal's services. Frequently the asker finds himself obliged to resort to the intercession of worthy people or of his wives.

"The stallion used under saddle should not mount more than five or eight times at the most.

"Mating should take place in the spring, otherwise the foal will be a weakling.

"The Arabs say that a stallion has more vigor and is swifter than the mare.

"Eminent men like stallions being used for stud, as they are vigorous and better runners than the others.

"In general, stallions are rare among the Saharians. They are found only in the homes of the chieftains and wealthy men, who have the means of taking care of them properly. It would be dangerous to turn these stallions loose to graze. On the contrary, the mare requires little care and is, therefore, the usual mount of the Saharian. We are of the opinion that the mare should be ridden while in foal, always taking care to avoid tiring her unduly. If the mare were too well taken care of, if she were to stay picketed in front of the tent and be abundantly fed, the result would be the handicap of her getting fat. The uterus with the foetus would be compressed, could not expand gradually, and would hinder growth.

"During the last three months of gestation, the wealthy require little of the mare; they do not ride her; they leave her on the grazing grounds. However, the poor man's mare works up to the last month.

"A mare that has just foaled is given a good nose bag full of parched barley, and a wide bandage is wrapped around her to support and reduce her belly. Not until the following day, in the morning, can she be given water warmed on the fire to drink. The new-born is made to swallow one, two, or three hen's eggs and then, before he gets to his feet, the soles and walls of his hoofs are rubbed with salt dissolved in a preparation of *bou-nafâa*. This will give him hard, resistant hoofs. Then the foal gets up, staggers about, and looks for his dam; twelve hours later he goes out with her and follows her to the grazing grounds. The moment the foal is born, the master of the tent hastens to set his ears, gathers the hairs of the forelock together, and carefully massages the mane and neck from bottom to top.

"If it is cold, both mare and foal are put inside the tent.

"Seven days after foaling the mare is made to swallow a pound or a pound and a half of rancid unsalted butter. It is a purge that cleanses her stomach.

"The greater the value of the mare, the sooner the foal is weaned, but in no case shall he nurse longer than six months. In some places the Arabs believe that a long period of nursing makes a colt ill-tempered and hard-mouthed.

"Whenever possible and according to the season, the foal is given camel's, cow's, or ewe's milk; this makes his coat finer and glossier.

"To permit a stallion to sense mares in season, even at a great distance, is dangerous. The Arabs are so convinced of this that in their camps they seek means of not even leaving the mares downwind.

"It is not rare to find tribes that believe they can overcome sterility in a mare by giving her to the stallion, for good or ill, twenty-five times in one season.

"Man's greatest good is a fertile filly. God has told them to multiply and they have multiplied."

THE TRAINING OF THE COLT

*The horseman "makes" a horse
as a man molds a wife.*

AFTER BEING WEANED the colt still follows his dam to the grazing grounds, thus obtaining that exercise as vital for his health as it is necessary for the development of his faculties. At night he returns to lie down near his master's tent, and there he becomes for all the family the object of the greatest care. The women and children play with him, they give him couscous, bread, farina, milk, and dates. This daily treatment is the reason for the docility which is so much to be admired in all Arabians.

Frequently it is found that year-old colts will grow wolf's teeth and then they lose weight quickly, eating little. However, the teeth are pulled and they regain their health. If by the time a colt is fifteen or eighteen months old he does not have great suppleness in his shoulders, one does not hesitate to fire the scapulohumeral joint; and this is always done in the form of a cross whose four extremities are joined by a circle. Care is taken before beginning this operation to make an outline with tar if the horse has a light coat and with calcimine if he has a dark coat.

If the colt's knees should be badly shaped or have a tendency to bony tumors or swelling, firing would be done on three parallel lines.

Lastly, as soon as one fears having noted the colt becoming stiff, be it in the fore, be it in the hind legs, one fires the fetlocks, but only on the anterior surface, which proves that the Arabs know the tendons and look out for them.

Cautery is usually done with a sickle. For this operation one avoids as much as possible the great heat of summer. The best time is during the end of the autumn or at the beginning of the spring, when the air is cooler and there are fewer flies.

It is necessary to begin the colt's training at eighteen months, first because it is the only way to accustom him to docility, and second because the growth of his spleen[1] is retarded, this latter, according to the Arabs, being a very important thing for the future. If he is ridden later than eighteen months, to the eye he will appear to be strong, but in reality he will be less able to withstand fatigue and hard gallops.

"Every horse that has been toughened brings good fortune."[2] And

[1] *Spleen*: the term is employed in this chapter in its archaic sense, not in the anatomical sense used today. In stressing the need to begin the colt's training early, reference is made to retarding the growth of his spleen, or be it, his mettle, fire, ardor, impetuosity, or the like, until he was completely docile; not cowed, but docile. [Translator's note]

[2] During my long career among my tribes, among my friends, or among my servitors, I have seen more than two thousand colts raised, and I affirm that all those whose training did not begin very early and in accordance with the principles referred to were never anything but rebellious horses, disagreeable mounts, and unsuited for war.

I affirm, moreover, that when I made long, swift journeys at the head of twelve or fifteen hundred horsemen, the horses in good flesh, or even those on the thin side but accustomed to fatigue from a very early age, never abandoned my banner, while those horses which were fat or had been broken in late, always lagged behind. My conviction, with regard to this matter, is so ingrained by long experience that not long ago, finding myself in Cairo in need of buying some horses, I roundly refused all those animals which were presented to me for my inspection which had been broken in late.

"How was your horse trained?" was always my first question.

"Sir," one inhabitant of the town answered me, "this chestnut was brought up in my house, as one of my children, always well fed and well looked after, as I didn't begin to ride him until he was fully four years old. Look and see how fat he is and how sound his legs are."

"Very well, friend. Keep him; he is your pride and that of your family. It would be a disgrace upon my white beard to deprive you of him."

"And you?" I next asked an Arab whom I recognized as a son of the desert, as he was so burnt by the sun. "How did you train your horse?"

"Sir," he answered, "from a very early age I accustomed his back to the saddle and his mouth to the bit. With him I made long journeys, very long journeys. He has spent many days without water and many nights without food. It is true that his ribs show, but if you were to join some path-finders, he would not bring

God knows, the Arabian horse is tough! He travels, so to speak, all the time. He travels in search of food and goes great distances to find the water he needs. That sort of life makes him calm of temperament, untiring, and thus fitted for doing any kind of work demanded of him at any time.

At eighteen to twenty months old then, the colt is ridden by a child. The child takes him to water and they go to the grazing grounds together. In order not to injure the bars of the mouth, the child guides the colt with a rope or with a gentle enough mule-bridle. That exercise suits them both: the child becomes a horseman and the colt becomes accustomed to carrying a weight in proportion to his strength. He learns to step out; nothing frightens him; and thus it is, say the Arabs, that they arrange matters in order never to have restive horses.

It is at that same age that the colt is first hobbled. The hobbles are then very close together, because without that precaution the young animal could twist his legs and do damage to his breast or shoulders, be it upon lying down or upon getting up. The hobbles should be left a little loose in order not to cause an obstructive edema (*louzze*).

This method of hobbling is undoubtedly the best, because on account of it one does not hear talk about those loose horses which bring trouble to the camp, are the despair of their riders, and are the cause of innumerable mishaps. As the horse is obliged to stoop and lean forward in order to graze, one would think that in the long run his stance would be ruined, but this fear is unfounded, for the breast develops and the legs are strengthened. All Barb horses stand very well and have admirable lines to their backs and loins. The Arabs severely criticise our custom of tethering horses with ropes, because, they say, in addition to the vices to which this might lead and the accidents which could occur, it prevents the animal from resting. It is a fact that with hobbles the horse stretches out his head and neck and composes himself for sleep after the manner of the saluki sprawled out in the sun. With hobbles many stable vices, caused by the use of

---

shame upon you. I swear it to you by the Day of Final Judgment, when God shall be the Judge and the angels witnesses."

"Tether this dapple-gray in front of my tent," I said to my grooms, "and make this man content."

(Sid-Hamed-ben-Mohamed-el-Mokrani, Caliph of the Medjana, chieftain of one of the most illustrious families of all Algeria. He is at the present time on a journey to Paris, returning from Mecca. 15th February, 1853.)

a rope disappear completely, because the animal cannot then turn foxy, or get loose, or jump into the manger or lie on top of it, or begin crib-biting, or paw, or entangle himself, or acquire the habit of weaving. There are great advantages.

The colt being hobbled outside the tent, a little Negro, switch in hand, is put over him to get him used to keeping quiet. This young slave is charged with the duty of correcting the colt gently should he try to kick anyone passing behind him or try to bite his neighbors. He is thus watched over until he attains a state of complete tractability. When the colt is sent out to graze, he is hobbled on the lateral, that is, the rope is attached to the fore and hind leg on the same side, and care is taken to see that the rope is very short. It has been noted that when the colt bends down to graze, the method to which we are referring forces the vertebral column to remain straight and be more convex than concave. If, on the contrary, the hobble rope from one leg to the other were very long, nothing would hold the spinal column in place and it could easily become curved.

At the age of from twenty-four to twenty-seven months a start is made upon bridling and saddling the colt, but not without taking great precautions. The saddle is never put on until the animal is completely accustomed to the bridle. For several successive days a bit wrapped in unprocessed wool is placed in his mouth; the wool is used as much to avoid hurting the bars of his mouth, as to get him to retain it because of its salty taste, which he enjoys. He is very close to being "made" when one notes that he champs it. This preparatory exercise is performed morning and night. The young animal is thus well enough trained before being ridden at the beginning of autumn— when he will suffer less from the flies and the heat.

In some tents of distinction, before the colt is made to carry a man, he is quietly led about for some fifteen days carrying a pack-saddle loaded with panniers full of sand. Thus he goes gradually from the first weight of the child he has carried to that of the man who is soon to ride him.

The colt is now thirty months old. His spinal column has gained strength. Hobbles, the saddle, and the bridle are now familiar to him. Then a rider gets on him. The animal is still very young, but he will only be required to go at a walk and a very soft bit will be put in his mouth. All that is wanted is to accustom him to the habit of docility. Also the rider, without spurs, having a little switch in his hand and taking care not to overdo in the use of it, will go to the market, to visit friends, to see the herds, the pastures, and will attend to his affairs without demanding anything more than sweetness of temperament and obedience. This can most frequently be achieved by speaking to the colt in a low voice without violent gestures, and by avoiding any opportunity for balking, which could result in a struggle from which the rider could not come off the victor except at the expense of the colt.

Frequently one sees the common folk riding their animals before these are thirty months old and, when they are reproached, they answer: "You are quite right, we know that very well. But what can one do? We are poor and we are forced to do it thus or to go on foot and we prefer the former, in spite of the possibility of unfavorable results. In our lives so full of danger, the present moment is everything."

Seeing the Arabs abuse their colts, riding them at two years old, demanding a considerable amount of work from them, making forced marches, and even using them for pack animals without any regard for either their age or their strength, many people have concluded that the Arabs do not have any knowledge of equestrian principles and they have even denied to the Arab any love for the horse. Those people did not choose to reflect that, as much to save their families as to save their possessions—and often because of wanting to obey the laws of the Holy War—these same Arabs have to, if you will excuse the expression, make arrows out of any kind of wood. They are forced to make use of their horses because of necessity, because of the circumstances which impel them; but they know perfectly well that it would be preferable not to do so.

It is also at about the age of thirty months that the colt is taught never to run away from his rider, when the latter has dismounted and even never to leave the spot where the reins have been thrown over his head, leaving them to trail on the ground. This lesson is given the greatest of care, for it is very important in the life of the Arab. During this lesson they use the same method as was used for getting the colt used to the hobbles. A servant stands by the colt's side and, by stepping upon the reins each time that the colt tries to go off, makes him feel a disagreeable jerk on the bars of the mouth. After many days of this, the colt will finally stay in the same place where he was left and there he will wait for his master for days on end. This principle is so widespread throughout the Sahara, that the first care of a man who has killed a rider, if he wants the dead man's horse, is immediately to throw the reins over the animal's head. By this means, the horse is kept from moving, and the victor has time to rifle his victim. Without this precaution, the horse would at once rejoin his *goum*.

Here is something which we have all seen:

An Arab arrives at the marketplace. He dismounts among fifteen or twenty horses and mares. You would think that he would have some-one hold his horse—but no. He throws the reins over the horse's head, lets them fall to the ground, puts a rock on top of them, and goes off calmly to attend to his affairs. Two hours later he returns and retrieves his horse, which has not moved from the spot to which it probably thought that it was tied; the rider mounts and goes.

From thirty months to three years the application of the preceding principles is continued to confirm in the youngster that docility so essential to warfare. Moreover, he is taught to be very quiet while being mounted and to achieve this aim, very gentle methods are used. The Arab in his adventurous and perilous life, has need, above all else, of a horse that allows himself to be easily mounted. The lessons continue for as many days as may be necessary; but they are short, in order not to bore the colt. At first, the rider will have two men helping him, one of whom will hold the reins and the other the stirrup. The rider will, by being patient, succeed in attaining an absolute immo-bility on the part of the horse. Only horses that are ailing or that have bad conformation do not learn these lessons.

When he is three to four years old, more is demanded of the horse, but he is well fed. He begins to be ridden with spurs; he is confirmed in the preceding lessons and now adds courage and learns not to be frightened by anything. The sounds of the animals that live with him in the camp, those of the wild animals that prowl about at night, and the shots that are heard constantly, have soon inured him.

If, in spite of all the training of which we have spoken, one comes across a horse that rears from laziness or malice, one that kicks, bites, or does not wish to leave the tent or the other horses, one that is easily frightened by anything whatsoever, to the point of refusing to pass by it, then the rigor of the spurs is applied. The points of the rowels are sharpened and lightly bent into the shape of small hooks and the horse is raked on the belly and flanks producing bloody scratches which end up in inspiring such a terror in the horse that not infrequently one sees him piss under his rider, become as gentle as a sheep and, doglike, follow at his master's heels. Horses which have received this punishment very seldom relapse into their former bad ways. To augment the severity of the spurs the Arabs go to the length of putting salt or gunpowder on the still bleeding wounds which they have inflicted.[3] They are so convinced of the efficacy of this punishment that they do not believe a horse has been truly trained for war unless the animal has undergone this severe test. In a word, among them the lesson of the spurs is to the horse what the lesson of a spiked training collar is to hunting dogs among us.

At the same time that the horseman makes use of the spurs to punish a decidedly restive horse, he beats him just behind the crownpiece of the bridle with a stout short stick which he always carries when he wishes to correct this type of horse.

In some places to keep a horse from rearing, the Arabs put an iron ring in the ear. When the animal rears he is given a heavy blow on the ring. The pain which the blow causes soon makes the animal give up that defense.

The Arabs say that spurs add a quarter to the horsemanship of the rider and a third to the vigor of the horse and they try to prove it by means of this fable:

"When animals were created they had the power of speech. The horse and the camel vowed never to do each other harm and always live sensibly together.

"One day, an Arab thrown into the abyss by war, saw to his despair that the camel upon which he depended to save his fortune was run-

---

[3] In his *Riders of Many Lands* (pp. 399–400), Theodore Ayrault Dodge, American cavalry officer travelling in the Near East in the 1890's, had this to say concerning the practice of severely roweling the horses:

Not a few [horses] have the curious marks on barrel and haunch and arm, which, by a queer superstition, are often inflicted on Arabians "to make them gallop faster," as they say; though what this means I am unable to tell, unless they give each two or three year old one special test (as is done in racing stables), and select those who show up the best; and to make them go the faster use a knife-blade rowel. Others explain the cuts in a different way, but it is a blind matter at best . . . The cut on the barrel is a long and semicircular one from below upward, as if made by the heel armed with a vicious spur. Into the cut is rubbed (again they say) powdered glass to make an ugly scar . . . On a white horse the scar I have described is peculiarly distressing. The other cuts are straight horizontal ones half-way up the buttock and arm. There seems to be neither rhyme nor reason in the trick. We brand a bronco to mark ownership; these cuts are a mere outcome of silly superstition. [Translator's note]

ning away. No time to waste! 'Bring me my horse!' he yelled, and launched himself in pursuit of the camel. He urged his horse, but to no avail. The horse would not respond, remembering the promise he had made to his friend. The Arab then put on his spurs which were in his *djebira*.[4] The horse, feeling his flanks raked, launched himself, put on a burst of speed and in an instant caught up with the fugitive.

" 'Oh, traitor!' said the camel. 'You have violated our pact; you swore never to do me harm and you have just finished putting me in the hands of my tyrant.'

" 'Do not accuse my heart,' answered the horse. 'I did not want to gallop, but such are the "thorns of misery" that they have brought me to you.' "

It is not easy to make good use of Arabic spurs. The horsemen who possess the knack of knowing how to use them are numbered even among the Arabs themselves. Some do not know how to do anything other than urge the horse by constantly punishing his sides, but without inflicting wounds. Still others do not know anything other than the *tekerbeđa*—that is to say they know how to strike their iron spurs noisily against their iron stirrups to excite the animal. Only the most expert know how to rake their spurs to cause those bloody scratches of which we have already spoken. When it is said of a rider that he rakes his horse from the navel to the backbone, that indicates the highest degree in the art.

During my sojurn in Mascara, how many times have I had Arabs say to me, in order to praise the horsemanship of the Emir Abd-el-Kader: "He crosses his spurs over the horse's loins!"

These spurs are dangerous when worn by inexperienced horsemen, because frequently they gouge the horses on the stifle and ruin the animals, if the cuts are deep. When the horse falls, the spur could also penetrate his body. For this reason the Arabs customarily wear their spur straps quite loose in order to mitigate with their looseness the effects of their own inexpertness. Too, having the straps thus, they can easily rid themselves of the spurs when, in combat, their horses are killed and the riders are forced to flee on foot to save their heads. This latter reason also makes them prefer heelless loose slippers to boots for serious combat.

---

[4] *Djebira*: a type of pouch or scabbard attached to the pommel of the saddle, in which the Arabs carry their powder, their papers, *etc.* There are some *djebira* with marvellous embroidery work. The *djebira* is also called *grab*.

The Arabs consider our spurs to be entirely insufficient. What result, in a case of life or death, would you obtain from an already very tired horse? "Such spurs are good for nothing but to tickle the horses and make them restive. With our spurs we suck the horse dry; as long as he has any life left, we seek it out; the spurs are not impotent except in the face of death."

The Arab personally trains his horse, because in the Sahara practice, traditions, and example are the riding masters; the title of horseman is not earned until after a man has undergone great tests of skill. To be reputed as such it is not enough for a rider to know how to ride a horse over easy terrain; he is required, weapon in hand, to get the best out of a horse at fast paces, over broken and wooded country—in a word, difficult. Such a one, they say, is a horseman with a firearm; but so-and-so is naught but a horseman in the use of the heel. The perfect horseman is he alone who can combine the weapon and the heel. A difference has even been marked between him who rides a horse well over dry terrain and him who rides a horse skilfully over slippery ground. To the Arabs there is the horseman of the summer and the horseman of the winter.

What lessons this apprenticeship carries! We could not mention them all, but there is one which they neglect: they are indifferent as to the lead in which their mounts gallop. The Arabian horse always has agility and lovely shoulders which, thanks to the habit the colt acquired of grazing among the hills, in the woods, and on uneven ground, have developed more surely than by the lunge line and manège. And too, the horse is always evenly balanced, because the rider follows all his movements so well that he is never out of harmony with them.

I would add that the Arab has a perfect seat, and even if he does use very short stirrup leathers, he makes up for this drawback with very long spurs which, with the least movement of the legs, touch the horse's flanks, forcing the animal to bring his hind legs under his center of gravity, to be in hand, and to carry his head just as well as the carriage which could be achieved by our best principles of horsemanship.[5]

[5] "Today we went out on horseback with our host Youssouf-ben-Bender and went towards the desert. He was accompanied by his sons and grandsons, all mounted on magnificent horses, while the servants rode dromedaries. During

All Arabian horses have good mouths. The adage says: "The horse-man 'makes' a horse as a man molds a wife."

But it is not enough to have calmed a horse, to have broken him. When by means of good treatment, of daily contact, of expertly administered punishment, he has become docile, when above all else he has a good walk, his education is still not complete. It is as well to perfect his education and one does so with the following exercises.

Departure at a gallop from a standstill. To achieve this the Arabs use almost the same methods that we do, with the sole difference that the *tekerbeḏa* of which we have already spoken implements the aids and it would take a horse completely lacking in aptitude not to be able to do what is asked of him.

Launching. The horse is launched against a wall, a tree, a man, and is stopped short. Gradually the point is reached when he is made to come to a dead stop from a full gallop, on the brink of a river, a ravine, or a precipice;[6] a marvellous faculty frequently used to great advantage in war.

---

this outing we encountered an Arab who caused me great astonishment. Without saddle or bridle, with just a small halter whose noseband was a kind of little steel chain and carrying in his hand a small switch with a curved tip which he used to guide his horse, he would launch the animal from a halt into a fast gallop, make a very close turn, and at that gait make flying changes on a straight line. It was unbelievable and I doubt that our *écuyeres* or most celebrated sports-men could ever do anything better. What struck me above all was the simplicity of the methods used by that son of Ishmael to achieve what he demanded of his horse. In Europe we study the play and functions of the muscles, only to run counter to them. In Arabia they are studied also, but in order to get the greatest advantage from Nature without violating it. And another aspect—it is not just one Arab that rides well; without exception they are all good riders, all love horses passionately, all concern themselves with training them. In the camp the dweller in the Nedj does not sleep unless his head is resting on his horse's shoulder and every horse lies down at his master's command. The latter thus finds a softer pillow than the ground and in this way prevents his horse from being stolen while he sleeps." ("Journey in Upper Asia," by M. Pétiniaud)

[6] Bonnemain, lieutenant of the local native regiment of Spahis, a Frenchman . . . a horseman of consummate skill . . . gave my friends an exhibition they will never forget. He and his mount were as one, like a Centaur of old and to entertain them he gave a demonstration of every maneuver known to the desert cavalry.

His parade ground was a small plateau bounded on one side by a precipice so sheer, so deep, that the river Rummel at its foot looked a mere thread of silver. A height to make a chamois giddy! Bonnemain rode his horse at full gallop to-

If a young horse is not willing, hesitates, and, above all, is obstinate about leaving other horses, a defect which can have fatal consequences for an Arab, the animal is corrected by means of this maneuver: several mounted men are placed in two rows at a distance of three or four paces from each other. Then the horse to be corrected is ridden down between these two hedgerows. If he stops, the riders then lash him with switches while his rider makes vigorous use of the spurs. The most stubborn animal cannot endure fifteen days of such lessons.

Wheeling. This exercise consists of making sharp turns to right or left, more frequently to the left, at the instant that the rider has fired his gun. In the beginning, just as the bullet leaves the weapon, one moves one's hand swiftly to the rear and to the left, on giving at the same time a blow with the other hand on the right side of the neck; the horse understands and very soon he obeys the mere inclining of the rider's body. This lesson is given with great care and is of enormous importance to the Arab, ever exposed to individual combat.

Sprints. First the horse is galloped only over flat ground, being urged on with a switch and spurs, for just short distances at the beginning. Then he is made to gallop neck-and-neck with an old horse of certain repute; the colt becomes animated and seeks to keep up in the contest. These repeated exercises also serve to give the rider an exact knowledge of the aptitudes of the pupil, of that which later he can undertake with him. They are not without danger, but "the angels have two special missions in this world: presiding at the racing of horses and at the union of a man to a woman." It is they who preserve horse and rider from all accident and take care to see to it that the conception may be happy.

Jumping. And, lastly, the colt should be taught to jump. One brings to such a task a great deal of patience and progression. One does not give that lesson but two or three times each day. One does not, at the beginning, go over any but small obstacles—the only way not to disgust the horse—and one does not confront him with large obstacles until he is docile and well trained. For the Arabs jumping is undoubtedly an obligatory complement to the education of the colt,

---

ward this precipice, reined him in at the very brink, made him rear and turn a half-circle on his hind legs, his forelegs beating the empty air above the void like a compass tracing an imaginary arc in space. It was incredible! Sublime! (Dumas, *Adventures in Algeria*, p. 168)

but they are far from attaching the same importance to it as do Europeans. Their country is in general difficult, crossed by gullies, strewn with large boulders and with thorn thickets. They allege that if they wished to jump every obstacle they encountered in war or in the chase, they would be jumping incessantly which would tire their horses horribly and could not but fail to ruin them in the long run. As a consequence they go around obstacles, descend perpendicularly, climb up the steepest slopes; and that custom makes their horses so handy that after a long gallop, the animals arrive, all things considered, sooner than if they had tried to jump everything in front of them.

The incitement. The horse is urged to rear up against that of the opponent so that both animals will bite each other. One reins in and presses with the legs while making the repeated sound *"cheït,"* and a satisfactory result is obtained sooner the more irascible the animal. The Arabs contend that horses thus trained have frequently in individual combat unseated the adversary. Thanks to this training, after forays the horses will often accelerate the pace of the captured camels. I saw a horseman of the *makhzen* thus quicken the pace of the animals that lagged behind. His horse chivied and bit them with an air of pleasure.

Renowned horsemen do not limit their horses' training. Apart from the foregoing maneuvers, so necessary in combat, they teach them to show off in gatherings and *fantasias.*

The caracole. The horse walks, so to speak, on his hind legs and scarcely has he set down his forefeet when he raises them anew. Hands, in conjunction with the use of the legs, very soon bend to this exercise the horse that has aptitudes.

The ballotade. The horse springs into the air with four feet off the ground; at the same time the rider tosses his weapon into the air and skilfully catches it. To obtain this action, one holds in, urges with the legs, gives when the horse raises himself and collects when he lands. There is nothing more picturesque than this exercise. The horses leave the earth, the weapons fly, the wide folds of the long burnnoose float and wave in the wind, thrown back by the vigorous arms of the sons of the desert; this is, properly, the enchantment and triumph of the *fantasia.*

Kneeling. The mounted rider makes his horse kneel. This is the *ne plus ultra* of man and horse. Not all horses are fitted for this exercise.

One prepares the colt by tickling him on the coronet, by pinching him on the forearm, by forcing him to bend the knee. Later on, the horseman will derive benefit from these preliminaries; he will not have to do more than remove his feet from the stirrups, stretch his legs forward, turn out his toes, touch the horse's forearms with his long spurs and, when at weddings and gatherings, the bullet is sped, his horse will kneel and he will hear the young girls applaud and pierce the air with their shrieks of joy.

Then, after the horses have been trained for all these gymnastics, come the following sports:

The game of the cummerbund. When the horse is fully trained, then at family parties or religious solemnities, the mounted rider at full gallop picks up a cummerbund spread on the ground. The most skilful pick it up in three different places.

Target Practice. The target is ordinarily a rock or a sheep's shoulder blade. The horseman starts from far off in order to place his horse well. He fires when some fifty or sixty paces from the target. The Saharian will remember these lessons when in the chase, launched at a gallop, he kills a gazelle or an ostrich.

It is not from an inhabitant of the Tell that one should demand such prodigies of mastery, skill, and horsemanship. You will never see him with the light clothing, the lovely and fine wool of the son of the desert, whom, moreover, you will always recognize by his sleek, tall horse, by his skill in handling his weapon, and by the graceful forward inclination of his body with which he increases the speed of his courser's gaits.

How many are there in the Tell who can gallop a stretch without dropping coins placed between the soles of the feet and the stirrups?[7]

"And you others, the Christians, go at a trot; so do we, but in ordinary times and to give our horses a breather. In war, we do not want any gait other than a walk or gallop. If we are not pressed, a walk will suffice. It is the everyday gallop. If we are in danger, a gallop will save our heads."

An Arabic chieftain would never keep a horse whose walk had not been well developed.

---

[7] Here again is a notable difference in the principles of equitation. Among us the stirrup should carry only the weight of the legs. Among the Arabs, to the contrary, all the weight of the body is on the stirrups at fast paces.

These exercises are not practiced by all Arabs. Each one chooses those which suit his position, his fortune, his tastes. But all conform to the principles which we have explained for the education of the colt. They consist of first reducing the young animal to the nth degree of misery in order to train him well later at the age of from three to four years. After these tests, one knows exactly what he is worth. These principles are, moreover, summed up in a proverb which is very widely known, which proves the importance attached to beginning that training at an early age. Here it is:

"Feed the yearling;
He will not sprain himself;
Ride him from two to three years old,
Just until he be submissive;
Feed him well from three to four years old.
Then ride him again immediately.
And if he is not suitable
Sell him without counting up the cost."

Now then, do not believe that it is alone the Arabs in our possessions in Africa who, if you will permit the expression (which is an apt one), are hell-bent on beginning the training of the colt very early. You would be in grave error. All Arabs, to whatever locality they may belong, practice the same principles. Do you want proof? Read what M. Pétiniaud, not an inexperienced man but a distinguished inspector general of studs, who has been commissioned by the government to travel throughout Upper Asia, there to buy horses of pure Oriental blood, has said. I shall let him speak:

After three years of travelling among the tribes who camp from Diyarbekir and Aleppo to the limits of Nedj, I returned to Baghdad last January. Among the papers waiting for my arrival, I found a copy of the *Journal des Haras*, which had an article about the horses of the Sahara.

The perusal of this too short paragraph which, however, showed a profound knowledge of the Arab and his horse, made me want to own the whole book. Upon my arrival in France you did me the favor of sending it to me and I thank you. No one could read with a greater interest than I a work which you could fittingly have titled *About the Arabian Horse of Asia and Africa*, because such is the spirit of tradition of that exceptional people, that in every line one recognized in the customs of the Arabs of Maghreb, the customs of their forebears the Koreyh and the Nedj—and that, after a separation of several centuries.

In 1851 I came down the Tigris from Mosul to Baghdad and I had in my hands a volume of Herodotus. All his descriptions of men and things were most timely. Thus he described two thousand, three hundred years ago, the customs of present-day Arabs, with the same fidelity that you, my General, have used in describing in Africa, the Arabs of Asia. Time and space are impotent in the face of the unchangeability of such customs: internecine wars, the chase, love for the horse, etc. I saw it all in Asia, exactly as you have described it in Africa.

Your work, which has the great merit of containing all truth and at the same time nothing but truth, will be called upon, in my opinion, to exercise a great influence on the training of horses in France. This book, full of charm, will develop a taste for horses among those who have not yet been concerned with the matter and our breeders will acquire useful instruction from the many facts you set forth.

They will learn not to reserve their admiration for a horse that has no other merit than that of being fat and at last they will understand the advantages which one can hope to gain from submitting a colt to healthful exercises during his early years. The horse is *in the work* [the value of the horse lies in his training]; thus it is necessary to accustom him to working early.

I noticed that all Arabs tire their horses mercilessly from two to three years old, only to then keep them well from three to four years old. They say that sustained work during the early years strengthens the breast, muscles, and joints of the colt, as well as ensuring in him a docility that will accompany him until he dies. They say, moreover, that once these severe tests have been undergone, his entire constitution should then be developed by means of rest, care, and abundant food because after that new period he cannot help but show how he will turn out for the rest of his life; that is to say, good or bad.

If he turns out well, he will be kept; but if he turns out badly the Arab will not hesitate to get rid of him, because in his eyes a bad horse is not worth the barley one gives him.

I hope that this digression will be pardoned for the sake of the reflections which it should suggest. But, is it not admirable to see a people spread over an enormous expanse of territory from the Persian Gulf to the Atlantic Ocean, without means of communication, without printing presses, without telegraph lines, without any of the means of modern civilization, but all speaking the same language, obeying the same law, and conserving by simple tradition, as well as we could do it by means of books, the usages, customs, and even the precepts of their forefathers? Seeing and questioning the Arabs of Algeria, I saw and understood the Arabs of earliest times. Is not that unity in analogous conditions worthy of admiration?

Upon the end of the horses' training, vices might appear in some of them. However, the Arab does not become needlessly alarmed, because, according to him, such vices cannot stem from any other cause but an excess of rest which makes the animals lazy from habit or flighty due to an excess of energy. The Arabs correct the animals with work, the fatigues of war or the chase. The comfortable build of the Arabic saddle permits the rider to remain in it despite the stubborn defenses of the horse. He does not become astonished or frightened and he always ends up by subduing the horse completely. You will never see an Arab get rid of a horse because he rears, bucks, or wants to go after a mare; they are pleased with this proof of vigor. The day will come when they will derive great benefit from it.

The Arabs say: "The horseman who has not known how to train his horse forks Death each day."

The man to whom the Arabs attribute the honor of having been the first horse trainer was Ishmael, the progenitor all Arabs have in common. They base this assertion on these words of God: "I gave him horses so that he would ride them"; and also on this celebrated sermon of Ishmael himself: "Horses, the night, and space are witnesses for me like the sword, pen, and paper." Always—as one can see—the influence of religious tradition.

With regard to bad vices such as biting, kicking, or striking with the forefeet, they are practically unknown because all efforts have been made to prevent them. The Arabs have the horse live close to the tent; they admit him, after a fashion, as a part of the family. Among the women, children, and slaves who spoil and caress him, he can do no less than acquire good ways and habits of submission. Moreover, this care, let it be well understood, is not only a matter of personal interest to the master that gives it: it is a religious duty. The Prophet has said: "The true believer who has trained his horse to shine in the Holy War shall have the sweat, the hairs, the dung, and the urine of that very horse intercede for him on the scales of well-doing on the Day of Final Judgment."

In spite of all those bonds which unite man to the horse, in spite of that solidarity which habit, interest, and religion give, a Moslem will never give his horse the name of a person. Those names were used by the saints and it would be a great sin, a sacrilege to use them for animals, even for the most noble of horses. They give names only to celebrated horses and that only in the large tents. The horses are named:

Rakib, the Pathfinder or Scout

Mansour, the Victor

Sabeur, The Patient One

Salem, the Savior

Kamil, the Perfect One

Sâad, Happiness

Maârouf, the Acquaintance

Aatik, the Noble One

Sabok, the Fleet, the Swift

Nadjy, the Persevering

Moubarek, the Blessed One

Guetrâne, Tar

Messaoud, the Happy One

Safy, The Pure

Ghrezal, the Gazelle

Naâma, the Ostrich

Mordjana, the Coral

El Aroussa, the Fiancee

Djerada, the Grasshopper

Ouarda, the Rose

Guemera, The Moon

Hamana, the Pigeon

Yakouta, the Ruby

El Guetaya, the Seamstress

Aâtifa, the Docile One

Leïla, the Night

The Arabs give the same names, more or less, to their slaves.

A general custom among the Arabs, which all those who fought in the African war were able to observe, is that of cutting the forelock, mane, and hairs of the tail of the horses. Here is the rule applying to this custom which may be considered bizarre.

When the colt is a year old his mane and tail are cut with the exception of a lock on the poll, one at the withers, and another on the dock. At the age of two years the operation is repeated and all the hair is cut off both mane and tail. At three years of age, a third shearing in the third spring. From three to five years old, all the hair is allowed to grow, only to be cut off again when the animal attains the age of five years. This last operation is called *el halafya*. After the animal is five years old, the hairs are never touched. It would be a sin, for it would have no object other than that of trying to deceive one's fellows with respect to the age of the horse.

Never is it omitted after each shearing to rub the sheared parts with sheep manure mixed with milk or with Prussian blue diluted in hot butter; this softens the skin and makes the mane heavy. This apparent oddity has many *raisons d'être*. It indicates, of course, at first glance the age of a horse until it is eight years old, for three years, at least, are necessary for the hair to have reached its full growth and then the horse may be called *djarr*: "he whose tail sweeps the ground." Next follows, and this is important in hot countries, habituating the horse to endure patiently the bites of flies; and lastly, one hopes to thus obtain thicker, longer, and silkier hair.

If the Arabs explain and justify that custom of cutting the hair of the horse until he is five years old, the same is not true of our custom of docking the tail. It is, in their view, an unspeakable barbarity; it is also the text of inexhaustible pleasantries. They rail us upon that subject even to the point of making the gravest of conjectures. I shall recount, in support of the foregoing, a fact of which I guarantee the truth:

In 1841 the column commanded by Marshal Bugeaud advanced toward Taguedempt to destroy the fort which, at great cost, had been built by the Emir Abd-el-Kader.

We camped at Oued-Khrelouk, one of the tributaries of the Mina. During the night we were awakened by the sound of a shot fired within the camp. We left our tents to go to the scene and find out what had occurred. An Arab was sprawled on the ground with a broken skull. He had a very sharp knife in his hand and, like all professional thieves, he was wearing nothing but a wide leather belt with a pistol.

The sentry who had fired on him, stated that having noticed a thorn bush move, stop, and move again he had, suspecting a ruse, fired from a distance of ten paces at the moment when the thief approached the horses of the sentry's captain.

At the recital of the old Africa hand, his comrades, furious, wanted to finish off the Arab; but the officers present calmed that first natural violent reaction and reported what had happened to higher authority. The Arab was taken to the ambulance and treated.

On the following day the column had to continue its march; the Arab was gravely wounded. There was no point in taking him along; killing him would have hastened his end by only a day or two and would not have done our cause any good. A greater advantage could be obtained from the occurrence; and the Governor General decided to leave him behind with a letter to the powerful Flittas tribe in whose territory we were. It was pointed out in the letter to that very hostile people that their hatred for us would, in the course of time, have dire results for them, that struggle [against us] was impossible, that France was powerful in men and wealth, and that the Emir Abd-el-Kader upon continuing the war could not help but bring upon himself untold disasters, and, finally, that the best thing they could do would be to separate their cause from his, if they did not wish to see their beautiful harvests destroyed and set on fire.

At daybreak the expeditionary column renewed its advance and the rearguard was not more than a thousand meters distant from the bivouac when Arabic horsemen were seen to arrive, dismount, and then take with them the wounded man we had left behind. On the following day we received the answer from the Flittas which was addressed to "General Bugeaud, Kaïd of the Port of Algiers,"[8] and couched, more or less, in the following terms:

You tell us that you are a mighty and powerful nation and that we cannot struggle against you. The mighty and powerful are just. However, you wish to conquer a country which does not belong to you and furthermore, if you are so wealthy, what do you want with a people who do not have anything but gunpowder to give you? Moreover, when He wishes, the Lord of the world knocks down forts and makes the weak triumph. Furthermore, you threaten us with setting fire to our harvests or having them eaten up by your horses and your pack animals, how many times have we not suffered similar misfortunes! We have had bad years; we have seen the locusts, the famine; and God, in the meantime, has not abandoned us, because we are believers, Arabs, and misery cannot kill the Arabs. "The Arab, his brother is the dog. The river cannot carry him away and misery cannot kill him." We shall therefore never surrender to you; you are the enemies of our religion—that is impossible. However, if the Almighty, in order to punish us for our sins and those of our fathers, should inflict upon us one day that horrible disease, we would then be most embarrassed, we are forced to admit it: among us the sign of submission is the presentation of a horse to the victors (*gada*), and we know that you love only those horses with docked tails and our mares do not make that kind.

Later on, however, the Flittas were, nonetheless, obliged to give us horses of the kind their mares did make; but the resistance of those warriors was stubborn. Since then they have always been the first

[8] It has been barely nine years since the Arabs recognized the supremacy of France over the port of Algiers. And one is astounded that there is not yet in Algeria a population of two million Europeans! What an answer to make to those who profess "the unintelligent domination of the saber," than that derisive address: "To General Bugeaud (to the representative of France), Kaïd of the Port of Algiers."

to utter the yells of war and revolt; it was they who killed our gallant general Mustapha-ben-Ismaïl.[9] It was they who received Bou-Maza;[10] it was they, in fine, who were the last to come to heel.

After this characteristic episode of our wars in Africa, I cannot bring the chapter on training the colt to a better close than by giving some entirely new data with respect to the treatment of the horse in Arabic surroundings. Such data will be right in their proper place here, and I hope that the role played by women in the life of the noble beast will not be found void of interest.

Frequently I have heard it asked whence came the sweetness, the good manners, and the intelligence which everyone is agreed are to be found in Arabian horses. Are these qualities inherent in Oriental breeds? Are they the result of training? A good climate is as favorable to the development of a breed as it is to its improvement. Experience proves it. A noble and generous breed is also more apt than another to give what is asked of it; but something must be asked. The most fertile of soils will not produce anything but thistles and thorns if it is not cultivated or if it is badly tilled.

[9] To the hatred of Mustapha-ben-Ismaïl for the Emir Abd-el-Kader, France owed the adherence, which was never given the lie, of that illustrious general of the powerful Douair tribe. For more than thirty years he was the Agha of the Turks. Thus when the son of Mahi-ed-din [Abd-el-Kader] at the age of twenty-five was proclaimed [leader] of the tribes of the Department of Oran, the old warrior refused to submit, saying that "never, with his white beard, would he go kiss the hand of a child."

The consequences of this enmity forced him to take refuge in the fortress of Tlemcen. There, for two years, he stood firm against the townspeople, devotees of the cause of him who took the title of Commandant of the Believers. However, at the end of his resources, he asked for and received the aid of Marshal Bertrand Clauzel, whereupon the column [under the command of Marshal Clauzel] raised the siege of 1836. From that time, at the head of *goums* of Douairs and of Zmélas, in all of whose vicissitudes he had shared, he participated, notwithstanding his advanced age, in all the combats which took place in the province of Oran.

France rewarded this energetic devotion with the rank of Field-Marshal and the Cross of a Knight-Commander of the Legion of Honor.

Mustapha-ben-Ismaïl was killed by the Flittas on the 19th of May, 1843, at the age of eighty while he was fighting in a rear-guard action. With some horsemen from his escort, he was protecting the immense booty taken from the Hachem-Gharabas at the moment of the pillaging of the *smala* [encampment].

[10] Bou-Maza or Bu-Maza ("The Goat Man") was a fanatical marabout or holy man who kept the tribes stirred up against the French during the conquest of Algeria. [Translator's note]

Starting at that point, the Arabs apply themselves with great intensity and persistence to perfect in their horses the gifts of Nature. Continuous training—daily contact with men, with animals, with external objects—is their great secret. That is what makes the Arabian horse as we know him; that is what has made him worthy of our wholehearted admiration. This admiration has not been general, I know. He was but imperfectly known. The Arabs have been accused of being ignorant, and of being torturers of horses, of riding them badly, of not giving that hand-care so highly regarded in Europe; they have been accused of abusing a horse's tender years, of constantly making his flanks and mouth bleed, etc. But the truth has come to light and when one has been able to prove that all the Arabs' horses were intelligent, obedient to hands and legs, easy to mount, and above all, impervious to all alarms, one is obliged to recognize that they have qualities which could not arise from any source other than that of a highly perfected training, very much based on reason.

Our horses are animals more or less submissive to man; they tolerate him, but they have neither love for nor confidence in those who ride them. In general, the slaves of man, they do not stick to one in particular because not one of us sticks to them and we do not look after them except as agricultural products which are sold for as high a price as possible, or as objects of trade with which to traffic, or as pieces of furniture to be exchanged at whim. Our dogs, on the other hand, love us so much, perhaps, because we do not sell them.

The Arabs seek in the horse a devoted friend. Among them, if I dare to express myself thus, he leads a family life in which, as in all families, the woman plays a big role: that of preparing by her sweetness, her vigilance, and her constant care the solidarity which should be established between the man and the animal.

On the road, in campaigns, far from home, it is the rider who looks after the horse; but at home, under the tent and at rest, it is the woman who directs, cares for, and feeds the noble comrade-in-arms who frequently enhances her husband's reputation, and contributes to the needs of her children.

In the mornings it is the woman who feeds him and looks after him. If the weather permits she washes his mane and tail. If the spot he occupies is on broken ground, uneven, covered with rocks, she puts him in a more suitable place for his rest and to preserve his legs. She pats him, lightly runs her hand over his neck and the sides of his head, gives him bread, dates, and sometimes even meat prepared and dried in the sun. "Eat, oh, my son," she says in a sweet voice, "one day you will save us from the hands of our enemies and you will fill our tent with booty."

It is still early morning when the Arabic woman goes to the pastures to gather for the animal she loves an ample ration of plants known in the desert for their nutritive and tonic value. On her return she sees children who have not yet reached the age of reason entertaining themselves by teasing or mistreating the horses hobbled in front of the tent. From the farthest point at which she can make herself heard, she calls and says: "Children, don't annoy the horses! You rascals! They are the ones that feed you. Do you then want God to place a curse on our tent? If you keep on, I shall tell your father."

In this respect the Arabic woman is so intransigent that she will not even excuse her husband if he does not care for his horse. The horse is her honor, he is her fortune; she is proud, jealous, and believes herself to be responsible for everything which concerns him.

Should it reach the point where the woman is forced to acknowledge that her remarks and observations are in vain, she will not hesitate to go to the chieftain of the tribe to make a complaint.

"Oh, my lord! You know that our horse is the pride and wealth of my family. Well then, my husband forces him to make useless journeys, mistreats, and abuses him. If even he would look after him at home—but no. His blanket is torn, his feed is not certain, and he does not even supervise the horse's drinking water.[11] Scold him, I beg of you. In the Name of God, make him return to the ways of our fathers; but above all, don't tell him that I warned you."

The Arabic chieftain in whose interests it lies to be followed in his adventurous existence by well-mounted horsemen, never fails to pay heed to the complaint. A little later he calls the culprit into his presence and warns him that if he does not mend his ways, he will take his horse from him and leave him on foot like a base infantryman; then he dismisses him, saying: "You have understood me. Go. Remember that in this world honor begins in the stirrup and ends in the saddle." Such a lesson always has a salutary effect, not only on the delinquent but also on all those who were tempted to follow the ex-

[11] Because many streams and watering places in Algeria were heavily infested by leeches, the Arabs exercised great vigilance over the water their animals were given to drink. [Translator's note]

ample, and it is so much so, that be it because of self-respect or because of fear of punishment the Arabs apply themselves to inculcating,
if not by willingness, then by force, love for the horse.

In the afternoons, sometimes early, sometimes late, according to the
season of the year, the woman busies herself with taking the horses to
water if the fountain is not far off and, in case it is, she herself goes to
fetch the water in goatskins. When the precious liquid is completely
lacking, the horses are given ewe's or camel's milk. Then the tent of
the Arabic chieftain presents a very curious spectacle indeed. One
can frequently see between the legs of the women or among the legs
of the horses, in the midst of a collection of children, picturesquely
dressed, at the side of falcons fluttering their wings and of salukis
straining, a gazelle or an antelope or an ostrich, which goes and comes
and jumps, begging for a little bit of that water which is so scarce in
the desert and which is going to be given, nonetheless, in abundance
to the family pet.

Night falls. What is that black dot on the horizon? It is the young
men of the *douar* [an encampment of tents pitched in a circle], who
are ashamedly returning to the tribe on hollow-flanked, unshod, and
exhausted horses. They have spent all day in the chase without eating
or drinking. Camels loaded with gazelles, hares, and bustards follow
them, but those spoils, appetizing as they are, will not save them from
the storm that awaits them.

"Young men," their mother says in an irate voice, "it is infamy to
thus ruin our horses for animals of little worth. You would do better
to save them for the day when the saliva drys in the mouth, for the
day when the goods are not enough to ransom heads."

During the times of great heat, the women put the horses inside the
tents to protect them from the sun. They are bathed, groomed, and
later, at night, the nose bags are filled with barley and hung around
the necks of those cherished animals. Each horse, and this is a very
important point, receives a ration according to his age, his temperament, or the work which he has performed. This attention, this daily
sweetness, as we have already said and as we never tire of reiterating,
make the horses loving and docile. They whinny with pleasure, they
gracefully turn their heads when they see the person who looks after
them approaching. She is always prepared at any time of day; and if
some surprise is expressed, the Arabic woman will answer simply:

"How do you expect our mares not to recognize the hand that caresses and feeds them! How often do they play in my presence? And then, rearing behind me they will place their forefeet with great delicacy on my shoulders. They will pick up by the fleece a little lamb and carry it about. They get into the tent to steal couscous. Those are memories that are very dear to us. And too, is it not I who upon giving them milk or barley, am then privileged to reduce their stomachs, develop their breasts, refine their heads, stretch their foreheads, and toughen their legs?

"Watch them graze at the side of a herd of gazelles and you will not be able to note any difference between them and those animals. The same grace, the same vigor in their leaps, the same swiftness at a gallop.

"Like the gazelles, do they not have prominent eyes, with large pupils, fine and confident ears, clean legs, rounded rump, and hard, trim hooves?"[12]

Observations of the Emir Abd-el-Kader

"The details given about the training of the colt are true, for that is what we do. Overtiring and long journeys are not suitable for the colt as they do not allow him to grow in height or strength. A colt less than three years old is like a young tree, everything that gets in its way keeps it from growing. But what does suit such a colt is exercise and a prudently gradual hardening to fatigue. He must be accustomed to the saddle and bridle. He should not be ridden by anyone other than a child or a wise man, whose weights are in proportion to the age and strength of the colt.

"A widely practiced exercise is the following:

"The colt is mounted by a child, switch in hand, who launches him into a gallop. When the colt tires, he stops, grazes, and lies down. The following day in the morning he is given barley and taken back to the departure point of the day before. Again he is made to gallop, but this time for a longer distance and so on until he makes a gallop of double the distance which he galloped the first day.

"The Arabs look for a good walk in a colt and demand three types of gallop from him: 1) a hand gallop which is used for pleasure rid-

---

[12] This role of the woman in the life of the horse is not well known except to those who, instead of going by outward appearances, have wished to plumb Arabic customs. It could then be contested, but not for that would it be less an expression of the truth.

ing; 2) a hard, decided gallop which is used in war or in the chase of wild animals; 3) a sprint or burst of speed used for racing or to save one's head. The latter should not be overdone.

"To sum up, the training of the colt must be begun very early. Such a custom is excellent and not to adopt it is a dishonor; it makes the horse unfit for war. The animal that is not trained from its earliest years is not docile, but difficult and clumsy; he sweats with very little work and is good for nothing.[13]

"It is necessary then to spare the colt, as I have said, everything which could impede his growth and the development of his strength, and aim at obtaining by means of work a limber horse inured to fatigue.

"The first horse that the Prophet had was named Ouskoub [The Torrent] because of his speed, for *sakab* is the name given to swiftly flowing water.

"Another of the Prophet's horses was named Mortadjez, because of the harmony of his neigh which was like a poem with the harmonious meter of Aadjaz. He was white and was also called the Graceful One and the Noble.

"A third was named Traînant, as if he swept the ground with his tail.

"A fourth was named El Hezzez, the fixed, the adherent, as if he were already fixed or adhered to the object which one wishes to attain. Others believe that this name was an allusion to the vigorous set of his legs.

"A fifth was named the Hill, be it because of his height, or be it because of his vigor and the soundness of his legs.

[13] Here is a practical precept which proves how right those men are who train their horses from a very early age, and which puts on trial those ordinary men who only know how to fatten horses and who will not allow the first training until the age of five or six years. It is undoubtedly due to such a system that all such animals, under the appearance of strength, are unspirited, unattractive, and unenergetic. Raised like beasts for slaughter they acquire all the characteristics of such.

Such a system gives them flesh and fat, but reduces bone and tendons, compresses the respiratory organs, and deprives them of all those faculties which later will be sought in them. And is it not also to this deplorable system of training that slowness [in being fit for] military service is due, as well as those respiratory ailments which affect our horses the moment we put them to work? (Observation of the Count d'Aure, ex-*écuyer-in-chief* of the Cavalry School, today Inspector General of Studs and of the Stables of the Emperor.)

"The sixth horse of the Prophet was named the Rose, because of the color of his coat, intermediate between chestnut and brown bay.

"Lastly, the seventh horse was named Swimmer; this name was given to him because of the beautiful movement of his shoulders and because on galloping he lifted his forefeet as if swimming.

"The first horse, Ouskoub, was the Prophet's favorite.

"He also had others named The Sea, The Wolf, etc., etc.

"I have wished, upon setting forth these indications, to show to the Arabs the rule to be followed for naming their horses, which should always be named after the horses of the Prophet.

"Djarada, the javelin; Dalim, male ostrich; Rakib, the sentinel (a nickname for the wild ass,) are also suitable names for horses.

"There are three conditions of horses:

Some are burdened with crimes and belong to Satan.

Others, save from eternal fire and belong to man.

Yet others attract rewards and belong to God.

"Laden with crimes and belonging to Satan is that horse which is trained from pride or ostentation, of which one makes use to bet or to gamble or to do evil to Moslems.

"Preserved from fire and belonging to man is that horse bred for stud, to save his master from poverty, for use in personal affairs, without straying from the path of God. Such a horse one may refuse to allow to participate in races or be used for stud.

"Lastly, that horse which attracts rewards and belongs to God. It is that horse destined exclusively to good works in the interests of religion.

"The grass which such a horse eats in a pasture or in a paddock, the water he drinks on crossing a river with his master, without the latter having had any intention that he should drink that water, the urine and the dung are inscribed by God in the ledger of good works.

"Scold your horses and they will avoid the faults which occasioned the scolding, for they understand the wrath of man.

"A man of a noble family of the Oued-Chélif (a river in Algeria) on departing for Mecca was accompanied for a short distance by some friends, who made up the escort. He was riding a blood mare which his family still owns. Suddenly she stumbled and to punish her, he lashed her with the reins. This agitated her so much that for a few moments she did nothing but rear and plunge to right and left. On returning from Mecca the horseman made use of the same animal and the friends who had accompanied him when he departed, went to meet him to welcome him back and scarcely had they reached the spot where the mare had been beaten, than she reared and went through the same motions as on the previous occasion when she had felt the lash. All were astonished by the extraordinary memory of that animal who, for an entire year, had kept the memory of the beating she had received and of the place where it was administered.

" 'Our noble coursers spend their time vying with each other in fleetness, the women use their veils to wipe off the sweat that runs down their faces; they strain their heads as if they wished to free themselves from the bonds that hold them captive and they are attentive to the least cry. On their backs are mounted ferocious lions.' "

FEED

Give barley and abuse; morning grain
goes to the manure pile; but that of the
evening goes to the rump.

IN THE SAHARA, if horses are frequently given ewe's or camel's milk, do not think that this is their only drink. Milk more often takes the place of barley which is scarcer than water, the latter being comparatively easy to find.

Arabs are convinced that milk maintains health and makes the flesh firm without increasing fat. Needless to say, the wealthy who own many camels are less avaricious of milk than the poor to whom it is a resource barely sufficient for the needs of their families. The latter stretch it with water when they can. During the spring the Arabs give ewe's milk; at other seasons of the year they add camel's milk.

In Souf, Tougourt, Ouargla, Metlili, Gueléâa, and in the Touât where there are more camels than there are horses and where grain is scarcer than in the first zone of the desert, dates frequently take the place of barley. When they are dried they are fed to the horse in a nose bag; the horse upon eating them skilfully spits out the pits. In certain localities, the pits are separated from the dates, crushed in a mortar, and given to the horse, mixed with dates which have also been lightly ground. Dates are also given to horses before they are entirely ripe and then they are eaten, pits and all. As they are still tender, they cannot cause harm. When the Arabs want to mix dates with a drink they do it thus: after the harvest they take three or four pounds of fresh dates and beat them in a large container of water until the dates become a sort of paste; this is thoroughly mixed and given to the horse. A diet of dates fattens horses, but does not strengthen their fiber.

Here, by season, is the obligatory regimen of the horses in the first zone of the Sahara:

In the spring, generally, the horses are unshod and turned loose in pastures which at that season are found to be abundant in succulent and aromatic herbs known by the generic term of *el aâcheub*. They are hobbled. Care is taken to keep the horses away from the places where *ledena*, a velvety plant with leaves like a rat's ears, grows. It is found growing very close to the surface of the ground, ordinarily covered over and hidden by sand. It causes, in a horse that eats it, colics which more often than not are fatal.

Those personages who have many servants and experienced horsemen never give green feed to their war horses.

Rich or poor, no one feeds barley; it is replaced by ewe's milk, very abundant at that season. It keeps the horses in perfect condition.

Horses are watered only once a day, at two o'clock in the afternoon.

In the summer, the Arab journeys to the Tell to lay in a stock of grain. There the Arab is surrounded by dubious strangers and sometimes by enemies. One takes care about sending horses out to pasture. They run the risk of being stolen. In addition, no one would be displeased to have them at hand in case of what might happen. The Arabs buy barley straw and barley from their hosts. It is the time of year in which the animals find abundance.

I have said barley straw, because the Arabs would never agree to feeding their horses on the new wheat straw; it causes jaundice, they think, when one feeds it before winter.

Apart from the distrust of doubtful neighbors or the possibility of bothersome eventualities, another reason exists to prevent the Saharians from sending their horses to the pastures at that season. The stallions would there find themselves mixed up with the mares, the sight of whom would remind them of their springtime love affairs. At each step they would rub their nostrils in the mares' urine and they would contract a grave malady called *kuerrefa*. The stallion loses flesh; his coat becomes staring; he neighs incessantly, sucks wind, and refuses to eat. To cure him he is removed from the presence of the mares and his nostrils are rubbed with tar mixed with onion juice. The Arabs fear this disease so much that a rider in the desert would prefer to allow his stallion to mount ten times rather than allow him to come in contact with the mare's urine.

If for some reason or other, it is not possible to go to the Tell to buy grain and the slopes do not produce anything but sun-dried plants, then the Arabs journey close to the mountains of the Sahara where there are greater possibilities of finding water in ponds or even marshes. Should that recourse fail, then they go to camp close to the *kuesours* or desert hamlets[1] where they lay in a supply of straw for cash or by trading. In either case, only the mares are sent to the pastures; the stallions are picketed in front of the tents for fear of *kuerrefa*. The animals are watered twice a day, in the morning at an early hour, and in the afternoons after the setting of the sun, for experience has shown that at these hours, the water is healthier and cooler. At this time barley is indispensable.

No matter how hot it is, the Arabs do not give their horses that mixture of bran and barley flour, stretched with water, which we call *barbotage* [mash] and of which we make so much misuse. To it the Arabs attribute the softening of the flesh, which favors the formation of fat—and that they avoid above all else. When their horses are heated, they lessen their work, giving them, if possible, *kuecil* or green barley; and if they do not have any, they bathe the horses to refresh them. As far as barley is concerned, they want it plump, without a bad odor, without the earth which gets mixed with it in the silos, and without those black and withered grains which have been struck by the southern winds.

In the autumn, the stallions return to the pastures where *chiehh* is found; that marvellous resource of the Sahara—where in order to praise a man who is capable and yet modest, it is said of him: "So-and-so is like the *chiehh*; he is capable and therefore one does not speak of him."

So much for the daytime. At night the horse is given, by handfuls some *seurr*, a species of thorny bush which is cut off close to the ground, flailed to remove the dry thorns which might injure the animal's throat or stomach lining and which contains many nutritive ele-

---

[1] *Kuesours*: singular *ksar*, hamlet, village, or town of the desert.

ments. The Arabs prepare, moreover, another plant very similar to the wild bramble which is called *âdem*.

Water is given only once a day, about two o'clock in the afternoon, because that hour would appear to be the best at a time of year when the temperature goes lower and lower; then the water has had the chill taken off.

Wealthy people feed barley; the poor cannot always do so.

In the winter, the horses continue to go to the pastures which are then abundant in grasses according to the rainfall; there can be found *chiehh, âdem, derine,*[2] and others which suffice largely for their nourishment.

At night the horses are given *bouse* which the Arabs term brother to barley, so much do they appreciate its nutritive properties. The *bouse* is none other than *alfa*[3] which, after its ears have formed, has been pulled up and has come loose from its wrapping. When it has been garnered in small bundles it is cut in pieces and takes the place of chopped straw. Furthermore, the *alfa* is utilized in another way: the roots are dug up with a hoe and their red covering is removed. The animals eat the peeled roots with avidity. This fodder then takes the name of *gueddeine* or *zemouna* according to the locality. It is nutritious, but does not do away with the need for barley.

Hay is unknown in the desert. The Arabs could, if they wished, make great quantities for the winter; but they dislike it, saying that it only serves to make the horse bloated, softening the flesh, and in the long run to cause inflammatory diseases. Water is given only once a day, as in the autumn. A proverb among the Arabs is "the morning grain goes to the manure pile, but that of the evening goes to the rump." The Arabs assert then that if a horse drank his fill the night before and ate well during the night, there is no need to give him

---

[2] *Derine* is the *Stipa barbatta* of Desfontaines. This plant grows abundantly in the Sahara. The inhabitants of that none too productive soil go great distances to garner the seeds of that cereal grass, and often bring back large loads. Those seeds, which are callel *el loul*, have the same use as wheat. Flour is made from them.

[3] *Alfa*: this plant is very widespread in Algeria. It is a great resource in the feeding of horses. On our marches the horses frequently did not have anything but that plant to eat. It is the esparto or Spanish grass (*Stepa tenacissima*). The stalk does not grow to a height of more than ten or twelve centimeters. Another variety is the *Lygeum spartum* which serves in the Orient to make the handicrafts called *sparterie*. In some places in Algeria the natives make mats out of it.

anything in the morning, especially when one starts off early. Also in our camps, sometimes filled with from fifteen to eighteen hundred Arabic horsemen on expedition with us, what took place before our eyes? The following: all the veteran officers of the Army in Africa can bear witness to it. Contrary to our custom, until the moment of departure utmost calm reigns in the Arabic camp. Not one moment is wasted that can be used to rest the horses. They are neither watered nor fed. Only, but a short time before departure, they are rubbed down with rough cloths; their blankets are exchanged for the saddles; they are bridled; tents are struck; morning prayers are said; and departure is made exactly at the appointed time. Several times it occurred to me to express surprise over this system, but always did the Arabs answer me: "Why do you do for your horse what you will not do for yourself? When you get up from the table at ten or eleven o'clock at night, can you be ready the following morning when the day breaks?"

With this regime the horses are kept lean, agile, and they are always ready to walk, gallop, or to perform, in sum, all the rough service demanded of them in the Sahara. They gain flesh in an astonishing manner, when instead of a few fistfuls of barley and some grazing on slopes burnt by a blazing sun, they encounter the feed of the Tell. What would happen if they were looked after like the European horses? Instead of being in hard flesh, they would be fat and would look well—but not to the eyes of the Arabs, who do not admire the type of beauty generally gained at the expense of the attributes of a war horse.

Be that as it may, even if the Arab is too true a horseman not to adhere to these ideas, he is also too great a lover of pomp, applause, and the *fantasia*, if I may be permitted to employ a term already popular in France, not to permit himself, when he can, the luxury of a horse for show and parade. Thus it is not unusual to see well-to-do Arabs leave their pet mares, for three or four months, tied in front of their tents without riding them. The mares then get fat and are not used except at fiestas, weddings, and on all occasions when the chieftains wish to show off.

For the chase, forays, and long punishing gallops the Arabs have horses of less evident worth, but of which they are sure; and they do not hesitate to tire them.

The mares to which we have just referred are most luxuriously caparisoned. The saddle pads and headstalls are embroidered with fine gold, the stirrups are silver or gold plated and the saddle cloths, *beda*, made of felt are as lovely as woven material; those held in the highest esteem are made in Ouargla.

Observations of the Emir Abd-el-Kader

"A certain morning, on sallying forth, one of his comrades found the Prophet wiping his horse's head with his mantle.

" 'Why with your mantle?'

" 'Oh, what do you know!' exclaimed the Prophet. 'Perhaps the Archangel Gabriel willed me to do it for his sake last night.'

" 'Well, at least, let me give him his feed.'

" 'Ah!' said the Prophet. 'You want to get all the rewards for yourself, because the Archangel Gabriel informed me that each grain of barley which I might give my horse will be counted as a good deed.'

"The inhabitants of the Sahara give their horses camel's milk, which has the especial property of making them swift, to the point that even a man, so people of good faith tell, who drinks it and it only for a sufficient length of time, acquires so much speed that such a man has been able to vie in swiftness with the horse. In practice camel's milk strengthens the brain and the tendons and makes the fat that softens the muscles to disappear.

"In certain parts of the Sahara, nobles and horsemen of great renown never give green feed to their war horses. Milk, barley, and the plants known by the names of *chiehh, derine, bouse,* and *seuliane* constitute their only diet. This diet does not expand the stomach and it does not fatten like green feed which bloats the alimentary tract, as much by reason of the enormous quantities which the horse must consume to satiate himself as by reason of the water it contains.

"In summer, water is not given to horses except at three o'clock in the afternoon. In winter, they are watered earlier—from midday to one o'clock in the afternoon, because that is the time of day when in the open air the water has lost its chill. These principles are explained in the following proverb, which is known to the least desert horseman:

" 'During hot weather[4] delay the hour of watering
And advance the hour of the nose bag.

[4] The Arabs mean by "hot weather" from April through September, and by "cold weather" from October through March.

During cold weather, advance the hour of watering
And delay the hour of the nose bag.'

"Among the tribes of the desert beginning with the month of August and continuing for forty days thereafter, water is given only every two days. The same system is followed during the last twenty days of December and the first twenty days in January.

"During the time of cold weather the wealthy give as much barley as a horse can eat and they cut down on the ration during the time of heat. Milk and *bouse* can take the place of barley.

"It is a rarity to give feed in the morning. The horse works on the feed of the night before and not on that of the same day.

"On looking at two horses, one from the Tell and the other from the Sahara, the man who has not delved deeply into the subject, would always prefer the former, which he would regard as being beautiful, stout, sleek, and fat, and he would contemptuously regard the second, which he would calumniate, fool that he is, for all the qualities which combine to make his strength; that is to say, the clean dry legs, lean belly, and bare ribs. Yet, meanwhile, that desert horse who barely knows what barley, green feed, and hay are, who only knows *chiehh, bouse,* and *seuliane,* who has never drunk anything but milk, who from a very early age has galloped in the chase and foray, will have the speed of the gazelle and the resignation of the dog; while the other [horse] will never be anything more than an ox at his side.

"The greatest enemies of the horse are rest and fat."

9

GROOMING, HYGIENE, AND PROPORTIONS

A noble may, without blushing, do manual
labor for the benefit of his horse, of his
father, and of his host.

GROOMING IS UNKNOWN in the Sahara. Horses are merely rubbed
down with woolen cloths, and the Arabs rug them with very good
blankets, *djellale*, which envelope the croup and breast. In truth, little
need is felt for this labor, the horses always being placed in healthy
positions on high ground and sheltered from drafts. The Arabs who
have seen us groom our horses, morning and night, with minute care,
allege that the continual rubbing of the hide, especially with the
currycomb, lessens their health, makes them delicate, very sensitive,
and, therefore, incapable of enduring the hardships of war or, at least,
more subject to diseases.

When it is hot and if it can be done, the horses are bathed, morning
and night. Frequently in winter they are tethered inside the tents,
which are very spacious, to protect them from the sun and the rain.

The principle is to have them clean. One day a horse was taken to
the Prophet. He examined the horse, got up and without saying a
word, he cleaned the horse's head, eyes and nostrils with the sleeves
of his tunic.

"What! With your garments!" onlookers said to him.

"Certainly," he replied, "and it was the Archangel Gabriel who more than once has reprimanded me and ordered me to proceed thus."

In winter the horses are blanketed night and day; in summer the blankets are put on at ten in the morning only to be removed from three in the afternoon until eight o'clock at night, at which hour they are put back on for the remainder of the night to keep the horses from a chill and from the dew which, according to the Arabs, is even more dangerous when the skin has been heated all during the day by a blazing sun.

The following proverb explains how much the Arabs dread the cold of summer nights:

"The cold of the summer or the slash of a saber."

If the Arabs do not, like us, attach much importance to grooming they are, on the other hand, very painstaking and meticulous in the choice of feed and above all the water which their horses drink. Many times, in the early days of the conquest [French domination of Algeria], while on a campaign, after many long days of hot marching with a wind from the south which choked us and blew sand and dust into our faces, when horsemen and infantry—both exhausted—rested, although continually harassed by the alarms which the enemy that circled and recircled in the vicinity gave us, I saw natives go as far as a league from camp to water their horses from a pure spring that was known to them.[1] They would rather risk their lives thus than bear the shame of giving water to their horses in the brooks of the camp where the passage of men and pack animals had left polluted pools.

I do not believe that it is necessary for me to examine the question of grooming among the Arabs in detail, for I could add nothing but repetitions and it seems preferable to me to remind the reader of all the details scattered throughout the preceding pages, especially the principles set forth in the chapter on the training of the colt. If I have expressed myself well, I shall have shown how every horse-owner among the Arabs is an attentive, watchful—I was going to say devoted—master, who follows and directs the progress, corrects the faults, and perfects the aptitudes of his pupil from the very beginning. This training takes in everything, as well as what I would term bringing out moral attributes. This education modifies, improves, and augments the physical attributes.

[1] One of the reasons for this was explained in Chapter 7, note 11. [Translator's note]

All is calculated and foreseen: drinking water, feed, exercises, shelter—all are tempered according to ages, places and seasons. Everything is the object of unceasing and constant care.

Once again, the matter does not reduce itself to knowing if the care is fully understood, if it is wrong, or if we are mistaken. However, after having asserted that in Arabic life the chief and almost sole preoccupation is the training and care of the horse, I have observed that the Arab does not go by chance, his passion is not blind and unreasoning, as those who observe him from afar and with a quick glance believe. Any man could convince himself, who studies the Arab's life with diligence and who analyses his daily acts under a microscope, if I may express it thus, that it is conducted or guided by a traditional and purposeful behavior. In a word, this training and care of the horse is subject to constant and sure rules, which all have as their ultimate purpose endowing the horse with vigor, bottom, and health.

What other thing is that but hygiene?

The Arabs, Ben-el-Ouardy says, have always preferred beautiful horses to their own children, and they are so fond of showing off on festive occasions or days of combat that they would go hungry before allowing the horses to suffer thirst or hunger. In difficult and burdensome circumstances, in years of famine above all, they go the length of giving the horse preferential treatment before themselves or their families. The sayings which are quoted apropos of this statement, as well as the ballads composed by their poets, prove it.

Here are some verses addressed by the sage Ben-Sassa to the great tribe of the Beni-Aâmer. We reproduce them in all their originality:

Beni-Aâmer[2] why do I see your horses
   Gaunt, changed by misery?
   Such condition cannot suit them.
Although Death has an appointed time which nothing can delay,
   The horses are your safeguard,
      Give them the goods which you prefer;
      With pure barley fill their nose bags
      And garnish their hooves with iron.

      Love horses, care for them:
      Only in them lie honor and beauty.

[2] *Beni-Aâmer*: a very important tribe situated to the northwest of Oran.

On caring for them you care for yourselves.
The Arab who does not have a good horse cannot aim at good repute.
For me, on this earth, I do not know of any other good fortune,
  And, if I have strength in golden *soulthanis*[3]
I would not rejoice except to share them with him.
  I would also support my family,
  And should they make me lack
  I shall know how to lower my pride
To the extent of arrogantly demanding alms for my friend.
All the treasures of Karoune,[4] without a horse
  Could not make me happy.

Should the North wind blow,
And the sky open over the earth,
Shelter your horses from the cold rain,
Warm them; they deserve these attentions.
For games, for war,
Deck them in the most luxurious of saddles,
With bridles embroidered in gold, with superb saddle cloths,
And the Prophet will love you.

Take thought also for the mares of your poor servitors
  Who, in spite of all their labors,
  Have not been able to satisfy their needs,
  Give them a generous hospitality,
Share with them the daily bread.
  Associate them with your families;
  Many of your sins will be remitted.

  The sabers are drawn,
  The warriors are in ranks,
The horse will become more precious than the wife.
  The fire of combat has been lit,
  I take him toward the midst of dangers,
  He protects me with his head, with his croup,
    And makes my enemies fly.

---

[3] *Soulthanis*: pieces of gold struck in Moslem countries and worth ten to twelve francs.

[4] *Karoune*: an Indian prince who lived before the birth of the Prophet and whose wealth was proverbial.

May God preserve this maned horse[5]
Whose eyes are flaming!

Love horses, care for them,
Only in them lie honor and beauty.

One sees, therefore, that in the Sahara, the horse is the most beautiful creature after man; the most noble occupation is that of breeding him, the most wonderful pastime is riding him, and the best domestic task is taking care of him.

The Arabs believe that they can determine beforehand, by means of certain methods, what will be the height and the attributes of a colt when he matures into a horse and the rules vary in different localities.

Here are those most generally recognized:

To measure height one takes a cord or a soft rope and places it behind the ears, over the poll, joining the two ends just under the upper lip. This measure once fixed is then applied to the distance which separates the foot from the withers; it is believed that the colt will grow the length left over.

When one wants to judge by his proportions the worth of a horse, one measures with the hand from the tip of the dock to the middle of the withers and one counts the number of palms [handbreadths]; then one begins to count from the middle of the withers to the end of the upper lip, passing between the ears. If the two measurements are the same, the horse will be a good one, but of average speed. If the rear measurement is longer, the animal is mediocre. But if the measurement from the top of the withers to the end of the upper lip is greater than the other, ah! Then the animal, you may rest assured, will have great qualities. The longer he is in the forehand, the more valuable he is. One can, say the Arabs, with such a horse go far, expressing thus the speed and bottom which such conformation assures.[6]

---

[5] "This maned horse"; a reference to the practice of cutting the hair of the mane until the horse is five years old. Therefore an animal with a mane, ridden into battle, would be eight years old at least, as it requires three years for the mane to reach its full growth. The Arabs did not consider a horse fit to be ridden into combat until he was at least eight years old. [Translator's note]

[6] "This simple procedure is of undoubted veracity. In effect, if the measurement from the middle of the withers to the tip of the dock is shorter, it is proof that the loins are short, the back straight, and the withers 'reversed.' If the measurement forward is longer, it is proof that the withers will be 'reversed,' the shoulders sloped, and the neck long. I tried this out in the cavalry school on more

With a little practice one can train one's eye and there is no necessity for measuring—a horse goes by, one swiftly compares the forehand from the withers forward with the hindquarters and, save for details, he is judged.

Observations of the Emir Abd-el-Kader

"On passing in front of a horse the Prophet began rubbing his head with the sleeve of his tunic, saying: 'God has been angry with me on account of horses.'

" 'Good fortune is fastened to the horses' forelocks,' and it is because of them that their owners may count on the help of God; also you should wipe their forelocks with your hands.

"A sage has said: 'A noble works with his hands, without blushing, under three circumstances: for his horse, for his father, and for his host.'

"One way of judging a horse is to measure him from the root of the mane close to the withers, to the end of the upper lip between his nostrils; then one measures from the root of the mane to the tip of the dock; if the forehand which one has measured is longer than the hind part, one can be sure that he will have excellent quality.

"To find out if a young horse will continue to grow or not, the Arabs first measure from the knee to the highest point of the withers, then from the knee to the top of the coronet (as far as the wall of the hoof); if these measurements are between them in the ratio of two-thirds to one third, the horse will not continue to grow. However, if this proportion does not exist the horse will continue to grow, for it is absolutely indispensable that in a grown horse the height from the knee to the withers represent double the length of the part of the leg from the knee to the hoof.

"In the desert the currycomb is unknown, but the horses are groomed with the nose bag, which is made of horsehair, and they are frequently bathed when the weather permits.

"The horses are generally given milk to drink, but if this becomes scarce, one does not hesitate to traverse long distances in search of water that is clear and pure.

---

than one hundred horses whose qualities were known to me and never did the measurements give the lie to the opinion I had of each animal." (Evaluation of the Count d'Aure)

"One sees to it that the barley is plump, very clean, without a bad odor, and completely free from the dirt which of necessity gets mixed in with it in the silos, as well as being free of those black and withered grains which have been struck by the southern winds.

"The horses are rugged with good blankets that protect their loins, bellies, and breasts. The rugs are manufactured within the tribes. Those that are carefully made are waterproof.

"There are certain colors [of horses] which should be equally protected from heat and cold. Experience has shown that this is necessary with all light-colored horses, beginning with the white, for their delicacy of skin makes them very sensitive.

" 'In the sun he melts like butter,
        In the rain he dissolves like salt.'

"Dark coats do not require such care.

"When it is very cold or very hot, the horses are made to enter the tents.

"In the Sahara the nights are always cool and summer or winter one must rug the horses.

"No precaution is neglected to avoid the stoppage of transpiration. After a long gallop, one does not unsaddle until the horse is dry; feed is not given until his breathing has returned to normal, and, more often than not, he is watered with the bridle on.

"Finally, care is taken to select good campgrounds. A dry terrain is desirable—free of rocks which could be a hindrance—on which the horse is placed in such a manner that his forehand is on ground a little higher than his hindquarters, and that, as much as possible, he is facing his master, who watches over him night and day as one of his children.

"To place a horse with his forehand lower than his hindquarters is to ruin his shoulders.

"The *djellale* should always be well cared for. A horseman comes very close to being disdained by the Arabs when they can say of him:

" 'His horse drinks muddy water
        And its blanket is full of holes.' "

10

COLORS

Always choose solid and dark coats
and distrust those which are light
and washy.

COLORS. The most highly regarded colors are:

The white (*el biod, el cheheub*). "Take the white like a silk flag, without bare patches, and with a black ring around his eyes."

The black (*el kahal, el deheum*). "He should be black as a night without moon or stars."

The bay (*el ameur*). He should be almost black (*semm*) or golden (*koummite*).

> "The mahogany bay
> Says to an argument: 'Come no closer.' "

The chestnut (*el cheggeur*). "Desire him to be toasted [liver]. When he flies under the sun, he is the wind. The Prophet was fond of chestnuts."

The dappled dark gray, which they [the Arabs] term the gray of the wild pigeon (*zereug el goumery*). "*If* he is like the stones in a river, he will refill the camp when it becomes empty, and he will save us in combat on the day when the firearms clash."

Grays are, in general, esteemed when their heads are less dark than the rest of their coats.

The wolf-color (*el khedeur*), the green [a dun]. One would desire him to be dark with a black mane and tail.

White, that is the color of princes, but cannot stand the heat.

The black brings good luck, but fears rocky ground.

The chestnut is the swiftest; if someone assures you that a horse flew, ask what color he was, and if you are told chestnut, believe it.

The bay, he is the hardiest and the most sober. If someone tells you that a horse leapt to the bottom of an abyss without injuring himself, ask what color he was, and if you are told bay, believe it.

Ben-Dyab, a chieftain renowned throughout the desert, who lived about the year 905 [counting from the Hegira], found himself one day being pursued by Saad-el-Zanaty, sheik of the Oulad-Yagoub. He turned towards his son and asked: "Which of the enemies' horses are in the lead?"

"The whites," answered his son.

"That is well. We'll get on the sunny side and they will melt as if they were made of butter."

A little later, Ben-Dyab turned to his son and demanded:

"Which are the horses now that are closest to us?"

"The blacks," his son shouted at him.

"Good. We'll take to rocky ground and will have nothing to fear; they are like the Negress of the Sudan who cannot walk barefooted over pebbles."

They changed their course and very soon the black horses were outdistanced. A third time Ben-Dyab asked:

"And now which horses are in the lead?"

"The liver chestnuts and the brown bays."

"In that case," yelled Ben-Dyab, "Sweat, my children, sweat and heels to our horses, for those [horses] could easily overtake us, if, during the entire summer we had not given barley to our own.[1]

---

[1] What a charming tale! Every bit of it is true. Experience and observation do no more than prove it.

Thus the pure-bred breed in England [The Thoroughbred], so famous for its speed, derives its origin from three Arabian horses, of which two were chestnuts, the Darley Arabian and the Byerley Turk. The Godolphin Barb was a bay. Eclipse, the fastest of known horses, was a chestnut. Rubens, Plenipotentiary, Tigris, and a thousand other celebrated runners were chestnuts. The rest were bays. Very rarely does one see on the racecourse a gray horse, and I am not aware that any horse of that color has ever won a race.

I stop here, for, if one should wish to take from the work of General Daumas everything that is good; everything that is true and instructive, it would be necessary to copy the entire book. I should not take more than that which ought

The colors held in contempt are:

The Pied (*el begâa*). "Fly from him like the plague, he is the brother of the cow."

> "The couscous comes when he has departed
> And quarrels begin the moment he appears."

The yellow dun with a flaxen mane and tail [the *isabelle*]. A chieftain would not ride such an animal and there are even tribes who would not permit him to spend the night in one of their camps. They call him "The yellow of the Jew (*sefeur-el-ihoudi*)." That color brings misfortune.

> "The iron gray
> And the yellow of the Jew
> If his master returns (from combat)
> Cut off my hand."

The gray roan (*el hamary*). He is termed *megheredeur edeum*, a sea of blood; his master will be taken prisoner and will never fight again.

Hold in high regard a horse without white markings on his legs and with a white star on his head (*ghora*) or with a simple stripe (*syâla*). The stripe must reach down to his lips—his master will never lack for milk. It is a felicitious indication. It is the image of the dawn. If the star is broken and irregular it will please no one, and if the animal has, in addition, an off-fore with a white sock, no man in his right mind should mount the animal, no connoisseur would even want to own him. That horse slays like subtle venom.

Should the horse have white leg markings, desire three white marks, with the exception of one off-foot, the fore or the hind, it matters not.

A good sign is a white off-fore with a white near-hind. One terms that:

> "The hand of the scribe
> And the foot of the horseman."

---

not to be unknown to a cavalry officer, that which could lend support to the precepts which I am seeking to introduce into the cavalry school. All that which deals with the subject of horse breeding, with hygiene, with mating, is also most worth while consulting. The work of General Daumas will be epoch-making and should be found, not only in the library of the horseman, but also in the library of every person who loves poetical, interesting and instructive works. (Observations of the Count d'Aure)

The master of such a horse cannot help but be happy, for he mounts on a white foot and dismounts on another (It is known that the Arabs mount on the off-side and generally dismount on the near).

Two white hindfeet are an indication of good fortune:

"The horse with two white hind-feet,
His master will never be ruined."

The same thing does not apply to a horse with two white forefeet; his master will always have an ashen face.

Never buy a bald-faced horse with four white feet for he carries his shroud with him.

The beliefs of the Arabs with respect to white feet are concentrated in the following little tale.

A certain Arab had a pure-bred mare and before she foaled many were vying for her product. Thus when the mare was about to foal, her owner convened all his friends. The foal's head came first and had a star in the middle of the forehead. The Arab rejoiced. With that mark his horse could surpass the dawn as the mark was on the forehead. Next came the near-fore and the wildly enthusiastic owner asked one hundred duros for his foal. The off-fore came next, with a white sock and the price went down to fifty duros. Then came the near-hind, with a white sock. The Arab, delirious with joy, swore that he would not exchange his foal for anything in the world. But then came the fourth foot, also with a white sock. In his fury, the inhabitant of the Sahara ordered the foal to be thrown on the dungheap, because he could not bring himself to keep such a beast.

WHORLS

The horse has forty whorls; of these forty, there are twenty-eight which, in general, are considered as being of neither good nor bad augury; only to twelve whorls is an influence attributed. It is agreed to regard six of them as increasing wealth, bringing good luck, and six others as causing ruin, bringing adversity.

The whorls that are of good omen:

The whorl which is found between the ears; the whorl of the crown piece of the bridle. The horse is swift on the race track.

The whorl on the sides of the neck, the finger of the Prophet. That horse's master will die a good Mohammedan and in his bed.

The whorl of the Sultan. It lies along the length of the neck following the windpipe: love, riches, and prosperity. The horse that has this mark makes three daily prayers: "May God grant that my master consider me as being the most precious of such precious things as he may possess in this world." "May God give him good luck so that mine may also be good." "May He grant him the mercy of dying a martyr on my back."

The whorl on the breast will fill the tent with booty.

The whorl of the girth increases herds and flocks.

The whorl situated on the flank, the whorl of the spurs. If it has an upward inclination towards the back, it will save the rider from any mishap in combat. If it has a downward inclination towards the belly, it is a sign of riches for the horse's owner.

The whorls that bring misfortune:

The whorl which is found above the eyebrow. The horse's master will be killed by a blow on the head.

The whorl of the coffin. It is found close to the withers with a downward inclination toward the shoulders. The rider shall die on the back of such a horse.

The whorl of lamentations. It is found on the cheeks: debts, wailing, ruin.

The whorl of theft: it is found on the fetlocks. Day and night the horse says: "Oh, my God! Grant that I may be stolen or that my master die."

The whorl to one side of the tail. It presages trouble, misery, and famine.

The whorl found on the inside of the buttocks: wives, children, and livestock will all disappear.

I have given the classification generally adopted, but it is not absolute, it varies from one place to another. Each tribe increases or diminishes the number of its good or bad whorls.

As one can see, I have not spoken of any but the principal colors, as I did not wish to go into the question of the mixtures of coats, which would have carried me to great lengths. Although the subject is full of prejudices and superstitions, it has been established that the Arabs like solid, dark colors. They judge light and washy colors, together with white markings on the head, body, and legs, when such markings are long and broad, to indicate a degeneration in the species and be signs of unsoundness.

Each Arab has his favorite color. Some like blacks; others grays; these, bays; those, chestnuts; etc. Their predilections or antipathies are, generally, motivated by family memories or traditions; so-and-so's forebears had great successes with this or that color and suffered reverses with others One sees, then, an Arab refuse a good horse, giving as his only reason: "He is not my color."

Observations of the Emir Abd-el-Kader

"*Colors.* The most highly regarded horse is the black with a star on his forehead and white markings on his feet.

"Next comes the blood bay with a black mane.

"Then comes the bright chestnut (*alezan cerise*) with a red mane.

"Horses of other colors are all placed on the same line, with the exception of the pied which the Arabs do not want at all.

"The Prophet has said: 'If you wish to go to war, buy a horse with a star on his forehead and three white feet, but that the off-fore be not white.'

"The horse with four evenly white feet is like a man who sways gracefully on walking, the sleeves of his mantle floating in the air.

"The Prophet has said: 'If after having gathered together in one place all the horses of the Arabs, I were to make them gallop together, it would be the chestnut that would out-distance them all.'

"According to these traditions, the black horse has the supremacy because of the loveliness of his form and his attributes; the chestnut for his speed.

"The Arabs have this proverb: 'If you have a chestnut, use him. If you have nothing but a poor chestnut, use him anyway.'

"In a vast arena destined for races, feast your eyes on the assembly of noble coursers.

"You will see the one which by arriving first at the finish line has dissipated his master's cares.

"Then the one that arrived second follows the first one very closely, both having reached the finish line without slackening their pace.

"Each horse of a noble strain captivates the eyes and shackles the glances of the enthusiastic spectator.

"One of a rose color. His skin resembles the red tint which the setting sun leaves on the horizon; another a white color, like a shooting star hurled at evil jinn.

"A third, a blood bay with a black mane, of incomparable beauty and tall body. One recognizes in him traces of his uncles, paternal and maternal, famous in racing annals.

"One also sees a bright bay whose coat is like gold.

"Then a chestnut who pleases because of his resplendent mane.

"Or another, black like the night, solely adorned with a white star on his forehead which shines like the first glow of dawn. Oh! He is blessed, the horse with a star and white socks.

"The Prophet detested a horse with four white socks.

"The horse with a white stripe that does not reach the upper lip, accompanied by a white off-fore, carries the worst of all auguries and he who sees him prays to God to spare him from the evil that he presages; he is like an hour's poison (that which carries off its victim within the hour).

"The swiftest of horses is the chestnut;
The most enduring the bay;
The most spirited the black;
The most blessed is he that has a white forehead.

"*Whorls.* The Arabs distinguished forty whorls on the horse. There are twenty-eight which are of no importance in their sight and are, therefore, of neither good nor bad omen. It is to only twelve of the whorls that they attribute an influence admitted by tradition and confirmed in their sight by observation.

" 'Horses are eagles mounted by horsemen; long like lances, they come cleaving the air like the falcon who falls on his prey.' "

CHOICE AND PURCHASE OF A HORSE

> By the Head of the Prophet, you would
> never ask how much my horse had cost
> had you seen him charge the enemy.
>
> Ruined [man,] son of a ruined [man], he
> who buys to cure.

IN THE SAHARA horses famous for their blood and speed sell easily and for high prices.

There are causes which will render a horse totally unfit for use in war and these are:

A narrow and sunken breast accompanied by thin, straight shoulders. One cannot imagine the importance the Arabs attach to the development of the muscles of the breast.

Thick low withers. Never will you be able to set a saddle properly on such a horse, nor will you be able to make bold use of him to gallop downhill.

Curb (*bou-chiba*). "The father of whitening"—of the chin, it goes without saying.[1]

[1] It is interesting to note that Bruno and Beatriz Premiani in their work *El Caballo,* in a plate illustrating the external diseases of horses indicate a sore (which they term a splint) in the chin groove. As in Argentina exactly the same type of bit is used as in Algeria (having been brought by the Spaniards, who in turn took it from the Moors after their conquest of Spain), it would seem more than a coincidence that the writers in those two countries where such a bit is in

Bowed tendons, when very pronounced.

Thoroughpins.

Spavin, especially when it borders the vein.

The formations called *louzze* (sidebone) and *fekroune* (ringbone).

Splints close to the tendons.

Long, weak pasterns.

Short, straight pasterns (*terrekuib el ghrezal*, the straightness of the gazelle).

Windgalls going up the length of the tendon.

A long and hollow back.

A horse that cannot see at night or when there is snow. He can be recognized by the way in which he lifts his feet as soon as darkness falls. One can make sure, furthermore, by presenting a dark surface to him in daylight. Should he walk over it quietly, the case has been proved. The life of the Arab is spent in making night marches to surprise the enemy or to fly from him. What would he do with such an animal?

Pegged shoulders.

Now here are the defects or blemishes which, although generally feared, do not prevent a horse from entering into circulation:

Narrow nostrils—the animal with such a defect will leave you in the lurch.

Long, slack, and floppy ears.

A thick, short neck.

Pay little attention to a horse that never lies down.

Hold in little esteem those horses that switch their tails on galloping.

Disdain those horses that scratch their necks with their feet, those that lie on their shoes, those that overreach, those that brush, distrust them.

---

common use should make mention of this specific type of lesion. Of many authorities, writing in English, whom I have consulted, only one, Francis Dwyer in his *On Seats and Saddles*, mentions this type of unsoundness specifically. He refers to it as a sore produced by badly fitted curb chains or straps.

This, to me, would seem to prove that, while the action of the Arabic ring-curb bit on a horse's mouth may, as General Daumas claims in a later chapter, not be as severe as some think, the ring itself, resting in the chin groove, is most deleterious in its effect on that portion of the lower jaw. It would, of course, render an animal unfit for use in war as, maddened by pain, it would be unmanageable. [Translator's note]

To find out if a horse will interfere, place your two closed fists together between the horse's forelegs, just below the brisket. Should the inside walls of the forelegs touch your fists, you may be sure that the animal has too narrow a chest and cannot help but interfere.

Be suspicious of the horse that wets his nose bag on eating his barley—that gives the appearance of tasting water with the point of his lips; whose anus is open and flatulent, signs of softness; or whose dung is not compact.

An ambler ill becomes a chieftain; he is the horse of those "who drum their heels" to carry messages.

Beware of the horse that "denies the spurs" (kicks at the boot), bites, "escapes the stirrups" (is difficult to mount), or who runs away from his rider who has dismounted. These are grave defects for war.

Leave the deaf horse for the packsaddle; you will know him by his expressionless, dangling, and turned-back ears and, moreover, by the fact that he does not respond to any clicking of the tongue.

By means of sight, sense of smell, and hearing the horse can, if not save his rider from great danger, at least warn him of it. He says: "Save me from that which lies in front. I will save you from what lies behind."

The lion and horse were vying to find out which one had better vision. The lion saw, on a dark night, a white hair in a little milk and the horse saw a black hair in a little bit of tar. Witnesses ruled in favor of the horse.

The greatest virtue in the horse is resignation. A perfect horse is one that unites strength to that quality. A horse is strong when one can count from the hoofprints of the hindlegs twelve to fourteen feet to those of the forelegs in the first bound of the gallop; if he has exceeded this, he has superior force; the animal that does not clear more than eight to ten feet is a clumsy animal.

A very fiery horse cannot have resignation to fatigue; thus he will be that horse whose legs are tall, who has too long a neck, and whose haunches are too powerful to be in harmony with the other parts of his body; or, perhaps, that horse whose heels lack strength. Such a horse, after a long gallop, will be leg-weary; he does not know how to stop at the wish of his rider; he takes a few steps more, as if he could not help himself.

The horse that has neither resignation nor mettle is easily recognized; the shape of his body is not uniform. His breast is narrow, he

"The horse walks, so to speak, on his hind legs." (Courtesy of Photo Keystone, Paris.)

"A horse which can, in a country generally very difficult and broken, walk, run, climb, and descend, endure unheard of privations, and do his campaigning vigorously—is he or is he not a war horse?" A French trooper on a grey Barb. (From T. A. Dodge, *Riders of Many Lands*; courtesy of the Hall of the Horsemen, The University of Texas at Austin.)

"Which do you like better, being mounted or dismounted? 'May God damn their meeting point!' answered the horse." A Spahi trooper and his horse. (Courtesy of the Service Cinéma des Armées, Paris.)

"Religion, war, the chase, love, and horses, inexhaustible topics, turn these talks into real schools, in which the warrior molds himself." Spahis gathered around the fire in front of their tents. (Photo by M. Recoupé.)

EUG. TITEUX

"Called to the honor of serving France, the native Algerian troops were not long in covering themselves with glory." Two Spahi troopers of about 1845; the mounted man from the 2nd Regiment, the man on foot from the 3rd Regiment. (Courtesy of the Hall of the Horsemen, The University of Texas at Austin.)

"In combat always ride a sweeper with his tail. The day on which riders are so hard pressed that the stirrups clash, he will get you out of the melee." A rider from the 2nd Regiment of Spahis, 1845. (Courtesy of the Hall of the Horsemen, The University of Texas at Austin.)

"The saddle enhances the horse." A Spahi and his Barb, the horse showing a spur scar on its flank. (From T. A. Dodge, *Riders of Many Lands*; courtesy of the Hall of the Horsemen, The University of Texas at Austin.)

"All the world's blessing shall depend from the forelocks of our horses."
(Courtesy of the Service Cinéma des Armées, Paris.)

"The Arab is too great a lover of pomp, applause, and the *fantasia* not to permit himself, when he can, the luxury of a horse for show and parade." A *fantasia* rider.

"Love for the horse flows in Arabic blood; the noble animal is a comrade-in-arms and the friend of the chieftain." A caliph in Tunisia.

(From T. A. Dodge, *Riders of Many Lands*; courtesy of the Hall of the Horsemen, The University of Texas at Austin.)

"The horses leave the earth, the weapons fly—this is the enchantment." (Courtesy of the Hall of the Horsemen, The University of Texas at Austin.)

" . . . the sweetness, the good manners, and the intelligence found in Arabian horses." (Courtesy of the Service Cinéma des Armées, Paris.)

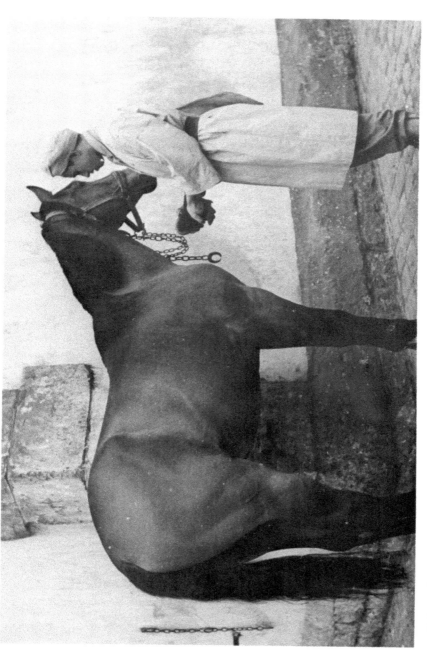

"The mahogany bay says to an argument: 'Come no closer'. A good Barb horse. (Courtesy of the Service Cinéma des Armées, Paris.)

"An Egyptian ass—the merchants call these animals the 'wealth-getters'." A well-bred saddle ass, Cairo. (From T. A. Dodge, *Riders of Many Lands*; courtesy of the Hall of the Horsemen, The University of Texas at Austin.)

"The *mahari* has the elegant ears of the gazelle, the supple neck of the ostrich, the lean belly of the saluki." Racing camels, or *mahara*, on the desert. (From T. A. Dodge, *Riders of Many Lands*; courtesy of the Hall of the Horsemen, The University of Texas at Austin.)

"They would rather risk their lives than bear the shame of giving water where pack animals had left polluted pools." Troopers water their horses with care (the trough is an amenity which was probably not available to such men during the mid-1800's). (Courtesy of the Service Cinéma des Armées, Paris.)

"A horse is truly noble when he glows with pride in the midst of gunpowder and dangers." (Courtesy of the Hall of the Horsemen, The University of Texas at Austin.)

"The drinker of the wind is well proportioned; his ears are slender and mobile; his bones are heavy; his jaws are lean; his nostrils are as wide as a lion's mouth; his eyes are beautiful, black, and prominent. His neck is long; his breast is thrust forward; his forearms are long like those of an ostrich and as well muscled as those of a camel; the veins of his legs are barely perceptible; the hoof is of a black, solid color; the hairs of the mane and tail are thick and fine; his flesh is firm." (Courtesy of the Service Cinéma des Armées, Paris.)

"Gallop, gallop, my beloved steed! And follow the enemy in his rout." (Courtesy of the Hall of the Horsemen, The University of Texas at Austin.)

lacks wind. Strength and good wind are the two foremost qualities of the horse; the lack of one of them influences his resignation and could diminish his mettle.

Look for bottom and speed in a horse. The animal that has only speed and no bottom must have a blot somewhere in his origin and the horse that has only bottom and no speed must have some defect, apparent or hidden.

Reject a weedy horse [one that "shows too much daylight"], with a narrow breast, flat ribs, and thin legs, that jigs incessantly while stargazing. When one lets him have his head, he seems to say, "Hold me back," and when one reins him in, "Let me go."

However, if you find during the course of your life a horse of noble origin, whose eyes are large, sparkling, and wide-set, whose nostrils are black, dilated, and close to each other, whose neck, shoulders, haunches, and thighs are long, while his forehead, loins, flanks, and legs are broad; with his back, cannons, pasterns, and dock short; the whole accompanied by a soft skin, silky mane and tail hair, powerful respiratory system, and good feet with the heels far from the ground; make haste to buy him if you can persuade his master to sell him to you and thank God, morning and evening, for He shall have sent you a blessing.

Never acquire a broken-kneed horse, one that is ill or wounded, should someone say to you that he has nothing but a temporary ailment. Remember the proverb of your fathers:

"Ruined [man,] son of a ruined [man],
He who buys to cure."

It is not rare to see Arabs buying mares on halves. Here are the most usual arrangements in such dealings:

One Arab sells to another a mare for one hundred duros, for example. He receives only fifty duros and he himself enters into the bargain for the other fifty; the buyer rides the mare and makes use of her for war, the chase, or journeys, and has her bred.

If the buyer takes part in a *razzia* [foray] three-quarters of the booty belongs to him and the other fourth to his partner; if the mare is killed in a military action or on an expedition made with the consent of both partners, the loss will be the same for both of them. However, should the death occur in a *fantasia,* at a wedding, or at some fete, the buyer takes the loss alone and reimburses the seller with fifty duros.

Should the animal unexpectedly die in front of the tent or under her rider while he was defending his wife, his children, and his livestock, that would be an act of *force majeure* and no reimbursement need be made.

Should the mare foal a colt, the latter would be taken care of until he is a year old and then he would be sold and what was paid for him would be divided between the two partners.

Should the mare have produced a filly, when the latter is a year old, she would be appraised and the seller would have the right to choose between mother and daughter, giving or receiving the difference in the amount of the appraisal.[2]

This type of transaction is never carried out with stallions. The Arab who wishes to sell a horse will never agree to being the first to name a price. He who is interested in the animal, says:

"Sell. You will gain."

"Buy. You will come out ahead," answers the seller.

"No. You speak. Is he bought or bred?" the buyer asks.

"Raised in my tent like one of my children," says the seller.

"What have you been offered for him?" the buyer inquires.

"I have been offered one hundred duros."

"Sell him to me for that price. You will come out ahead. Tell me then what you want for him."

"Look at what is written by God," replies the seller.

---

[2] "Kuwait is the port of the Nedj; it is here that the big affair of the mares begins, the most important [business] affair in the country and one for which witnesses and scribes are called in who are to draw up the bills of sale or attest birth certificates. The ways of possession are most diverse: I shall speak only of the one in most common usage. 'To the one, the tether, to the other, the womb.' The mare cannot be with two owners at the same time, she is 'tethered' to one of them; that is the consecrated expression. To the party to whom she is "tethered," by rights belong all the colts which might be foaled. But, should a filly come along, the owner of the womb is free to choose the mother or the daughter. It is incumbent upon the owner of the womb, seconded by two witnesses, to decide within three days. Should he choose the mother, he will accord thirty-one days of milk to the filly. Should he decide to the contrary, the owner of the dam cannot refuse him the thirty-one days of milk, recognized as being indispensable to the young animal. When the mare has again become the sole property of one owner, the former associate employs every means imaginable to repurchase a moiety in the mare. 'The filly is ailing; he knows of a stallion of the purest of blood, but will not point him out until after the deed of association has been renewed; etc.'" ("Journey in Upper Asia," by M. Pétiniaud)

"Come now. Let us chase away that first buyer and here are ten duros over."

"I accept. Take your horse and may God grant that you be happy on him as many times as he has hairs on his back."

When one desires to avoid the action of redhibitory cases, one adds, in the presence of witnesses: "Separation between us begins now. You do not know me and I have never seen you."

A horse may not be ridden on trial until an agreement has been reached on the price. Always, before the deal is closed, the horse is tested against another animal with a certain repute in the locality. Such a test has one peculiarity: the riders must mount barefoot and not boot the horses during the trial.

Horses with well-established reputations in the locality are never sold by bargaining.

It is a deadly insult to an Arab to ask him: "Do you want to sell your horse?" before he has made known his intention of doing so. "Do you think that I am in want," he asks, "that you dare to make such a proposal?"

Some tribes are particularly given to horse trading; among them the Beni-Addas are frequently cited as being the most renowned of the Arabic horse-dealers. Of them it is said:

> "Among the others
>   The horses are carrion,
>   Among them brides.
>   Among the others they sleep,
>   Among them they dance."

On the other hand, the Arab is not a horse-trader after the manner of the European; he does not use ginger, he does not employ cunning to conceal the blemishes of his horse. He simply shows him. However, he replaces cheating, which he disdains, with a flow of words which can beguile [the unwary]. His inexhaustible eloquence overflows with metaphors and hyperbole. Thus on showing his horse, he will exclaim:

"Look at his back and feast your eyes!"

He will continue:

"Do not say that it is my horse, say that it is my son."

"He attracts at first glance."

"He is as pure as gold."

"He has such good sight that he sees a hair in the night."

"On a day of gunsmoke, he delights in the whistling of the bullets."

"He overtakes the gazelle."

"He says to the eagle: 'Descend or I shall come up to you.' "

"When he hears the shrieks of the young girls, he whinnies with joy. When he is in the presence of the girls, he begs with a forefoot."

"When he gallops he brings tears to the eye."

"He is a horse for black days when the smoke of gunpowder even darkens the sun."

"He is a pure-bred mount."

"He is the leader of horses!"

"No one has possessed his equal; I depend on him as I do on my heart. He does not have a brother in this world. He is a swallow."

"He is always attentive to his rider's heels; he understands just as well as a son of Adam; he only lacks the power of speech."

"He has so gentle a walk that one can carry a cup of coffee on him and not spill it; a nose bag fills him; a sack covers him."

"He is so light-footed that he could dance on your beloved's breast without hurting it."

> "The master of true beauty sells,
> The master of the swift takes oaths."

Ben-Yousseuf, after having given twenty camels with their young in exchange for a desert mare, answered his father, who had reproached him severely, with: "Why are you angry, sire? Has not this mare brought me the swiftness of the *volte-face* and softness of hide of the jerboa; of the hare its movement of the neck; of the ostrich its speed and eyesight; of the saluki its leanness of the barrel as well as the cleanness of the limbs, and of the bull its courage and the width of the head? She can do no less than make the faces of our enemies blanch. When I pursue them, she will be right on their heels and if I were to be pursued, the eye would not quickly perceive where I might have gone."

One sees, and I have already indicated this, in outlining the portrait which the Arabs paint of the pure-bred, that they regard highly the resemblances it bears in its conformation, to certain animals. A horse should combine in himself all the attributes to be noted separately in the gazelle, the saluki, the bull, the ostrich, the camel, the hare, and the fox. Thus he should have the length and cleanness of the limbs of the gazelle, the lines and strength of its rump, the convexity of its ribs, the shortness of its forelegs, the darkness of its eyes, the narrowness of its armpits. Of the dog he should have the following: the length of the lips and tongue, the abundance of saliva, the length of the lower part of its forepaws.

The Arabs even come to regard that closeness [in conformation] of the horse to the saluki as a means of guiding inexperienced buyers; at least, that is what one last anecdote, widespread among them, seems to me to prove:

"Meslem-ben-Abou-Omar, upon learning that one of his relatives was going to make a journey to Egypt, wanted to take advantage of the opportunity to acquire one of the horses famed in that country. His relative was not knowledgeable about horses, but he was a great hunter and had many very good hounds. Meslem, upon sending his servant to his relative with the order, told the latter that the shape of the horse that he desired should correspond to that of the best of his hounds. He was brought such a horse that the Arabs could not find his peer."

Merou-ben-el-Keyss replied one day to friends who accused him of not understanding anything about horses or women:

"Yes, I have ridden horses,
Sober, strong, and swift for gallops,
Whose haunches were powerful,
Tendons dry and croup rounded,
Forming a rivulet toward the tail:
Their hooves were hard, they could go without shoes.
By God! I thought myself to be mounted on an ostrich.

"To find high grass
Which grows in solitudes dangerous to traverse,
In the solitudes defended by the points of lances
And by the courses of torrents
I have often galloped
When the birds were still asleep in their nests.

"To chase the zebra with the white skin
Whose legs are striped like stuffs from the Indies,
Or to overtake the antelope that lives in wild places,
I have ridden horses with flesh made firm by gallops.
It is God Who makes them for the good fortune of the believers!

How many times have I not leaned my heart
On that of a young woman with a swelling throat
  With legs ornamented with golden bracelets.

"In our cavalry invasions
When eye should meet eye,
How many times have I not also said:
  'Gallop, gallop, my beloved steed!
  And follow the enemy in his rout.' "

The value of a horse lies in his blood line.

Observations of the Emir Abd-el-Kader

"A poet, in answer to a king who wanted the poet's horse, Sakab, said: 'Sakab is not for sale or exchange; I would recover him at the cost of my life; my family would die of hunger before he would be permitted to suffer.'

"An Arab said: 'My countrymen reproach me for having debts, and yet I contracted those debts for a pure-bred horse, with rounded lines, that does them honor, that is a talisman for my goum, and to whom I have given a slave as a servant.'

"A certain Arab one day sent his son to buy a horse in the market place and the son upon departing asked his father what attributes the animal should have. The father answered:

" 'His ears should move constantly backwards and forwards as if he were listening to some sound; his eyes should rove with a watchful look as if he were occupied with some object; his legs should be well set on and well proportioned.'

" 'Such a horse,' his son made answer, 'would never be sold by his owner.'

"Many Arabs have genealogical tables in which they certify, by means of witnesses who give faith, as to the birth and description of a foal so that when an owner wishes to sell his horse he has but to show his table to prove to the buyer that he is not being deceived.

"I have seen among the Anézé, a tribe which extends from Baghdad to Syria, horses so highly priced that it was almost impossible to buy them, particularly for cash. Those horses are customarily sold to personages or great men of affairs who liquidate in thirty or fifty installments of a year each the almost fabulous price of such a horse, or else they bind themselves to pay a lifelong income to the seller and his descendants.

" 'I surprise them in the morning, when the bird is still in its nest and when the water of the dew makes its path to the streams.

" 'I surprise them with my sleek courser, who because of his fleetness overtakes the tawny beasts and hunts without cease the gazelles at all seasons and far from our dwelling.

" 'He has the flanks of the gazelle, the legs of the female ostrich, the straight back of the wild ass keeping watch from a hilltop.

" 'His croup, resembling a sand dune which humidity has made compact, corresponds to withers rising above his back like the pack-saddle on the camel that holds the litter in place.

" 'The eminences behind his ears are rounded like spheres, the reins and the bridle seem to be attached to the end of a trunk of a palm tree denuded of its fronds.

" 'Tethered at the side of other horses, he bites and rages in his jealousy, as if he were urged by some demon.' "

12

FARRIERY

The farrier and the cobbler
should not pay taxes.

CONTRARY TO GENERAL OPINION, the Arabs of the Sahara ordinarily shoe their horses—be it on the forefeet, be it all round, according to the nature of the terrain in which they live. Those who dwell in rocky lands, the greater number, are those who shoe their horses all round. We shall cite principally the tribes of Arbâa, Mekhadema, Aghrazelia, Saâid–Mekhalif–Oulad-Yagoub. Oulad-Naïl, Oulad-sidi-Cheikh, Hamyâne, etc.

It is a universally accepted custom to remove the shoes in spring when the horses are turned out in the green pastures. The Arabs allege that one should take care not to interfere with the renewal of blood which takes place at that time.

Each tribe has a separate camp, called the maestro's *douar*, which is for the blacksmiths. Blacksmithing being a profession entirely and especially dedicated to that indispensable complement of the Arab, the horse, it should be the object of an especial regard; also many and invaluable privileges are accorded to the smiths. However, I am not sure if, in the concession of those privileges, one should see only the homage paid to a purely equestrian art or whether, in the attention which is paid to the only craft that exists in the desert, there may not be a trace of the stimulation given to the skilful and wise craftsmen of Arabia, Egypt, Africa, and Spain by the Arabs of bygone days, those brilliant conquerors of the Goths, the contemporaries of Haroun-al-Raschid.

The Arabs of the Sahara say that the first farriers arrived among them from the edges of the litoral as well as from Fez, Tunis, Mascara, Tlemcen, and Constantine, and that their profession and their knowledge have since been perpetuated in families from one generation to the next.

Farriers have to be something of armourers, shoers, and honers, to mend bits, spurs, knives, rifles, sabers, and pistols; they make the horseshoes, the needles, the sickles, the axes, and the hoes.

They enjoy the following exemptions:

They do not pay taxes and when the members of a tribe journey to the Tell to lay in a supply of grain, they make up a quota for them, which is shared with the cobbler who does not pay taxes either. They do not have to share their couscous or shelter with anyone, which is to say that they are exempt from having to furnish that hospitality which, in certain cases, devolves upon everyone.

The sustained work which their profession demands, the inevitable contingencies to which the urgent necessities of their fellows make it liable night and day, the late hours they have to keep, give them a right to a benefit known as "the custom of the maestro." Upon returning from the buying of grain in the Tell each tent [household] makes available to them a *feutra* of wheat and barley, and one of butter, and in the spring they receive, moreover, a fleece. If a camel is butchered, its owners set aside for them the part included between the withers and the tail, with the exception of the hump, which part is ordinarily full of fat and the most sought after.

Whether or not the farrier takes part in forays or expeditions, he has a right to a share of the booty—generally to a sheep or to a camel, according to the size of the prize. This custom is called the "horseman's sheep."

Lastly, the most important privilege of the farriers, the irrefutable mark of the protection which they enjoyed in bygone days and a mark of the esteem in which they are still held, is the gift of life in combat. If the farrier is mounted with weapons in his hands, he runs the risk of being killed, like any other horseman of the *goum*. But if he dismounts and kneeling, imitates, by alternately raising and lowering the two corners of his burnoose, the motion of the bellows of his forge, his life will be spared. Some horsemen have, more than once, saved their lives by means of this stratagem.

The farrier can only enjoy this privilege as long as he lives inoffensively, absorbed in the duties of his profession. However, should he make himself known for his prowess in war, he renounces all the privileges of his profession and enters the common herd.

That privilege has a very great drawback. When the farrier has become wealthy, an uneven quarrel is picked and he is stripped, one way or another, of part of his fortune to prevent him from leaving the locality.

A maestro, whose tribe has been pillaged by the enemy, goes to seek the victors and, with proof of his profession, has returned to him his tent, tools, and equipment.

His equipment consists of a bellows, which is simply a goatskin with three orifices, of which two are on top on the same line, and the third on the opposite side. Through the latter projects the barrel of a rifle or pistol which conducts the air to the fire. The women who are charged with the handling of this bellows, kneel down in front of the charcoal, placed in an excavation, and take in either hand one of the top holes which they close by gathering together the walls of the skin which forms them. Then, alternately lowering and extending their hands, they make an "in and out" movement which creates a sufficient, if not very effective, draft. The Arabs of the Sahara prefer this form of bellows to any more perfected type, because it has little volume and is easier to carry on their nomadic wanderings.

To the bellows is added an anvil, a hammer, rasps, tongs, and a vise. These instruments generally come to them from the coastal region; but there are, nevertheless, some which they make themselves.

They used to get the iron in the large markets of the central desert, in Tougourt from the Beni-Mezabe, in Timimoun, according to how close they happened to be to those points with respect to their localities. They are beginning to buy from us. They themselves make their charcoal with *arar, remt, senoubeur,* or *djedary*; this latter being the most highly regarded.

The horseshoes are prepared in advance; a sale is sure, the Arabs always laying in a year's supply which consists of four pairs of shoes for the forefeet and four for the hindfeet of their horses.

The nails are also wrought by the blacksmiths.

When a horseman goes to the smith, he takes or does not take the shoes. In the first instance, the smith is paid by his privileges; the horse shod, his master mounts and says, simply: "May God be merciful to your fathers," and departs. The blacksmith continues with his work.

If the rider does not take the shoes, he gives two *boudjous*[1] to the smith who has shod the four feet and thanks are reduced to the simplest of the Arabic formulas of affability: "God give you strength."

In the Sahara horses are cold-shod, for the Arabs say that in the hoofs of the horse there are delicate parts, such as the frog, the heels, etc., and that it is always dangerous to heat them, even though it be no more than by nearing a red-hot iron. That dislike of hot-shoeing, caused by the injurious action of heat on the delicate parts of the hoof, is ingrained in them to such an extent that in camp, when they watch us shoe our horses, they say: "Look at the Christians adding fuel to the flames." In a word, they cannot understand how, especially on marches, in which movement carries the blood to the horse's foot, one can augment by nearing [artificial] heat that natural heat.

The horseshoes are made of a soft and malleable steel and are very light. The shoes have the points joined. Shoes for the forefeet have only three nails in each side and the ends are free, nails never being driven into them. According to the Arabs, nails in the ends impede the elasticity of the hoof and will make the horse experience exactly the same sensation when he sets his hoof down on the ground, that a man experiences with shoes that are much too short; this is the cause of a multitude of accidents.

The Arabs do not rasp the hoof. They do not pare it down. The hoof rests freely; rocky terrain and constant work are enough to wear away the hoof as it keeps growing over the shoe. They do not see the necessity for trimming the hoofs, except when the horses have been tethered in front of the tent for a long time without working or when they have remained in the Tell. The Arabs then use only sharp knives which they never fail to carry.

Their system, moreover, has the advantage that an unshod horse can continue on his way because the sole of the hoof is strong and hard. "Among you," say the Arabs, "with your custom of trimming the hoof, if a horse casts its shoes, you have to stop or watch him bleed, limp, and suffer, etc."

---

[1] An old Algerian coin.

The horseshoes have closed ends because the horse can only feel in the soft part and not in the hard and it is the frog that must be protected from injury. The ends must follow the curve of the frog.

The heads of the nails are given the shape of the heads of grasshoppers, this being the only way, according to the Arabs, that enables the nails to last until the end without breaking. They approve of our method of introducing the nails into the holes and clamping them down on the outside which prevents the horse from cutting himself. However, the scarcity of iron obliges them to clamp the nails on the hoof so that they may be used a second time, remaking the heads.

When a horse forges, his heels are trimmed and light shoes are put on his forefeet and heavier ones behind. Care is taken not to leave a horse with one foot shod and the other not. If during a journey the horse casts a shoe on a forefoot and the rider does not have a spare, he puts a shoe from a hind foot on the forefoot and removes the shoe from the other hind foot. If the horse were to be unshod on one forefoot, the Arab would take the other shoe off rather than leave him as he was before. If a horse, after one of those long, swift rides which the horsemen of the desert know how to make, should have to be shod, it is not unusual to see that a piece of felt is placed between the shoe and the hoof.

This necessity for shoeing horses of the Sahara, due to the nature of the terrain and the long journeys, has made the convenience to be felt of accustoming the colt to allow himself to be shod easily. He is given couscous, sweet biscuits, and dates, and he allows his foot to be lifted and tapped. Afterwards, his neck and the sides of his head are stroked, he is spoken to in a low voice and thus soon he learns to lift his feet at the slightest indication. The small amount of difficulty encountered later in shoeing, thanks to that training, has probably inspired this Arabic hyperbole: "The instinct of a pure-bred horse is so marvellous that scarcely will he have cast a shoe than he will indicate it by holding up the unshod foot."

At least, that exaggeration shows how easily the horses allow themselves to be shod and how, in the desert, every horseman should, while on a journey, be able, and know how, to shoe his horse. This is a point of great importance and being an excellent rider and having expertly trained a horse is not enough to earn one the reputation of being a horseman. It is necessary to know how to shoe in case of need. Thus when he embarks upon a long journey each horseman carries in his saddlebags shoes, nails, hammer, tongs, some rags or thongs, and an awl, to repair his gear.

Should his horse cast a shoe, the rider simply dismounts and opens his saddlebags. He unwinds his camel-hide thong, passes it around the *kerbouss* [pommel] of the saddle, then around the pastern, and ties the two ends together at the desired length so that the horse will raise his foot. The horse does not move and the rider shoes him alone. Should a hindleg be involved, he rests it on his knee and shoes without assistance.

In order not to make a mistake, he passes his awl through the holes to make sure in advance of the proper place for the nails to go.

When, by chance, the horse is difficult, he has a comrade help him to shoe the hindfeet. The comrade pinches the horse's muzzle or ears. To shoe the forefeet, he simply places the rump of the horse opposite a thorny bush or makes a twitch out of a nose bag filled with earth.

The Saharians find our horseshoes much too heavy, and allege that on long, swift marches they tend to tire the joints of the legs horribly or to be the cause of many diseases of the fetlocks. "Look at our horses," they say, "see how they cover the ground or the sand leaving it behind them, how light and swift they are! How easily they lift their feet! How they relax or contract their muscles! They would be as heavy footed and tortured as yours if it were not that we use light shoes which do not weigh down their feet, whose material, when it wears down, blends with the sole and becomes one with the hoof."

When I pointed out that I had not noticed in our horseshoes the drawbacks they had pointed out, they replied: "How can you note them? Traverse like us, in one day, the distance you cover in five or six days' march and then you will see. Fine marches you Christians make with your horses!"

13

TRAPPINGS AND TACK

The *koheul* adorns the face of the maker of children,
A tribe embellishes a parade,
And the saddle enhances the horse.

I HAVE POSTULATED that the Arabic saddle gives the rider such a firm seat that he is not at all concerned with certain vices of the horse, which make us feel uneasy. I shall say a word about the saddle here, although today it be well known to all.

The Arabic saddle consists of a wooden tree with a long *kerbouss* in front and a wide cantle behind, high enough to protect the kidneys. The whole is covered and held together without nails or pegs by an unadorned camel's hide which gives a great solidity. The bands rest on the horse's back; they are flat and wide, freedom of the withers and loins being well understood, and the seat is wide and roomy. This seat is extremely hard, and it takes a great deal of use to accustom oneself to be able to endure it. The chieftains cover it with a cushion of wool, but the common horsemen make it a point of honor to ride on the bare wood, alleging that the use of cushioning is an excess of softness which, as well as lessening the rider's points of contact, cannot help but be conducive to sleep during long marches and consequently exposes him to causing his horse saddle sores. Riding without padding is even more meritorious, because, more often than not, especially in summer, the Arab rides without drawers.

The tree is concealed by a *stara,* a covering of red morocco leather which the poor use without any adornment whatever, and by a *ghrebaria,* a covering of material in wool or scarlet velours, embroidered with gold or silver thread and adorned with fringes, which the wealthy and the chieftains use.

The breast plate is very wide and fastened on after the manner of that on our French saddle; the ends are provided with strong buckles of iron or inlaid silver and are attached to the saddle by small straps ingeniously placed to keep the saddle level.

The Arabs do not want cruppers on their saddles. They say that cruppers check the horse's forward movement, due to the hindrance they cause the animal. They only put them on pack mules and donkeys, and then not under the tails.

The stirrups are large and heavy. Their side walls narrow from the bottom to the top until they join the upper part which bears the rings of the stirrup leathers. The Arabs use short stirrup leathers and put their feet all the way home in the stirrups which thus protects the foot from bullets and falls. These stirrups can be very painful for those who are not accustomed to using them, for when one stands up in them, the eye rests against the bone of the foot. In time, the skin becomes calloused and a type of splint is formed which prevents further sensitivity of the part. By these exostoses those who are horsemen are distinguished from those who are not, to such a degree that in the Department of Oran a certain bey upon inflicting an exemplary punishment upon a tribe that had risen in revolt, ordered that among those who had fallen into his hands all who were marked by the *maâzia* be executed. He knew that thus he would not punish any other than the horsemen. Among the wealthy the stirrups are gilded or plated. The Turkish chieftains used to use stirrups made of gold or solid silver.

The stirrups are supported by stirrup leathers, placed behind the girth, which are no more than plaited thongs of morocco leather or camel hide folded seven or eight times and are therefore very strong. The nobles have their stirrup leathers made from silken cords, but no matter how strong they may be, because they might not be able to hold up under a form of horsemanship in which full body weight is customarily borne entirely on the stirrups at fast paces, *maoune* or stirrup supports are added.

As saddle blankets for their horses, the Arabs make use of felt pads which are attached to the saddle in order to make it possible to saddle in a hurry. They are seven in number, dyed blue, yellow, and red; the blue must cover the others. The Arabs add an eighth, but it is white and not affixed and can be washed or dried in the sun if the horse has sweated. When these felt pads are well cut, their distinct colors, which may be seen showing one above the other, form an ornament of quite good taste; and they save the horse from saddle sores. One tries to place them so that they will cover the loins slightly.

The girth, which is narrower than ours, is placed in front of the stirrups. The Arabs, as a matter of principle, do not girth their horses tightly; they can follow this practice without any inconvenience because their saddles are always firmly set.

The bridle is made of very wide straps, with blinders. Sometimes, but very rarely, it has a throat-latch. This is attached to the crown piece and worn loosely. The Arab of the Sahara does not like it at all, because if in combat his horse be laid hold of by the bridle, something which is not infrequent, the rider would not have the usual recourse of passing the reins over the horse's head and thus escaping from the enemy, leaving the latter a bridle as sole captive. The blinders have the advantage of preventing the horse from being distracted by objects around him and they are, perhaps, one of the reasons why the horse fears nothing.

The cheek and crown pieces of the bridle are embroidered in silk by the middle classes and in gold or silver by the wealthy.

The bit is sewn to the headstall and is never cleaned. The cheek pieces of the bit are wide, short on the vertical line and made *a la* Condé; the mouthpiece is smooth and the curb is an oval ring attached to the upper part of the port. The Arabic bit has no freedom of tongue and the length of the bars of the curb is much less than that of the French bit; it is therefore much less severe than one would have thought up to now. The advantage which it offers in war is that it does not have a curb chain or hooks which frequently cannot easily be replaced, something which has not been sufficiently appreciated.

The reins are long. Two knots are made in them. One is made at the length which permits the rider to keep the horse at a walk without interfering with his liberty of movement and the other at the point where it has been determined that the horse, after having collected the muscles of his neck at the gallop, will be in hand. The reins are held in the whole hand, and when necessary one makes use of the length left over as a whip to animate the horse.

The Arabs repudiate the snaffle which, according to them, only serves to confuse the aids. Rarely fighting with sabers, they have never felt the need of it.

The Arabs of the Sahara use a riding crop to correct a horse while they are training him or to animate him in the chase or in war. They call it the *souâte*. This crop is made of five or six plaited thongs hanging from a ring attached to an iron rod, six or seven inches long, which has another ring attached with a keeper, so that the crop dangles from the wrist. Around the metal part, but an inch shorter, is a hollow cylinder, also made of metal, whose diameter permits easy play. The Arabs make use of this crop by swinging the arm, and it has such power that after some time it is enough to make it rattle to have the horse burst into a breakneck gallop. The sound produced by the contact of the cylinder, be it with the rings, be it with the rod that joins them, reminds the horse of the *tekerbeâa* of which we have already spoken. In the desert, a club, an elbow's length which terminates in a quite thick head, studded with nails and worn on the wrist by means of a thong, is carried on the *kerbouss*. Some replace it with a longer cane ending in a hook in order to pick up booty lying on the ground without having to dismount. The Arabs call it the *aâraya*, the despoiler. The Arbâa and the Harares never ride without carrying these canes.

Spurs have a single shank and are heavy, solid, and long; they are attached by a single crossed strap and are worn very loosely. We have given the reasons. One cannot wear them while on foot.

Each Arab carries as a complement to his tack, hanging from the pommel of the saddle, a pouch called *djebira* or *guerab*. The *djebira* has several compartments in which are carried bread, biscuits, a mirror, soap, cartridges, shoes, flint stone, a pen, and paper. Some *djebiras* are richly adorned; I am convinced that it is from the East that we have derived the saddlebags of our Hussars. The men of a tribe on an expedition also carry hanging from the cantle a type of saddlebag which they call *semmâte*; this is shorter than ours in order not to tire the horse's flank.

The Arabs, except for the great lords, do not carry holsters on their saddles. They carry their pistols at the waist or in a heart-shaped hol-

ster which is worn on the left, bound by a thong over the back and
by a wide belt. The Arab prefers this method of carrying his pistol
because he has discovered the advantage of having it on him when he
finds himself obliged to leave his slain horse.

Those who do not use throat-latches on their bridles adorn their
horses ordinarily with lion's fangs or wild boar's tusks or with talismans which they hang around the neck with silk or woolen cords.

According to our ideas, the more stripped a pure-bred horse, the
more the beauty of his conformation leaps to the eye. The Arabs are
not of the same opinion as we and they say:

"The koheul[1] adorns the face of the maker of children,

A tribe embellishes a parade,

And the saddle enhances the horse."

During my stay in Africa I saw many horses that were unsalable
under an English saddle, be much admired when they were decked
out with Arabic tack, so that I came close to sharing the native opinion. Many times I convinced myself that the Arabs were correct, when,
after they have bought horses from Europeans, they have saddled
the animals with their own saddles, and made the vendors rue the
sale; for, too late, the latter discovered a hitherto unsuspected beauty.
It is true that all the luxury of the Arab lies in the trappings of his
horse, for if the Prophet strictly forbade gold on garments, on the
contrary, he ordered it on arms and on horses. He said: "He who has
not hesitated to spend [money on] the maintenance of horses for the
Holy War, will be considered after his death to be the equal of him
whose hand has always been open," that is, someone who has given
a great deal of charity. Also, it is not unusual, even in hard times, for a
chieftain to acquire a saddle for two or three thousand francs.

If Arabic tack is not beyond reproach in all its details, there exists,
nevertheless, an indubitable superiority over our light cavalry saddle,
the so-called Hungarian type. In effect, the seat of the Arabic saddle,
is it not better adapted than that of ours? The latter is uncomfortable,
wearing, separates the horse from the rider, and prevents the latter

---

[1] Koheul: sulphur of antimony, which is used to tint the eyelids. When a
woman has ornamented her eyes with koheul, decked herself with henna, and
chewed a twig of souak—to sweeten the breath, whiten the teeth, and make the
lips purple—she is more pleasing in the eyes of God for she is more loved by
her husband.

from having a good seat. The other, on the contrary, brings the rider close to the horse, something whose importance should be known to all. It permits the rider to have a good seat; by reason of its structure it permits many points of contact, because it affords the chance to grip strongly with the thighs.

Is not the girth better situated on the sternal or true ribs, than on the false or asternal ribs which play such a great part in the act of respiration? Is not the play of the lungs then freer?

Do not short stirrups, placed behind the girth, have the advantage which ours lack, of forcing the rider, no matter what his build, to carry his legs close to his horse's sides? Do they not also afford a greater firmness, permitting one to stand in them, as much to make use of one's weapons as to ease the fast paces of the horse?

The breastplate can be put on easily and without waste of time; it does not interfere with the shoulders and does not cause galls on the withers like ours does, whose eternal tension on the under part of the pommel has such dire results for our horses.

All that is useless and tires the horse needlessly is excluded from the tack. The Arabs do not understand our housing at all. They ask if the horse has not already enough to carry into combat without overburdening him?

I do not know if these observations are judicious, but I do know that the Arabs very quickly acquire a good seat and confidence on a horse, while we take several years to produce a mediocre rider. Our men are, however, well built and vigorous. From where, therefore, does such an inferior state derive? It comes, in my opinion, from our tack which requires long pelves, flexible loins, and a privileged conformation. In a word, Arabic tack suits all pelves, all loins, all stomachs, all thighs, and serves the old as well as the young, and makes [riders] out of everyone, whereas we cannot achieve this except for a numbered few.

Undoubtedly we have great improvements to make in our tack. A people cannot be condemned not to ride horseback for the sole reason that the saddle used is not suited except to a few.

14

GENERAL PRINCIPLES
OF THE ARABIC HORSEMAN

Rest and fat are the horse's
greatest enemies.

WHEN YOU MOUNT A HORSE, always speak these words: "In the Name of God." The grave of the rider is always open.

A true horseman should eat little and above all drink little. For if he does not know how to suffer thirst, he will never make a warrior; he will be nothing but a frog in a puddle.

Buy a good horse, for should you pursue you will overtake and if you are pursued the eye will not quickly perceive where you passed.

Prefer the mountain horse to the plains horse and the plains horse to the swamp horse which is only good for carrying a packsaddle.

In combat always ride *a sweeper with his tail* (a horse eight years old, at least). The day on which the riders are so hard pressed that the stirrups clash, he will get you out of the melee and carry you to your tent, even if traversed by a bullet.

When you have just bought a horse, study him carefully, give him barley gradually until you arrive at the amount demanded by his appetite. A good horseman should know the measure of barley which suits his horse just as well as he should know the charge of powder which suits his firearm.

Do not allow dogs or donkeys to lie down on the straw or barley which you feed your horses.

The Prophet has said: "Each grain of barley given to your horses will be worth an indulgence to you in the other world."

Give barley to your horses; deprive yourself to give them more, for Sidi-Ahmed-ben-Youssef has added: "Had I not seen the mare make horses, I would have said that it was the barley."

He has said further:

> "Under the spurs
> There is naught but barley."

Water only once a day, at one or two o'clock in the afternoon and do not give barley until the evening at sunset; this is a good custom for war and besides, it is the way to make the horse's flesh firm and hard.

To prepare a too-fat horse to withstand the fatigues of war, thin him down by exercise, but never by depriving him of feed.

As long as your horse, on being exercised, sweats all over his body, you may be assured that he is not in hard condition, but you may depend on him from the moment that he sweats only around the ears and breast.

Do not leave your horse beside others which might be eating barley without his also being given some; that would make him fall ill.

Never water after having given your horse barley, that would be to kill him: *medroube be chaïr* (stricken by barley).

Never allow a horse to drink after a fast gallop, you run the risk of seeing him struck by water: *medroube bi el ma* (stoppage of perspiration).

After a fast gallop, water with the bridle, feed with the girth [*i.e.,* the saddle still in place] and you will always find yourself well off.

Be clean and bathe yourself before mounting your horse. The Prophet will love you.

Whoever commits some folly on the back of his horse is not worthy of owning him, and, moreover, he will be punished: his horse will be wounded.

Never sleep on your horse's back; the rider's sleep causes saddle galls or tires the horse.

When you gallop your horse you must rate him in order to be able to depend on him; you should make use of him as one makes use of a goatskin full of water. One opens it gently and upon closing the mouth tightly one easily conserves the water it contains. But if it is opened abruptly the water escapes in a single gush and there is none left to slake thirst.

A rider should never gallop his horse while ascending or descending, unless forced to do so; he should, on the contrary, slow his pace.

"Which do you like better," someone asked the horse, "being mounted or dismounted?"

"May God damn their meeting point!" answered the horse.

When you have a long way to go, rate your horse with intervals at a walk which will allow him to get his wind. Repeat this process until he has sweated and cooled three times; let him urinate, adjust the girth and then do as you please, for he will not leave you in the lurch. A horse thus treated is called *el aoud cheheub*.

When, on a march, you have a very strong head wind, arrange matters, if possible, to spare your horse from it; you will save him from illness.

In bivouac, if your horse is in such a position that he cannot evade the wind which blows with violence into his nostrils, do not be afraid to leave the nose bag on; thus you will save him from worse accidents.

If you have put your horse into a gallop and other horsemen are following you, calm him, do not urge him on; of his own accord he will animate himself quite enough.

If you are pursuing an enemy and he commits the error of pressing his horse, hold your own in and you can be assured of overtaking the fugitive.

Never strike a noble horse, that would be to vilify him and then his mettle would revolt and make him resist. Words or gestures will suffice to correct or animate him.

When the horseman after having travelled through hills on a narrow track for a long time, reaches a level stretch, it is a good idea to give the horse a short gallop.

Upon going out the horseman should never fear to play with his horse for a few minutes for upon doing this the legs limber up and the calmness of the animal is assured for the rest of the day. In the same way, after a difficult and tiring march, upon arrival at the tent the horse should be made to perform some fancy figures. The women of the camp will applaud, saying: "There's a son of a so-and-so." Moreover, you will realize what your horse is worth.

The rider who does not teach his horse to have a good walk is not a horseman and inspires pity.

Whoever may be able to do so and does not halt to let his horse urinate, sins; his companions should also halt; it is a meritorious act.

When, in war or in the chase, you have made your horse sweat and you come upon a little stream, do not be afraid to let him take seven or eight swallows of water with the bridle on; it will not harm him in the least and will permit him to continue on his way.

When you dismount think of your horse before yourself. It was he that carried you and it is he that will continue to carry you.

After a long gallop either unsaddle your horse immediately and throw cold water on his back, taking care to walk him about, or leave him saddled until he is completely dry and has eaten his barley; there is no middle way.

When after a long journey in winter, in rain and cold, you reach your tent at last, blanket your horse well, give him parched barley and hot milk, but do not water him that day.

Never give grain or water to your horse immediately after a prolonged gallop, for you will cause inflammations or blemishes on his legs.

Do not gallop your horse, without urgent necessity, during the great heat of summer. Remember the dictum of your fathers:
"The horse says:
'Do not make me gallop in summer
If you want me to save you on a day of sword-play.' "

When, in a case of life or death, you feel that your horse is blown, take off the bridle even if only for an instant and give him, on the croup, a blow with a spur hard enough to draw blood; he will urinate and may still be able to save you.

When after a fast gallop you can give your horse a breather, the moment to continue on your way is when his nostrils begin to run.

Would you like to know, after a day of hard gallops and great fatigues, whether or not you can still depend on your horse? Dismount and pull him by the tail strongly toward you. Should he resist, standing firmly without being shaken, you may count on him.

It is also a very good sign when upon arriving home the horse urinates with such force as to crack the ground and the urine forms a lot of foam.

On expeditions, when after great fatigues you have but a moment to rest, use as a pillow some bridles of your brothers and you will never be abandoned or forgotten, no matter what might come to pass.

A horseman should study his horse's habits, know his character profoundly. He would then know if, having dismounted, he could have every confidence in him, if he were quiet among mares, or whether he would have to be watched and hobbled. None of these details is too insignificant in the presence of the enemy.

The best time to demand a great deal from the horse is in the spring, before the arrival of the great heat and in the autumn before the arrival of the great cold.

The horse lies in his training [without training, he is useless].[1]

> Yes, spur your horses.
> Learn, and teach them, what will be of use to you.
> In this world, of necessity, some day or other,
> A man will encounter his demander.[2]

Observations of the Emir Abd-el-Kader

"The Arabs have preserved the custom of racing which they practiced even from the time of idolatry before [the coming of] Mohammed.

"The new faith has not modified this custom, it has become legitimate and by setting a religious seal on it, a new value has been affixed to it.

"*Training.* For racing the Arabs subject their horses to a prior regimen before beginning training (*tadmir*). Thanks to this treatment they acquire an extreme swiftness.

"Here is what the *tadmir* consists of:

"It is begun by increasing the horse's grain ration so that he will get fat; after having achieved this result and to thin him down, the

---

[1] "I repeat, all these precepts are full of reason, sense, and truth; nothing should be disdained, not even those which have a sort of triviality, such as the following: 'Do you want to know, after a day of gallops and fatigues, whether you can depend on your horse? Dismount and pull him strongly by the tail; should he resist without staggering, you can count on him.' The Norman herdsman who, of all Frenchmen, is the one that makes most demands on his horses, in view of the fact that in one day he often covers twenty-five leagues on his running-walker [*bidet d'allure*] knows the procedure well and uses it to learn if he still can, after a long day, count on his mount.

Our riders should know by heart all these precepts of the Arabic horsemen, never forget them, and put them into constant practice; *they should be the catechism of the horseman.*" (Observations of the Count d'Aure)

[2] The demander of his life.

ration is gradually reduced for forty days until the minimum necessary amount is reached. During these forty days, the horse is made to
take progressive exercise. At the same time and from the first day of
the reduction in grain, the horse is rugged with seven blankets and
one is removed every six days. The sweat melts all the fat, relieving
the horse of an unnecessary weight, tones all the muscles, and leaves
nothing but firm flesh. With that treatment the horse attains, according to his breeding, the greatest degree of speed.

"Thus prepared he is taken to the race-course (*djalba*). To the
course come horses from all localities and the public also attends in
great numbers. Never, unless it be at the time of a congregation of
pilgrims, is such a large number of people seen. All the nobles and
the chieftains attend. We have gone to races and in spite of the fact
that it was still early, the public was as numerous as at pilgrimage
time.

"Never are horses prepared by training raced against those which
are not. They are ranked by categories; to each category is assigned a
distinct goal. The trained horses have to run a far longer race.

"The race course, in this case, is called El Midmar and the sage
Bokhari said on the subject: 'The Prophet made trained horses run
together and fixed a distance of seven miles for them, while he fixed
a distance of only one mile for ordinary horses.' (This "mile" is really
equal to one kilometer.)

"The horses run in fields of ten. But before they are allowed to be
off, and to avoid false starts, here are the precautions which are taken:

"A rope is uncoiled which touches the horses' breasts. The ends of
this rope are held by two men on each side of the line of horses. This
rope is named *el mikbad* and *el mikouas* and, concerning it the
Prophet said: 'The horse gallops according to his breeding; but when
he is behind the *mikouas* he gallops according to his owner's luck.' In
other words, in ordinary circumstances the speed of horses is in rela-
tion to the qualities of the breed, more or less good, with which they
are endowed; but in races success depends very much upon the skill
of the trainers, and frequently a horse of the purest of blood is beaten
by an animal less noble.

"To each of the ten horses which have raced a name is given according to its degree of speed. Thus the first one to reach the post is
called *Modjall* (Reliever), for he relieves his owner's heart of care.

"The second is named *El Mousalli,* from the word *salouan,* point of the buttock, because he follows the first horse so closely that he touches him with the end of his muzzle. 'I shall have to be *el mousalli* (the second) if I consent to your winning first prize.'

"The third is called *El Msalli* (The Consoler), for he consoles his owner who is made happy because there was only one horse between his and the winner.

"The fourth is named *El Tali*, or the Follower.

"The fifth is called *El Mourtah*, the fifth finger of the hand.

"The sixth is named *El Aâtif*.

"The seventh is named *El Hadi* (the Lucky One), because he has his share of triumph with the winner.

"The eighth is named *El Mouammil* (He Who Raises Hopes), because he made his owner hope to share part of the winnings.

"The ninth is called *El Lathim* (the Rebuffed), because he is humiliated or rejected on all sides.

"The tenth is *Es Sokeït* (the Taciturn One), for his owner suffers the utmost humiliation without saying a word. Shame shuts his mouth.

"Of these ten horses, seven each win a purse and the others do not get anything. At the end of the race course is a large tent where entrance is granted to the seven winning horses to shelter them, but it is ignominiously refused to the last three.

"In the Name of God, the Clement and Merciful.

"We have attended horse races and in spite of the fact that it was very early there was a great crowd as at the time of pilgrimages.

"Horses came from everywhere; but none know better than we the art of breeding and training them. We arrived at the crack of dawn with horses with hoofs as hollow as cups. The stars had announced their good luck. One ranked them according to the purity of their breeding—the noble beside the noble.

"Among them was a black with strong limbs and adorned with a white mark on his forehead—that star which shone on him equaled the splendor of Mirzam (a star in the constellation of Orion); when he felt the bit in his mouth, he pranced, leaping the lines drawn to mark the goal. Next was a brown bay with black mane and tail, endowed by Nature with admirable qualities, with a sleek coat, who also had a star on his forehead and a white mark on the upper lip. Then came a solid black without a white mark, but sharing the excellent qualities of the others. They were led out for the admiration of the spectators impatient to see them enter the lists.

"Riders strong as steel rods and of small stature mounted them; the riders' voices sounded like the roars of a lion. Seated on their horses they resembled starlings hovering over a mountain plateau.

"At last they were lined up in the midst of the conglomeration of people. A man, also a Moslem, acted as judge; he was chosen with common consent as arbiter and certainly his decisions were not blotted by partiality.

"The horses were loosed in the arena and scattered like pearls fallen from a necklace or like a covey of gray partridges (*ketâa*), spotted by a falcon which falls on them, attacking with fury. The black with the white star came in first.

"The bay with the black mane came in second and the solid black was beyond reproach; he came in third. The *Tali* was the fourth, he came next; but the inhabitant of Tahama was far from the inhabitant of Nedj. The fifth, *El Mourtah*, was not at fault. He galloped as best he knew how. *El Aâtif*, the sixth, came in still restless; and his fear failed to stop him on the way. The seventh was *El Hadi* and the prizegiver also gave him his reward.

"*El Mouammil*, who gave such hopes to his owner, came in eighth. He was seen to be downcast, the luckless one met the bird of ill-omen in his path. He allowed seven horses to get in front of him and came in eighth, but the eighth horse was not one of the winners. The ninth came in at last; he was *El Lathim*, the Rebuffed, and he received blows from everyone. At this point *Es Sokeït* (the taciturn) came in at a trot, his [jockey's] face contorted and humiliation on his brow. The man who rides him and who goes at the tail of the others is the object of reproaches from everyone; but even more so is his groom. If it is asked who is his owner no reply will be forthcoming from those whom shame has rendered dumb.

"He who did not send the most noble horses by birth to the racecourse should by now be repenting it.

"By attending we have experienced the greatest of enjoyment, not to mention the glory and the winnings which we have obtained. In exchange for the seven roses planted at the end of the track and plucked by the seven who came in first, we received magnificent presents such as it is fitting to offer: striped cloth from Yemen, dyed in various colors, and *haïks* in silk and wool. We carried all these showy stuffs whose borders were red like blood on our horses. Moreover, we were given pieces of money by the thousands; but that money we never keep, rather we distribute it among the grooms who look after our horses, notwithstanding that we look after them more than they do and with our own hands. These are the horses who drink only the purest of water and eat only the choicest of feed.

"Mohammedan law recognises three ways of offering prizes in horse races. The first is authorized unconditionally, the second under certain conditions, and the third is absolutely forbidden.

"1. A man, without pecuniary interest in the race, offers a purse, saying: 'He who wins will receive the prize.' Kings, chieftains, great personages, whose rank or fortune has them situated in an exalted position, offer, at times, prizes in this way, which is unconditionally permitted.

"2. An individual, interested in the race says: 'I offer a prize.' This is permitted on the condition that if the donor comes in first, the prize will be given to the assembly of persons.

"3. The third way is that in which each of the competitors offers a prize in favor of the one who gets ahead of him. This type of race constitutes real gambling and is, consequently, completely prohibited.

"With even greater reason the betting of outsiders on races is formally prohibited."

15

VETERINARY PRACTICE AMONG THE ARABS

> Among us, he who possesses the art of
> being able to cure horses owes to all his
> coreligionaries the full and continuous
> benefit of the gift which he has received.

I HAVE NOT THOUGHT IT FITTING to end the really important part of this book without giving some idea of the knowledge which the Arabs have of veterinary science; and outlining that idea is the object I pursue in the following pages. I reiterate that I do no more than set it forth, without making any pretense of teaching.

Just as I consulted competent authorities with respect to the book, I wished to appeal to a man of recognized knowledge, Monsieur Riquet, chief veterinarian, secretary of the Commission of Equine Hygiene, with respect to the special matter of veterinary medicine. Upon publishing the opinion of that renowned and skilled practioner, again I have no other purpose in mind than that of offering, after a fashion, a guarantee of the conscientiousness which has presided over my studies.

"Paris, February 17, 1851.

"My General:

"I read with interest the documents which you did me the favor of entrusting to my care and which are concerned with the principal diseases by which Barb horses are most generally attacked. I admit that I was struck with admiration of the spirit of observation of which the Arabs give proof in that which concerns disorders of the forelegs and hindlegs and of the simplicity of the curative measures taken. However, the same thing did not occur with respect to what concerns internal disorders, for ignorance of anatomy and of the various vital functions makes the Arabs believe in a thousand imaginary causes and so make use of treatments which science repudiates. Nevertheless, as nothing has appeared dealing with this subject and as in the list of diseases which your notes contain, there are several which are not found in our veterinarian nostologic picture, I am persuaded that the publication of the documents which you have collected among the nomad tribes of Algeria will be of interest to those persons who concern themselves with equine science.

"I have the honor, my General, to offer myself as your devoted servitor.

"Riquet

Chief Veterinarian, Secretary of the Commission for Equine Hygiene."

Before pointing out the different remedies which in the desert are used in diseases of the horse, we shall say a few words about the veterinarian art among the Arabs. That which among us is a complete science taught in schools and constituting a special profession is, among them, a multiple tradition, the parts of which cannot be gathered together except by consulting a great number of men situated in very distinct walks of life.

Within recent times works on this important subject existed, carefully preserved by the *tholbas*. Now the books have almost disappeared; but their spirit still lingers. That which was read is recounted and those whom an aptitude inclines toward curing horses find instruction in the words of priceless documents. These documents are a benefit which the student should render, in some way, to his entire country. Such is the religious love which surrounds the horse among the Arabs, that one could not find words sufficiently eloquent to vituperate the man who might turn his knowledge of veterinarian medicine to his own benefit. He who knows the art of curing horses owes to his coreligionaries the full and continuous benefit of the gift which he has received. Invested with a sacred function, he is ever at the disposal of anyone in need of his knowledge; and should it occur to him to put a price on the trouble he goes to, he would be called a usurer. His first duty is to be in a condition of absolute disinterest.

Another obligation, no less severe, for a man who knows how to treat horses is that of not hiding his knowledge. One could not reiterate enough times: the skill of a veterinarian is a blessing which does not belong to just anyone; it is a real national treasure spread among several persons in the form of a deposit. When one thinks of the role that the horse plays in the life of the Arabs there is nothing in the foregoing which should surprise one. For the disciples of Mohammed, the horse is a weapon of war and war itself a medium of religious propaganda. Therefore, it then constitutes a true, a veritable attack on the cult of his country when a man wishes to allow his talents to remain hidden or lie fallow or to exploit the knowledge which is so straitly joined to the interests of the Faith.

The only recompense which may be offered to a veterinarian is a generous hospitality. He will find in the tent to which he has been summoned abundant food for himself and for his horse; when he leaves it shall be said to him: "May God remember your fathers," and he will reply: "Abide with good."

Far from being a lucrative practice, this noble profession frequently proves to be onerous for the man who practices it. The veterinarian does not always go to the tents of his coreligionaries; frequently they go to his dwelling to consult him and he has to provide hospitality. Such a man, famous for his skill in curing horses, is ruined by the continual expenses which his profession imposes.

In spite of the absence of veterinarian schools in the desert, young men are frequently sent to some man of great renown for his skill in treating horses. These young men are destined to teach afterwards in the tribes what they have been able to learn about the diseases of horses. He who trains disciples does not receive any compensation in cash, but he may accept gifts of wheat, sheep, or garments. He does not bear the expenses of his pupils and they contract a debt of gratitude toward him from which they shall never feel themselves to be free.

There is only one instance in which the veterinarian may accept a testimonial of true munificence: when an Arab of high rank sees a horse for which he has a particular affection, attacked by some grave illness, he calls in for consultation four or five of the most renowned veterinarians. After they have reached an agreement on the treatment which should be followed, the duty of carrying out the prescribed treatment is entrusted to one of them and he who has been chosen remains in the tent of the personage until the horse has either recovered or dies. When the doctor takes his leave he is given a camel or a horse or clothing.

There is, if I am not mistaken, in the exact details which I have just given, a teaching more elevated than the very subject with which I am dealing. In these simple, dignified arrangements, prescribed in advance down to the last detail between the veterinarian and his co-religionaries, one can savor an entire facet of Arabic life. One finds in them a people who relate to a religious thought all the acts of their calm and perilous life. That said, let us return to our subject.

DISEASES OF THE EXTREMITIES OF THE LEGS

Corns (*rahsa*). Pare the hoof, reach the corn, expose it, and do not fear to make it bleed. Purulent, suppurant, or not, put resin, rancid grease, and tar on it, which one melts by the application of a hot iron. Shoe immediately, covering the entire sole and the frog with a piece of leather placed under the shoe. Next day the horse can travel.

Overreaches (*jelhag el djerida*: literally, "he reaches the stripe on his head"). For overreaches on the heel one applies to the bruised part a kind of unguent made with henna and powdered *zadje,* the fixative being rancid butter.

One regards overreaches on the tendons as being particularly dangerous, above all if they have caused an engorgement. The curative means is the application of a plaster of fine hulled wheat flour mixed with egg white. That plaster, spread on a strip of cloth three or four inches wide, should be fastened on above and below with a smooth band of cloth until it will stay on by itself. This will not take long to happen and when the time comes to take it off, one should not do so except with great care and by means of warm water.

Cracked heels (*seurr*). All muck, urine, in fine, all dirt, should be carefully disposed of.

Make applications of bran boiled in water to which a little vinegar has been added.

Or, apply to the crack an unguent made with henna and ground *zadje,* or fresh butter, and *toutya* reduced to powder.[1]

---

[1] *Toutya*: under this name, the natives designate copper sulphate (blue vitriol, blue sulphate) and the sulphate of zinc (white sulphate.)

Before making fresh applications the parts should always be washed with soap and warm water.

Founder. One calls a foundered horse *medroube be chaïr* (barley-stricken). When one has committed the imprudence of allowing a horse that has eaten a large amount of barley to drink, he becomes *medroube be chaïr*—barley-stricken. Haste must be made to bleed the forearms and the saphenas. Then, every morning for many days, one gives the horse a bath with cool water. He is kept in the bath from daybreak just until the sun begins to get hot.

To complete this treatment, one cuts down on the animal's feed and he is purged by mixing onion juice with his water.

Blows on the feet. For blows on the feet, with or without wounds, here is the curative means used:

Take the root of *bou-nafâa,*[2] stripped of its bark, cut it into little pieces, and boil it in oil just until the latter becomes impregnated with its properties to the point of turning reddish. Dampen in the oil thus prepared a rag containing rock salt and bathe the wounded part. For the time being it will swell and then return to its normal state.

Lacking *bou-nafâa,* apply to the wound a poultice made of grease, resin, and tar which have been boiled together.

DISEASES OF THE FLESHY PARTS OF THE LEGS

Capulets or Wens (kherradja). When the wen is recent and not very pronounced, one shaves off the hairs that cover it, makes light scarifications on the skin, and then applies heat by means of a small sachet filled with salt and soaked in boiling oil impregnated with *bou-nafâa,* stripped of its outer covering.

As I said upon indicating the curative means used in the treatment of blows on the feet, one can know that the *bou-nafâa* has ceded all its properties to the oil as soon as the latter turns red.

Care should always be taken not to inhale the steam of the *bou-nafâa,* as it could be harmful to the eyes.

---

[2] *Bou nafâa:* the father of usefulness, the most useful thing par excellence. This name is the synonym of *drias.* These two words are used interchangeably to designate two or three species of umbelliferous plants of the genus *thapsia* [meadow parsnip and allied genera].

The Arabs make great use of *bou nafâa.* It is used for engorgements, chronic ailments of the chest, the abdomen, etc., etc.

When the wens are old, very pronounced, and when the subcutaneous cellular tissue has passed into the stage of induration, it is necessary to shave off the hairs that cover it and make a longitudinal incision, laying back the skin on two sides, removing the hard tissue which covers the tip of the calcaneum, and join the edges of the wound; finishing the treatment by applying rancid grease, resin, and tar melted by the application of a hot iron. Suppuration sets in, quickly ceases, and at the end of fifteen or twenty days the horse is cured. Contact with water should be avoided.

Blood-spavins (*beïda*). The Arabs attribute blood-spavins and windgalls to two principal causes:

If the horse is young, he has been overridden or too abruptly halted; if he is old, he has frequently been watered after a fast gallop, lathered and with a full stomach.

Again according to the Arabs, blood-spavins have three "eyes." One is situated on the external surface of the hock, another on the internal surface, and finally the third also on the internal surface, below and behind the tibia. The third is the one most to be feared.

When the blood-spavin is uncomplicated, one fires it with an iron whose head is about the circumference of a twenty-five centime coin; and even if it has not yet appeared on the internal surface, it will not delay in so doing, say the Arabs, so as a precautionary measure one fires the corresponding place which is called *aâyn* (the eye).

When thoroughpin is involved the Arabs adopt another procedure: they fire just one point on the exterior part, then they apply one point of fire to the center of the internal tumor and then finish by applying points of fire very close together encircling the tumor. The number of points of fire is in proportion to the dimension of the tumor.

After that operation, one puts liquid tar on the points which were fired and then the hot iron is applied again, but more lightly, just enough to make the tar penetrate. Treatment must always end with an application of tar. Contact with water should be avoided.

In winter and spring, honey takes the place of tar.

There is another curative means very frequently employed in the treatment of blood-spavin and one which, almost always, I have seen give good results.

The hairs are shaved off the location of the blood-spavins, both on the exterior and interior parts. By means of scarifications the reddish liquid which they contain is made to come out and the wound is gently rubbed with that which the Arabs call *ras saboun* (the head of the soap) which is none other, I think, than a solution of potash. Or, after the scarifying, one applies heat with a small sachet of salt soaked in boiling oil. Great inflammation sets in, followed by suppuration and the cure comes quickly, without leaving any traces.

I have seen, when I was [French] consul in Mascara, the veterinarian of the Emir Abd-el-Kader obtain, by that method, a radical cure on a horse belonging to one of the Spahis who had accompanied me. The animal had his hocks at the time in such a condition as to make one despair.[3]

[3] Note communicated by General Yusuf [see letter on pp. 210–211]:

Operation for blood-spavin: the horse's four feet are hobbled, he is cast and bedded down on litter, every precaution being taken to prevent him from making any movement that might interfere with the operation.

The swollen part of the hock is then carefully shaved, freeing it of hairs, not only the affected part but also all the hair for a few millimeters beyond the circumference.

That done, a light incision in the shape of a cross is made on the blood-spavin and the edges of this artificial wound are lifted to facilitate the escape of the matter which flows out; that matter is yellowish mixed with a little blood.

When the tumor has disappeared, the incision is rubbed with mutton fat which one sprinkles with two or three pinches of powdered pine resin. The wound is then cauterized with a round iron rod, heated white hot; in that way, the resin upon melting, mixes with the fat and spreads with it over the incisions.

It is necessary that the iron rod which one uses for the cautery be round so that it will not tear the tissues with which it comes in contact.

The horse is then put on his feet and hobbled in such a way that he cannot scratch the wounded parts, which are covered with a piece of mutton spleen bound on with a strip of cloth. This is left on the wound until the maggots have entered therein, something which ordinarily occurs in four or five days. That period of time over, one allows the maggots to consume all the rotten flesh in the wound.

The maggots should be left just until one is sure that there is nothing left of the synovial matter which was in the tumor and that the organic tissues which were affected have returned to their normal state. Five or six days ordinarily suffice for that purpose; after which the wound is rubbed with tar and the horse is cured.

During the course of treatment one does not change the horse's feed at all, unless there are special circumstances which require it. One only takes care to avoid, as much as possible, flies and all accidents which could torment the animal. [*Note continued on next page.*]

Windgalls (*menafeuss*). When the windgalls are small and do not grow in volume, one worries little. One even says of them: "They preserve from faults."

However, when they are voluminous, hard, or when they spread upwards on the tendons, the Arabs take energetic measures against them. Here is the method most frequently employed:

The skin covering them is shaved. Then a longitudinal incision is made, care being taken not to let the instrument penetrate too deeply; then when the reddish liquid which the tumor contains has completely drained away, rancid grease, resin, and tar are placed on the opening of the wound and made to mix by the application of a red-hot sickle. Then comes inflammation, suppuration sets in, and the animal is cured in about fifteen or twenty days. Should the suppuration continue for a long time, liquid tar placed on the wound will suffice to stop it.

It is strongly recommended to avoid allowing the horse to put his feet in water during the length of time that the treatment lasts.

If it is a question of extenuating the dangers of the puffed-up windgalls that spread up the tendons, they are fired on two vertical parallel lines, joined by perpendicular lines. The pattern thus made looks like a ladder.

Firing is done with the point of a sickle, with successive applications (and as a last resort) of honey or tar, according to the season. Honey, it is said, is preferable in winter and spring for it keeps the wounds from all humidity.

Diseases of the Bony Parts of the Legs

Bone Spavin (*el djeurde*). Bone spavin, whatever its location, is always very dangerous, but it becomes, in the eyes of the Arabs, an insurmountable cause for exclusion from all service when it is found under the saphena or even close to it.

From all points of view it is better to practice this operation in cold weather, so that an incurable gangrene will not result.

If a thoroughpin is involved, one practices the operation on both sides of the affected hock.

The Arabs think that it is better if the horse can be left standing up during the operation; in that way the matter will drain more easily and one does not risk having it flow inwards, something which could happen if the horse were lying down.

The spavin is fired in such a way as to be encircled with points quite close to each other. The cautery is done three times and each time the traces of firing are covered with a layer of tar. In the center of the circle and on the spavin itself one also takes care to apply a point of fire, deeper than the others.

The Arabs refuse to try to cure stringhalt (*éparvin sec*). They reject, for war, a horse thus afflicted.

Splint (*aadom chiche*). The splint is only dangerous according to the place where it is found; the most grave being that which is close to the tendons.

The Arabs believe that the splint starts at the knee to descend progressively and successively toward the extremities. It is necessary, they say, to stop it at the moment of its appearance, because that disease of the bone will end up by reaching the fetlock and putting the animal out of service.

They attempt to stop it by taking a round loaf, just out of the oven, cutting it in two and applying it to the affected part.

Should that give no result, they sponge the splint with a small sachet full of salt which they soak in boiling oil impregnated with *bou-nafâa*.

The hair will grow back and the horse will not be depreciated.

They prefer this method to that of heat applied with an iron.

Ringbone and sidebone (*fekroune, louzze*). These ailments, according to the Arabs, come from the accumulation and duration of the blood in the part of the foot where they make themselves manifest. Too tight hobbles can cause them. At the moment they appear, haste must be made to bleed the horse from the veins of the pastern. This simple operation often suffices to arrest their development or even make them disappear.

Fekroune is the name given to ringbone. It is regarded as being the less dangerous. It is fired in such a way as to encircle it with points quite close to each other.

Louzze is the name given to sidebone which shows on the bone of the coronet and it is very dangerous because of the tendons which are in its vicinity. To cure it, three applications are made alternately of fire and tar. Moreover, care is taken to place another point of fire very deep on the internal part of the frog. This latter operation being regarded as absolutely indispensable.

However it may be, ringbones and sidebones, are very much feared and render an animal unfit for service in war.

LAMENESS OF THE JOINTS

Lameness. All lamenesses whose causes are apparent, say the Arabs, can be cured more or less easily. It is not thus with those arising from the scapulohumeral and coxofemoral joints.

Lameness of the shoulder (djebda, stiffness). To detect lameness of the shoulder, place oneself in front of the horse's breast, take in the hand the foot of the member which one thinks is affected and pull it strongly toward one. Should the horse, to avoid pain, yield, lean, or even come forward, you may rest assured that the evil lies in the scapulohumeral joint. If, on the contrary, he backs off, look for the cause elsewhere.

Lameness arising in the scapulohumeral joint is called *djebda* (stiffness).

Here is the treatment used in such cases:

Draw together the skin from the last third of the neck to the joint, take ten stitches in it with a needle and make a stout knot in the thread. This will set up an irritation favoring healing [this is a seton].

Lameness of the hip joint. One can always recognise that the site of the lameness is in the coxofemoral joint when after having forced the horse to climb a slope rapidly, one sees him suffer horribly and manifest his pain by violent efforts.

Now, one of two things: either he has naught but a strain of the round ligament (*medila*) and it will suffice to fire the coxofemoral joint; or, the head of the femur is dislocated and then, before firing, an effort should be made to get it back in place.

To obtain that result, the Arabs place the horse on an incline; he is tied to a stake by a hobble on the pastern of the affected leg. Then by means of whip lashes he is forced to bound forward. The efforts which the animal makes, as he is restrained are sufficient to reestablish the articulation. The Arabs also achieve their object by constraining the animal to lean only on the bad leg for an entire day. In the latter case, the means employed is the following:

Take a woolen cord and tie it tightly above the hock on the opposite leg to the affected one, which forces the animal to rest its weight on the latter because of the pain which the ligature causes.

DISEASES OF THE EYES

Inflammation of the conjuctiva, simple ophthalmia. Bathe the eye with oil after having spat it between the lid and the opaque cornea.

Cataracts (el beyad). Whatever its extent or its situation on the eyeball, if the cataract is recent, take the tobacco juice found in the stem of a pipe, moisten a piece of cotton with it, lift the upper eyelid, insert the cotton and lower the eyelid at once. The cotton will stay there until the horse himself rids himself of it. The next day, sprinkle the eye with salted water and repeat this operation for three successive days. Or,

Grind male coral until it is reduced to a very fine powder, then by means of a hollow straw, blow that powder into the eye. Or,

Mash the leaves of the dwarf palm or the leaves of the cedar and spit the juice into the eye. Or,

Finally, cast the horse and put human excrement in his eye. Repeat for three successive days. That procedure gave me good results on the expedition of Taguedempt.

In the desert, the horse is cast and the blood of a tortoise which has just been bled is put in his eye.

Paralysis of the optic nerve (el koholy). The Arabs know the paralysis of the optic nerve to which they give the name *el koholy,* but they abstain from treating it.

DISEASES OF THE STOMACH

Worms in the stomach (el merdjoune, el methiour). A horse that has in its stomach worms which are quite thick, short, white, with black heads and covered with hairs, is called *el merdjoune.* These worms pierce the membrane of the stomach and at the end of a certain length of time, which varies from six months to a year, the horse inevitably dies.

The Arabs believe that the malady is caused by horses having eaten grass which sprang up over the body of a serpent that died in the spring, whose putrefaction engendered the flies called *debabe.*

El merdjoune is recognized by the following signs: when the horse passes droppings, they are the usual color; in a few minutes they turn red. He urinates infrequently, but with abundance. His urine is oily and stays on the surface of the ground for quite a long time in foam. He loses his appetite.

This illness is among the principal causes for redhibitory action. At the end of a year, one may still choose experts, have the animal opened, and the fact sworn to.

To cure *el merdjoune*, the horse is made to swallow infusions of *zateur*.[4] The Arabs say that they were led to the use of this remedy by the hedgehog which hunts vipers, seizes them by the middle of the body with its teeth and kills them by blows of its quills on the head without receiving a single bite. Then it always carries the viper to the side of the *zateur*, which it starts to eat with avidity as if to preserve itself from all accident.

Colics (*el oudjâa*). If the colics cannot be attributed to any cause other than that of indigestion provoked by an abundance of water swallowed on top of too large a feed, one does not have much to worry about. It will be enough, say the Arabs, to make the horse sweat, which is easily accomplished by making him run a little, above all on first mounting. The exercise over, one takes care to cover him well, and if he passes droppings or stales, one may be assured that he is cured.

However, when the colics are provoked by the bad quality of the feed, especially by the dirt or dust which are frequently mixed with barley, they are regarded as much more dangerous.

To cure them, one resorts to fumigations, most frequently made with red pepper and fennel smouldered on hot coals.

In distinguished tents, one always finds, for the same purpose, rats which are termed *faret-el-khreïl* (horse-rats) which, after they have been bled, gutted, and heavily salted, have been slowly dried in the sun. When one wants to make use of them, one cuts off a little piece which is then smouldered over hot coals and the horse is made to inhale that odor. The odor is nauseous, the horse tries to escape it; but, for his prompt recovery, he must be constrained to accept it.

---

[4] *Zateur*: this plant is probably one of the euphorbias, belonging to the family of spurges. Euphorbium is a gum resin obtained from the concreted juices of several species of euphorbia indigenous to Morocco. Pliny, the naturalist, states that the name of the drug was in honor of Euphorbus, the Greek physician of Juba II (died *cira* A.D., 19–24), king of Mauretania. The drug was formerly valued for its drastic purgative and emetic properties. There is a treatise on it, *De Euphorbia herba*, written by Juba II. *Euphorbia resinifera*, a cactuslike spurge, yields a gum resin which is used as an emetic, cathartic, and vesicant in veterinary practice. [Translator's note]

Gastrohepatitis, jaundice (*bou sefir*: the father of yellowness). The Arabs allege that jaundice only comes in summer or autumn, for then the horses eat wheat straw too soon, which, according to the Arabs, should not be fed before winter.

A horse with jaundice loses flesh; his coat becomes staring; his skin turns yellow; he loses his appetite and lacks strength.

One knows that a horse has jaundice when in the hollows of his ears one finds small yellow stains, when the whites of his eyes turn yellow and, on turning back his lips, one finds the membranes of the mouth to be yellow, spotted with little buds; also, when under the tail the skin is yellow as well. Apart from these indications, the mare presents, in her case, yellow spots inside the vulva.

To cure the animal, one splits the skin between the nostrils in such a manner as to lay bare a thick shallow nerve, called the nerve of jaundice. When one has found it, one takes a needle threaded with some horse-hairs, pulls it toward one, dissects it, and then cuts it at the top and the bottom in such a way as to remove a length of half an inch. The blood flows; salt and tar are put on the wound.

To complete the treatment, scarifications are made on the inner part of the ears, on the lips, and also on the lower part of the dock. These scarifications are daubed with salt and tar. The cure will not be long in coming.

PLEUROPNEUMONIA

El mefellougue. When a too-fat horse has made too fast and too long a gallop, he splits, say the Arabs. He no longer eats, he no longer drinks; his flanks are hollow and his coat staring. Sometimes he urinates blood.

Here are the ways to cure him:

1. Make him swallow two or three ounces of henna mixed with luke-warm oil and that day do not permit him to drink. The following day allow him to drink through the bridle.

2. Take the part of the root of the dwarf palm which is called *el kuernafa*, pound it in a mortar, let it soak in water just until the latter turns red, and make the horse drink it. He will die or he will recover.

In many districts the horse is made to drink hyena blood mixed with luke-warm water. This remedy is regarded as being so sovereign that in each tent of distinction little pieces of *haïk* impregnated with hyena blood are always to be found. To make use of them they are soaked in warm water and when the water has turned color the horse is made to drink it.

Whatever the treatment used, the animal, until it is cured, is kept very warm.

SPECIAL DISEASES

Farcy (*el djedri*, smallpox). The Arabs call farcy *el djedri*, smallpox. They subdivide it, according to the danger it presents, into four categories, to each one of which they give a different name. These four categories are:

1. *Bou sebahh* (father of the rosary). These are the buds which follow the path of a vein, be it on the neck, on the body, or on the limbs, anterior or posterior. These are regarded as being easy to cure.

2. *Bou salem* (father of the saved). This is the farcy which appears on different parts of the body or legs, but at great distances from one another. Buds are rare and wide apart.

3. *El kholt* (the mixture). It appears on the anterior or posterior limbs, does not follow the paths of the veins and is scattered. It is considered dangerous and even after having been cured, always leaves traces.

4. Lastly *el ferg* (the disseminated). This appears all over the body, on the lips, the neck, and the limbs. The buds, which are small, appear and then disappear. The animal limps on one leg, that leg heals. A few days later he limps on the other leg. He always faces the sun, refuses to eat, loses a great deal of flesh and ends up by discharging bloody matter through the nostrils, which is a precursory symptom of death. One of the infallible signs of that dread disease is a cord without buds which extends from the ear to the breast, following the line of the neck. When the illness reaches that stage it is called *bou chekhare* (father of snores.)

To cure the *bou sebahh* it is enough to make, with a red-hot sickle, a line the width of and above the highest bud; all those which lie below will crack open of themselves or dry up. The Arabs allege that as farcy always goes from bottom to top, this is the only way to stop its spread.

Should the buds not crack open by themselves or if they do not dry up quickly enough, they can be quickly arrested by smearing them with honey and piercing them with a sliver of rose-laurel heated in the fire.

For the *bou salem*, a small gland to be found above and on each side of the nostrils is fired. The gland is called *oulsis*, and it is, according to the Arabs, the father of farcy. One goes just far enough to remove it and limits oneself to applying salt as the only dressing on the wounds thus caused. If necessary, the treatment is completed by firing the buds with honey and rose-laurel.

The *kholt*. This is treated by first making a transverse line with a sickle above the highest bud, to prevent it from spreading. Then all the buds are fired with honey and rose laurel. If this operation has been performed before the leg swelled, the horse will recover. If to the contrary, he will still recover, but he will never regain his normal condition, the farcy by then having gone into the stage of *rebou*.

With respect to the *ferg* which always leads to the *bou chekhare*, the Arabs have tried every means imaginable in order to cure it, and they have not succeeded. They are so convinced that it is incurable, that they force the owner of a horse thus attacked to destroy him. If the owner does not do so, he is forced, by law, to pay the price of such animals as might die by reason of his imprudence.

When firing, make an application of tar immediately, renew [the treatment], and end always with an application of tar. It is preferable to fire with rose laurel because its "bile" is, of itself, an excellent means of healing.

Exercise is strongly recommended for a horse that has been operated on for farcy.

The Arabs believe that farcy is contagious and that it has a great analogy to smallpox.

DISEASES UNKNOWN IN EUROPE

El Aâdeur (*pain*). When one unsaddles too quickly a horse that has been lathered by a long gallop, he can contract a grave disease which is called *el aâdeur,* pain.

It can be recognized by the following symptoms:

Small buds break out on the back, the ribs, the flanks, the belly, and the legs. Two or three days after their appearance, they break open and are immediately replaced by others. The matter which comes out is fetid; it resembles pus. These outbreaks of buds, alternated with healing, can go on for a year. They almost always lead to the death of the animal.

The *maadour* horse travels with his head held high, his hindlegs wide apart, his eyes haggard; he cannot bend his neck.

The Arabs declare that they cannot cure this disease; only they have noted that if the first buds spread from the back down to the feet, the animal sometimes pulls through, while if the buds appear on the feet and spread upwards over the flanks and ribs, he will undoubtedly die.

When a horse that has been purchased dies and it is suspected that he was *maadour,* the buyer demands an examination by experts; the body is opened and if in the artery lying below the spinal column pus is found, the seller is forced to make restitution of the price which he has been given.

Bou Dinar (father of the *dinar*[5]). The Arabs have given the name of *bou dinar* to a disease which reveals itself in splotches resembling coins, appearing on the skin from the neck to the flanks.

These splotches are swollen when the north wind blows; they disappear when the south wind blows. One has noted that, apart from their appearance, the lips of the vulva of the mare always become distended.

This disease follows when in order to obtain a mule, the mare has been given to an ass that was not healthy.

If the mare has conceived and her fruit dies, she will be saved. To the contrary, the sleet of winter will surely cause her death [if she is still in foal].

If, thinking that the mare did not conceive with the ass, she is

---

[5] *Dinar*: a Moslem coin. This disease is probably dourine (equine syphillis or *maladie du coït*). The symptoms described above are very similar to those given by Moore (Veranus Alva Moore, *The Pathology and Differential Diagnosis of Infectious Diseases of Animals*), who states that the disease "seems to have first been recognized in Algeria."

Dourine attacks both the horse and the ass, although the latter would appear to be more resistant to it. Moore states that the symptoms have been divided into three different stages. The secondary stage is that "in which the exanthematous eruptions appear in the skin—the so-called 'plaques' [The *dinar* of the Arabs]." Dourine is caused by the *trypanosoma equiperdum* (*Trypanosoma rougeti*) which is closely allied to the *Trypanosoma brucei* which causes African horse sickness or encephalomyelitis. [Translator's note]

given to a stallion, the stallion will contract the *bou dinar* and, if he does not die, his member will always be flaccid and dangling.

The Arabs believe that the disease is caused by those large flies (*debabe*) which, after having feasted on the serpents to be found in such large numbers in the spring, have become impregnated with their venom and have deposited it on the member of the animal.

In the tribe of the Beni-Selyman, alone, in 1846 more than forty to fifty mares afflicted by *bou dinar* died. The chiefs of the tribe were so convinced that the disease came from the cause mentioned above that they caused it to be published in all their domains, that under penalty of a very stiff fine, serpents should be very deeply buried.

The death of an animal from *bou dinar* is attested to by experts. It is a redhibitory case; the vendor must make restitution to the buyer.

When the spots have disappeared, one cannot affirm the presence of the disease except by an examination of the vulva of the mare; when it is opened, very red small inflammations can be found, resembling the bite of a flea.

NERVOUS AFFLICTION

Encanthis (el meghbla). When a horse has hypertrophy of the *caruncula lacrymalis* and the "nail" of that gland takes on the dimension of a small pea, it is known that the animal is suffering from encanthis. One is confirmed in this opinion if the horse alternately lies down and gets up and does not perceive objects around him.

To cure him the following operation is performed:

The horse is cast, a strong needle is threaded with two or three mane hairs, that which is called the "nail" is lanced, and the ends of the hairs are joined. They are wound around the little finger of the left hand, the index finger of the same hand is slipped under the lachrymal gland, and lastly the "little bean" which is in excess is cut horizontally. Without wasting a second, salt mixed with rancid butter is put in the eye which has been operated on and the horse will heal in no time.

On the first expedition to Kabylie, in 1844, I saw a horse of one of my *mekhazeni* thus operated on and cured. He was treated by the Kaïd of the Ysseurs, who laughed heartily at our incredulity and especially at the danger which we attach to such an operation.

Observations of the Emir Abd-el-Kader

"For recognizing diseases of the horse and treating them there are veterinarians of great repute in the Sahara, as well as in the Tell; and rare indeed is the tribe, however small, that does not have one or two. Of these veterinarians, some treat all diseases; but the majority only know how to cure a few. The lack of veterinarian schools prevents the Arabs from studying this science in a more complete form and I do not know of any clinics, either in the Sahara or in the Ghaib (Empire of Morocco).

"All that the person who wishes to study the science can do nowadays is attach himself to a competent veterinarian and observe his treatments. It frequently happens that in the beginning the pupil studies the art of curing with zeal, but achieving uneven results with the treatment he uses, his reputation is made only for being able to cure certain ailments, which makes him neglect the others.

" 'The most intelligent of men can make a mistake,
    The sharpest sword can fail to cut,
    And the most noble of horses can stumble.'

"Everything has its hazards:

"What is the hazard of sagacity? Anger.
    What is the hazard of the spirit? Pride.
    What is the hazard of wisdom? Forgetfulness.
    What is the hazard of talk? Lying.
    What is the hazard of doing good? Vanity.
    What is the hazard of generosity? Associating with misers.
    What is the hazard of force? Oppression.
    What is the hazard of religion? Neglect of religious observances.
    What is the hazard of a noble heart? The attraction of new ways.

"And the hazard to a horse, as well as being the principal cause of its illnesses? Rest and fat."

16

GELDING

The horse, the companion par excellence
of the warrior, the host in the large tent,
is that [horse] which possesses all the
plenitude and all the energy of his faculties.

IT IS SUPPOSED that the gelding of horses is known only in Europe, but
this is a mistaken belief, for that operation is practiced in the desert,
although it is not customary except among the poor. The horse of a
wealthy man is exempt from such mutilation. Why? That is easy to
understand. The stallion finds in the desert continual causes for ex-
citement; the air that surrounds him carries on it the whinnies of
mares and the scents of aromatic plants; shouts and perfumes act on
his senses and make him difficult to control. Only the wealthy can
afford the expense of the necessary constant vigilance, and he who
cannot look after his horse every moment finds himself obliged to
geld him.

This is how the gelding is performed: the horse is cast and a strong
tourniquet [ligature] is applied above the testicles. Then, with a very
slender sickle which has been heated to white-hot, an incision is made,
large enough so that the skin will peel back and allow the testicles to
appear. Once outside, they are tied off above with a silk cord. Once
again the sickle is employed to cut below the second ligature. As soon

as this operation is finished, some round iron instrument, such as a pistol barrel, is heated to red-hot, but not to white-hot. The parts which the sickle has just cut are cauterized with that instrument, care always being taken not to destroy the ligatures. After the cautery, the wound is plugged with a tampon made of salt which has been plunged into hot oil in which butter has been dissolved.

For the first three days after being gelded the horse should drink very little, and for eight or ten days he will wear a belly-band made of canvas or, lacking canvas, of wool. This bandage, which is tied over the loins, is to prevent all contact of the affected parts with the air. Feed will continue to be the same but fatigue nil.

The horse will be in complete repose for ten or twelve days and he will not be ridden for the first month, except with great precautions.

As some superstition must always attach to all the customs of the desert, care is always taken, immediately following gelding, to dig a small hole in the sand and to bury in it the cut-off testicles. Should some animal eat these bloody remains or should some enemy chance to see them it would be a sure cause of misfortune.

Horses are gelded from the age of two until they are eight years old. Fatalities are very rare, and only thoses horses in whose cases care is not taken to avoid contact of the air with the wound are likely to die.

In some tribes, instead of gelding with an edged implement, the operation is done with a mallet or wooden hammer. However, this procedure cannot be practiced on other than colts from six months to a year old.

Gelding is so generally practiced in the desert that even the camels are castrated. Gelded camels can endure fatigue with greater energy than entire camels because they do not wear themselves out by continual exertion with she-camels. But it should not be deduced from the foregoing that the stallion is not the animal held in the greatest esteem by the Arabs. Gelding is made necessary by poverty in the Sahara, but there, as in all parts of Africa, the stallion, by reason of the possession of all the plenitude and all the energy of his faculties, is, par excellence, the companion of the warrior and the host of the large tent.

Observations of the Emir Abd-el-Kader

"Among the Arabs, gelding of animals is little practiced, above all among the great personages, for it wastes the horse, diminishes his beauty, his agility, and the sheen of his coat. There are some who allege, furthermore, that gelding lessens strength and makes the flesh flabby. A gelded animal is ordinarily longer lived because it does not mate. That is the reason why mules live for many years and for the opposite reason birds do not live long. A gelding loses speed and vigor, for he is reduced to the condition of a mare and it is known that in all species of animals the female is weaker than the male. Is the woman as strong as the man?

"Mohammedan law prohibts the gelding of horses, for it weakens them and reduces their masculine nature to a feminine one, which is inferior. Therefore, it may be affirmed that if gelding is sometimes useful, it is not so for those horses ridden in times of war or destined to run in big races.

"Glory to Him Who created man and Who made for his benefit all beings, Who endowed him with reason, Who teaches him the advantages which may be derived from all things."

17

ADVANTAGES TO BE DERIVED
FROM THE NATIVE HORSE

In the country par excellence of equestrian life, it is necessary that the horse
become our instrument, that he cross over
from Arabic service to French service, and
that it be not only our colonial possession
but also our mother-country herself that
benefits from this priceless conquest.

WE HAVE STUDIED up to this point the horse in the hands of the natives;
that companion of the Arabic warrior has been shown just as he is in
that primitive and bellicose society in which he occupies by religion
and custom such an important place. But our work would not be complete if we passed over in silence the career which our domination
in Africa opens up to the equine species.

Everything which belongs to a land in which our flag flies should
be looked at from a new point of view—that of our national interest.
In the country par excellence of an equestrian life, it is necessary that
the horse become our instrument, that he cross over from Arabic
service to French service, and that it be not only our colonial possession but our mother-country herself that derives benefit from that
priceless conquest.

The horse indigenous to our African possessions belongs to the

Barb breed.[1] Barbs were the horses ridden by the intrepid horsemen who proved to be such rude adversaries for the Romans. Even should they lack the rounded contours, the harmonious beauty, the fluid elegance of the Arabian horse, still it can be said that their lean and vigorous lines reveal unquestionable qualities. Between the Barb and the Arabian lies the difference which lies between a glass etched in crystal by human hands and a glass cast in a mold. One has a rough finish while the finish of the other shows a polishing, a perfection which leaves nothing to be desired to the eye; but they are both marvellous horses for war.

The Barb deserves, perhaps even more than the Arabian, to have applied to him these true and concise lines of an Arabic poem which we have already quoted: "He can withstand hunger and he can withstand thirst." The expeditions of Hannibal in Italy in which the Numidian cavalry launched itself so well against the Roman cavalry is proof that he does not need the sky under which he was foaled to develop his full powers. The conquests made by the disciples of Mohammed regenerated—rather than weakened—the blood which flows through his veins. The equine species as it exists today in Africa presents a felicitous mixture of all the gifts which are the appanage of the horses in the lands of great extent and blazing sun.

The destiny of this noble and useful breed has ever been endangered by the war which, after the taking of Algiers, has continued without interruption and with violence at all points in Africa. Horses became scarce in Algeria and their blood degenerated somewhat; for the Arabs believe that they sin against Mohammedan law by sending

---

[1] If our personal opinion may be permitted, we would make it clear that one is disposed to establish a very sharp line of demarcation between the Barb and the Arabian horse. There is a more general term, which we feel should be applied to both; it is that of "Oriental breed." This "Oriental breed" is one great family of common origin, which was modified by spreading itself and changing habitat under the influence of the changes in climates little felt in other places. Strength, agility, vigor in conformation as in action, was the inheritance of the horse from the moment in which he found himself on this side of the Euphrates, the Mediterranean, and the Caucasus, where he dwells in the land of Islamism. He is ever the spirited calm horse, impervious to privation and to fatigue, living between the sky and the sand. Call him Persian, Numidian, Barb, Syrian, Arabian, Nedji, it matters little. All these terms are but given names, if one may express it thus. The family name is one: Horse of the Orient. The other family across the Mediterranean is the European horse.

to a Christian market an animal for which the Prophet himself commanded love and respect. Today the ravages of war are being repaired and religious prejudice is weakening. The natives have the custom of sacrificing their sectarian fanaticism to their commercial instincts. One sees many among them exchange some of their best horses for our silver.

The European horse has disappeared from our cavalry in Africa, where he could not second whirlwind charges or forced marches; he has been replaced by the horse native to the country.

Should an officer arrive in Algeria from the Continent, to take part in some of the [military] expeditions, his first care will be to procure native horses. He will take good care not to venture into the desert, much less the mountains, with horses that would be greatly applauded on the turf at Chantilly, Champ de Mars, or Satory.

Therefore, this matter is then no longer a topic for discussion; but rather, the question is how to regulate and develop the use of the horse in our African possessions. There is, nevertheless, a truth, lamentably still unknown in spite of the fact that the evidence is plain: no breeding establishment in France can meet the conditions requisite for out-crossing, production, and breeding, which the Algerian establishments do.

The management of a stud goes to seek, at great expense, even into the interior of Syria, stallions that an intelligent acquirer will often find up to the standard set, among the very varied specimens of Algeria.[2]

[2] This assertion will provoke many contradictions. It offends the ideas already held, but I shall answer only with facts:

In the stud of stallions at Mostaganem, M. de Nabat, former director of studs, has found a stallion which he evaluated thus: "of great and irreproachable beauty," and which he valued at forty thousand francs. This stallion, named El Azedji, came from the Azedj, part of the great tribe of Beni-Aâmer, Department of Oran.

In the same stud is the Pacha. The entries on him are as follows: "a horse of enormous strength and height, a true mount of ancient horsemen, a good sire, of a breed to be found in the locality." He was foaled on the rich plain of the Mina. He was presented to the stud by Marshal Bugeaud. And here is a further description of him: "very beautiful, very good, a lot of style and breeding, a rare stallion of incomparable value."

Le Saharien, foaled among the Oulad-Naïl, has a lot of blood and breeding. Of great worth.

Boghar, foaled in the environs of Boghar. Very beautiful, a remarkable stal-

Moreover, this is not the major drawback which must be overcome. The sky of Pompadour and Limousin is not certainly that which the horses need in the delicate years of their growth—those products of a hot country. Finally, out-crossing in France encounters innumerable difficulties because breeding among us is rare, doubtful, considered by some to be a risky speculation and by others as a ruinous game. In Africa on the contrary, horse breeding is simple—for all Arabs are breeders. Natural inclination, religious faith, national tradition, and private interests, all impel the owners of great or small tents to breed horses.

It is, then, in Africa that we could most suitably found studs destined for the improvement of our breed of horses. For that reason, the control of brood farms and studs, as well as that of remount depots, should come under one administration, that of the Ministry of War. As, because of the needs of our conquest, the army already has in our colonial possessions so many and such vast resources, everything concerning horses should be, without a doubt, its province. One should not forget the old axiom: "He who desires to raise a good crop should sow well." We should try to put into the same hands production and consumption. As in Algeria it is the army that consumes, let us entrust it with the care of production.

Moreover, the seed is already sown. Three studs whose administration is wholly military have been established since 1844. They are situated in Coléah, in the Department of Algiers; in Mostaganem, in

---

lion, of great distinction, of priceless worth and excellent get. In the Alélik stud is mentioned among others the Emir, foaled on the plains of Bone. Vigorous stallion. His get is magnificent.

As far as the mares are concerned I allege and can name many witnesses to support me, that in our raids on the tribes in the south we often captured thin, gaunt, and wounded mares, their appearance ruined by war. However, after a few months of care under French hands, those same mares aroused the admiration of the most knowledgeable of connoisseurs. One finds in them distinction, height, high withers, sloping shoulders, admirable lines to their backs and loins, wide haunches, and cleanness of leg. Some of those mares went to the 5th Regiment of Chasseurs, at the time garrisoning Hussein-Dey near Algiers, and wise devotees just come from France assured me that among those mares there were some that in England would be valued at fifteen or twenty thousand francs.

These noble animals will not come to seek us on the coast. It is necessary to go in search of them into the interior, frequently far away.

the Department of Oran; and in Alélik, near Bone, in the Department of Constantine.

The stud of Coléah[3] was formerly situated in Boufarik. It has twenty-five stallions of which two, above all, are outstanding: *Le Kabyle* and *Le Pacha*. I have already spoken of the latter. A dozen of the others have all the necessary qualities to get energetic and valuable offspring.

[Translator's note: As the rest of this chapter contains for the most part the author's suggestions as to suitable localities for the foundations of new studs, tables showing how the studs already founded were operating, and so on, I shall omit the greater part of it. The following are passages which might, however, be of some interest.]

The most important of the three depots is the one at Mostaganem; it is also a stud on a small scale.[4] It has twenty-six stallions, sixteen brood mares, thirty-four colts or fillies, and six jackasses. In general, these stallions are good sires. There are among them some excellent ones: Biscuit, Le Barde, Jupiter, l'Haamena, Auguste, Bordji, Djin, Massoul, Salem.

Ten of the Mostaganem-bred animals give great hopes. Among the broodmares, special mention should be made of: Diane, L'Arba, L'Oulassa, Daïa, Volonté.

They are from the Department of Oran or from Morocco.

The practicality of this establishment is each day more appreciated by the Arabs; also the numbers of [mares] served have not failed to grow year after year.

The depot of Alélik[5] has twenty-three stallions. The most beautiful are Saptaaba, Kamissa, Lutin.

There also, the natives appreciate the importance of that establishment for the betterment and conservation of the breed; each year they bring their mares in increasing numbers to the depot.

In this locality [Médéah] one could derive advantage from the tra-

---

[3] The Coléah stud is one of the many improvements which Algeria owes to the illustrious Marshal Bugeaud.

[4] It was M. le General de Lamoricière who, during his command of the Department of Oran, established the depot of Mostaganem.

[5] The initiative in the creation of this depot belongs to M. le General Randon, now commandant of the subdivision of Bone.

ditions and customs attached to that capital of the beylik of Tittery, with its numerous and wealthy Arabic towns. The tribes within a radius of twenty kilometers of Médéah are reputed to have something like one thousand horses: stallions, mares, geldings, colts, fillies, and foals. Among them special mention should be made of the excellent breed of mountain horses, raised among the Righa.

In Milianah resources are no less good than at Médéah. Since long ago the horses bred in the valley of the Chélif have been renowned, particularly those of Djendel. The chain of the Ouarsenis furnishes mountain horses.

The horses of the plain of Eghris, in the district of the Hachem, are famous.

In Sebdou one would be in touch with Morocco; the Angad, the Hamian-Gheraba (of the west) furnish a breed of horses most sought after by the natives. These tribes are certainly the least drained [by war] of those of the Department of Oran.

Tiaret receives the products of the great tribes of Oulad-sidi-Cheikh, of Hamian-Gheraba (in the east) . . . and of the Oulad-Yakoub-Zerara. The qualities of that southern breed are highly appreciated and when the nomads travel toward the Tell to lay in provisions, never do they fail to make important dealings in horseflesh.

After having attested to the immense equine resources which we possess in Algeria, I could not end this chapter more fittingly than by quoting the verses, in the Bible and in the Koran, devoted to celebrating the qualities of the horse. They now come to the support of that ancient and obligatory love which, throughout the course of this work, I have attributed to the peoples of the Orient for this noble animal.

The Bible, Job, Chapter 39, Verses 19–25:

Hast thou given strength to the horse? Hast thou clothed his neck with a mane? Dost thou make him bound like a grasshopper? His proud neigh inspires terror. With his foot he parts the earth; he animates himself in his force and goes to the encounter of the armed man. He laughs at fear; he is afraid of nothing and does not turn himself aside in the face of the sword; nor when the arrows of the quiver make a sound, nor by reason of the iron of the lance.

He animates himself and he cannot contain himself when the trumpet sounds.

When it sounds the charge, he says: "Let us go!" He senses war from far away, the command of the leaders and the cries of triumph.[6]

The Koran:

By the swift coursers whose high blowing is heard at a distance when they gallop.
By the coursers who cause sparks to fly from under their hoofs
By the swift coursers who gallop in the mornings,
By those who raise behind them a dense cloud of dust,
By those who penetrate the midst of the batallions,
Most certainly man is ungrateful toward his Lord.

---

[6] I am giving below the quotation from the Book of Job as it is found in the King James' version of the Bible. This is probably the rendering most familiar to English-speaking readers, and it differs enough from the version quoted by General Daumas to make a comparison interesting. [Translator's note]

The Bible, King James' version, Job, Chapter 39, Verses 19–25:

Hast thou given the horse strength? hast thou clothed his neck with thunder?
Canst thou make him afraid as a grasshopper? the glory of his nostrils is terrible.

He paweth in the valley, and rejoiceth in his strength; he goeth on to meet the armed men.

He mocketh at fear, and is not affrighted; neither turneth he back from the sword.

The quiver rattleth against him, the glittering spear and the shield.

He swalloweth the ground with fierceness and rage; neither believeth he that it is the sound of the trumpet.

He saith among the trumpets, Ha, ha; and he smelleth the battle afar off, the thunder of the captains, and the shouting.

THE OPINION OF THE EMIR ABD-EL-KADER
WITH RESPECT TO ARABIAN HORSES

Horses are birds without wings.

HAVING MET THE Emir Abd-el-Kader, while I was the French consul in Mascara from 1837 to 1839, and having seen him again in Toulon in 1847 when I was sent there on a mission at the moment that he set foot on the soil of France, I was able, in my numerous interviews with him, to appreciate his profound knowledge of everything that touched upon the history as well as the equestrian matters of his country. I have not hesitated, therefore, to ask his opinion upon an apparently scientific subject, which, nevertheless, could be of great interest, not only for the future of our colonial possession but also for that of the mother-country.

Here is the letter which he wrote to me on the 8th of November of 1851:

"Glory to the only God.
Only His reign is eternal.

"Health be with him who equals in good qualities all the men of his times, who does not seek anything but good, whose heart is pure, and who is true to his word, the wise, intelligent General Daumas from his friend Sid-el-Hadj, Abd-el-Kader, ben-Mahi-ed-Din.[1]

---

[1] No one is unaware of the custom of the Arabs of beginning their letters with flowery hyperboles. Upon setting them forth, I seek to do no more than give my readers some idea of Oriental style.

"Here are the replies to your questions.

"1. You ask me how many days can an Arabian horse travel without rest and without suffering too much. Know ye that a horse that is sound in every leg, that eats barley—the amount his stomach requires —can do whatever his rider asks of him. For that reason the Arabs say: 'Give barley and abuse.' But without abusing the horse one can make him travel daily sixteen parasangs [a parasang is an ancient Persian measure of length of about five thousand meters.] That is the distance from Mascara to Koudiat-Aghelizan, on the Oued-Mina which has been measured in *drâa* (elbows.) A horse traversing that road every day, who eats as much barley as he likes, can continue without fatigue three or even four months without resting one day.

2. You ask me what distance a horse can travel in one day. I cannot answer you precisely, but that distance should be close to fifty parasangs, such as the distance from Tlemcen to Mascara. We have seen a great number of horses do the distance from Tlemcen to Mascara in one day; nevertheless, a horse that might have done this journey would have to be looked after the next day and he could only travel on the second day a much shorter distance. The greater part of our horses go from Oran to Mascara in one day and they could travel the same distance two or three consecutive days more.

"Once we left Saïda at about eight o'clock in the morning in order to fall upon the Arbâa who were camped at Aaïn-Toukria, among the Oulad-Aïad near Taza, and we overtook them at dawn. Thou knowest the country and how much road we had to cover.

"3. You ask for examples of the sobriety of the Arabian horse and proofs of his ability to suffer hunger and thirst.

"Know ye that when we were encamped at the mouth of the Moulouya we made forays in the Djebel-Amour, following the route to the Sahara, pushing our horses on the day of the attack to a gallop of five to six hours with one breather and completing our incursion, going and coming, in twenty or twenty-five days at the most. During this interval our horses ate no more barley than that carried by their riders, about eight feeds. They found no straw; only *alfa* and *chiehh* or grass in the spring. Nevertheless, upon arrival among our own [people] we engaged in games on horseback the day of our return and showed off with a certain number of the horses. Moreover, those horses which could not perform this latter exercise were, nevertheless, still in a fit condition to travel. Our horses went without water one or two days and once no water was found for three days. The horses of the Sahara do much more than that. They go as long as three months without a grain of barley; they do not know what straw is until the day they reach the Tell and they generally eat only *alfa* and *chiehh* and sometimes *guetof*.[2] *Chiehh* is worth more than the *alfa*, and the *guetof* more than the *chiehh*.

"The Arabs say: '*Alfa* makes the horse go, the *chiehh* makes him fight, and *guetof* is worth more than barley.'

"Some years pass without the horses of the Sahara having eaten one grain of barley in a whole year when the tribes are not well received in the Tell. Then, at times, the Arabs give dates to their horses; this food fattens them, and the horses can then go on expeditions and fight.

"4. You ask why, while the French ride their horses at four years of age, the Arabs ride them from an early age. The Arabs say that the horse, like man, does not learn quickly except when young. Here is their proverb to that effect: 'The lessons of childhood are carved on stone; the lessons of maturity disappear like the nests of birds.' They add: 'The young limb can be straightened without much trouble, but the old trunk will never straighten up.' In its first year the Arabs teach the horse to allow himself to be led with a halter. The colt is then called *djeda*, and they begin to tether and bridle him. As soon as he is in his second year they ride him and make him go a mile, then two, then one parasang, and by the time he is eighteen months old they are not afraid of tiring him.

"After he has risen three they keep him tethered, stop riding him, rug him well, and fatten him, saying: 'During the first year tether him so that he will not suffer an accident; during the second year ride him just until his back acquires flexibility; during the third year tether him again; then, if he does not suit you, sell him.'

"If a horse is not ridden before his third year assuredly he will not be any good for anything except galloping, something which he does not need to learn, for it is his primordial faculty. The Arabs explain this thought thus: 'A noble horse does not have to learn to gallop.'

"5. You ask me why, if the stallion passes on to his get more attributes than the dam, mares are nonetheless higher in price than stallions. Here is the reason: he who buys a mare hopes to have, in addition to the services she can render to him, numerous foals; but he who

---

[2] *Guetof*: *Androsaemum officinale*. [Translator's note]

buys a stallion does not derive any more benefit than that of riding him, for the Arabs do not traffic with the services of their stallions, and they lend them for stud without charge.

"6. You ask if the Arabs of the Sahara keep stud-books to prove an animal's description. Know ye that those of the Algerian Sahara do not and those of the Tell do not concern themselves with such registries. Public knowledge is sufficient for them, for the genealogy of their pure-bred horses is as well known to all as is that of the owners. I have heard it said that some families have these genealogies written down, but I cannot name one of them. Such books are in use in the East as I mention in the little treatise which I am going to send you.

"7. You ask me which are the tribes of greatest renown in Algeria by reason of the nobility of their horses. Know ye that the best horses of the Sahara are the horses of the Hamyâne, without a doubt. They have nothing else but excellent horses, for they do not use them either for harness or as pack animals. The horses are not used for anything but expeditions and combat. They are the ones that best endure hunger, thirst, and weariness.

"After the horses of the Hamyâne come those of the Harar, the Arbâa, and the Oulad-Naïl. In the Tell the best horses by reason of their nobility, breeding, height, and beauty of form are those of the people of the Chélif, principally those of the Oulad-Sidi-ben-Abd-Allah (Sidi-el-Aaribi) near the Mina and also those of the Oulad-Sidi-Hassan, an offshoot of the Oulad-Sidi-Dahhou who inhabit the mountains of Mascara. The swiftest on the track, and also lovely in form, are those of the Flittas, of the Oulad-Cherif and the Oulad-Lekreud. The best for travelling on rocky ground, unshod, are those of the tribe of the Assassena, in the Yakoubia.

"These words are attributed to Moulaye-Ismaël, the celebrated sultan of Morocco: 'May my horse have been bred in Mâz and have drunk from Biaz.' The Mâz is a region of the Assassena and the Biaz is a stream known under the name of Foufet which flows through their territory.

"The horses of the Oulad-Khaled are also famous for the same qualities. Sidi-Ahmed-ben-Youssef said, apropos of this tribe: 'Long tresses and long *djellale* will be found among you until the Day of Resurrection,' thus eulogizing its women and its horses.

"8. You tell me that someone has maintained to you that the horses of Algeria are not Arabian horses, but Berber [Barbs]. That is an opinion that turns against the person who expresses it. The Berbers are Arabian in origin; a famous author has said: "The Berbers inhabit Maghreb. They are all sons of Kaïs-ben-Ghilan. It is further asserted that they come from two great Hémiarite tribes, the Senahdja and the Kettama, who arrived in the country at the time of the invasion of Ifrikech-el-Malik. According to these two opinions the Berbers are clearly Arabs; historians have established, furthermore, the affiliation of the greater part of the Berber tribes and their descent from the Senahdja and the Kettama. The coming of these tribes is prior to Islamism. Since the Mohammedan invasion the number of Arabs that have emigrated to Maghreb is incalculable. When the Obeïdin (the Fatimites) were the lords of Egypt, immense tribes went into Africa, among others the Riahh.

"The tribes spread from Kaïrouan [in Tunisia] to Marrakech (Morocco). It is from these tribes in Algeria that the Douaouda, the Aïad, the Mâdid, the Oulad-Madi, the Oulad-Yakoub-Zerara, the Djendel, the Attaf, the Hamïs, the Braze, the Sbéha, the Flitta, the Medjahar, the Mehall, the Beni-Aâmer, the Hamian and many others descend. There is no doubt but that the Arabian horses were also spread out over the Maghreb like the Arabic families.

"In the days of Ifrikech-ben-Kaif, the Arabic empire was all powerful. It extended in the west to the limits of Maghreb as in the times of Chamar the Hémiarite it extended in the east to China, according to what Ben-Kouteïba has set forth in his book titled *El Mârif.*

"It is very true that if all the horses in Algeria are Arabians by descent, many of them are beneath their true nobility because they are too frequently used in ploughing, or in threshing, for pack, for carrying burdens, and for other similar tasks; because the mares have been bred to donkeys; nothing of the kind was done among the Arabs of yesteryear. With respect to this it is said that it is enough that a horse walk over tilled ground for him to lose his worth. In that connection, the following story is told: 'A man was riding his pure-bred horse and was discovered by an enemy who was also riding a noble animal. One pursued the other and he was was giving chase was outdistanced by the one being pursued. Despairing of being able to overtake the other, he yelled: "I ask you, in God's name, has your horse ever been used for ploughing?"

" ' "He has done it for four days."

" ' "Well, mine has never done such a thing; by the Head of the

Prophet, I am sure of overtaking you." He continued the pursuit and upon twilight falling he who was fleeing began to lose ground and his pursuer to gain it. And he was successful in fighting with the man he had lost all hopes of overtaking.'

"My father, may God hold him in mercy, had the custom of saying: 'Heaven's blessing has been lacking on our lands since we made our horses beasts of burden and plough animals. Did not God create the horse for galloping, the ox for ploughing, and the camel for transporting burdens? Nothing is gained by changing God's ways.'

"9. You ask me what are our precepts for training and feeding our horses. Know ye that the owner of a horse will feed him little barley at the beginning, gradually increasing the ration in small amounts; and when the horse leaves barley, he then lessens the grain feeding and maintains him with that measure. The best time to give barley is when evening falls; except on a journey no benefit results from giving barley in the morning. To this effect it is said: 'The morning barley will be found in the dung-heap; the evening barley on the rump.'

"The best method of giving barley is to give it to a saddled and girthed horse, as the best method of giving water is through the bridle. It is said:

'Water with the bridle;
And barley with the saddle.'

"Arabs prefer horses that eat little always provided that they are not thin. Such a horse, they say, is a treasure without price.

"Watering at dawn makes a horse thin; water given at dusk will make him fat; giving him water at midday will keep him in condition. During the time of great heat which lasts for forty days, the Arabs only water their horses every two days. They allege that that custom has the best results. In the summer, in the autumn, and in the winter, they give an armful of straw to their horses, but the basis of the feed is barley in preference to any other kind. The Arabs say with regard to this: 'Had we not seen that horses come from horses, we would have said it is barley that sires them.' They add: 'Seek the broad and buy him; barley will make him gallop.'

"Here follow many of the sayings of the Arabs with respect to horses:

" 'Of forbidden flesh seek the swiftest.' That means: 'choose a swift horse.' Horseflesh is forbidden to the Moslems.

" 'One does not become a horseman until after one has frequently been thrown.'

" 'Well-bred horses have no malice.'

" 'A well-schooled horse honors his master.'

" 'Horses are birds without wings.'

" 'For the horse nothing is far away.'

" 'He who forgets the beauty of horses for that of women will not prosper.'

" 'Horses know their riders.'

" 'Love horses, care for them,' said Saint Ben-el-Abbas, whom God esteems for being agreeable. He continued:

'Do not grudge giving them attention.
For them honor and for them beauty.
If the horses are abandoned by men
I shall make them enter my house;
I shall share with them my childrens' bread.
My wives will dress them with their veils
And will shelter them with their covers,
And I shall take them forth daily on the field of adventure;
Carried by their impetuous gallop
I fight with the most valiant.'

"I have finished the letter which our brother and companion, friend to all, Commandant Sid-Bou-Senna shall get to your hands. Health."

This letter was written in the holograph of Abd-el-Kader. The original is in my hands and is certified by the Commandant of the squadron of artillery, Boissonnet, who for the past three years has carried out with distinction, close to the Emir, a mission as delicate as it is difficult.

I am indebted to Commandant Boissonnet[3] for the translation of this exquisite document.

[3] Today a colonel of artillery.

THE WAR HORSE

He can endure thirst, he can endure hunger, and he makes in one day, the journey
of five.

SOMETHING OF THE INTEREST which earlier was aroused by the Scandi-
navian sagas would now appear to be aroused by the poetry of Africa.
I see, with pleasure, this intellectual movement to which I cannot,
perhaps, have been a complete stranger. All that which the European
spirit carries to Algeria is favorable to that country in which useful
resources, long disputed and little known, and undiscovered riches
are becoming visible today.

Imagination is a force which the most practical thought should not
neglect. Whatever is taken under its protection will prosper, particularly in a country like ours. We believe then that again raising a corner
of the veil which covers a poem of which we have already made
known more than one passage does not place us farther from the constant goal of our labors.

The Arabic poem of which we are going to give a translation contains in the clearest manner of speech, the sentiments which concern
the Arabic soul: love for the horse, the love of women, and resignation to the will of God. It is needless to say that we have not brought
to our task any literary pretensions. We have simply tried to preserve
in French words African thought in all its profundity, as well as its
rare originality, and if we have employed some odd circumlocutions

and unusual imagery, we hope that the reader's taste will not be very offended. I could neither restrain nor weaken the breath of Oriental ardor.

Here is that poem. Let it be judged. It will explain its breadth better than any note, it will plead its cause better than any prologue.

"My horse is black like a night without moon or stars.
He was foaled in immense solitudes;
He is a drinker of the wind, a son of a drinker of the wind,
His dam was also of a noble breed.
Our warrior horsemen have named him Sabok[1]
The very lightning cannot overtake him;
May God save him from the Evil eye.
His ears rival those of the gazelle;
His eyes are the eyes of an alluring woman;
His forehead is like that of the bull;
His nostrils are like the lion's den;
His neck, shoulders, and rump are long;
He is wide in the back, legs, and flanks;
He has the tail of the snake, the hocks of the ostrich;
His vigorous heels are far from the ground.
I count on him as I count on my heart.
No one has ever ridden his equal.
His flesh is firmer than that of the zebra,
He has the collected canter of the fox,
The long and easy gallop of the wolf,
And in one day he makes the journey of five.
When he swims he bites the girth with his elbows and
One might call him an arrow launched by destiny,
Or even the startled dove that flies
Towards the water held in a hollow in the rock.
Yes. Sabok is a war horse!
He likes to pursue wild animals
And sighs only for glory and booty.
The voices of our virgins inflame his ardor
When I launch him into the midst of danger;
His neighs call the vultures and
Make my enemies tremble.

[1] *Sabok*: the Swift, the Overtaker.

On his back, Death cannot touch me
She fears the sound of his hoofs.
Aâtika[2] has said to me: 'Come and be without a companion!'
Docile now as the saber which is drawn from the scabbard,
Sabok responds to my spurs and divines my thought.
He cleaves space like the falcon returning to its nest,
And when I come to her whose eyes are languid;
Alone, in the midst of danger, patient and immobile,
He champs his bit until my return.
By the Head of the Prophet!
That horse is the resource of the caravans,
The ornament of a tent, and the honor of my tribe.
I am an Arab; I know how to command and fight;
My name protects the weak and afflicted,
My herds and flocks are the reserve of the poor,
And the stranger in my house is well received.
The Almighty has crowned me with blessings;
But time turns back on itself and goes backwards,
And should I have to, one day,
Drink of the two cups of life,
I shall show that adversity cannot humiliate my soul.
My virtue shall be resignation;
My fortune a disdain for riches;
My happiness the hope in the next life.
And should misery come to oppress my neck
Not for that shall I praise God the less."

---

[2] *Aâtika*: the Noble One.

LETTERS TO THE AUTHOR

"Paris, 4 February, 1851.

"I HAVE JUST FINISHED READING, my dear General, your work on the horses of the Algerian Sahara. This work, in conjunction with its undoubted historical interest has the merit of presenting, in a most alluring form, very opportune observations.

"Men who dedicate themselves to the study of equine science today recognize that the propagation of Oriental blood is the true principle of regeneration to which it is urgent to resort. This thought has already received an application. The management of studs is preparing to send to Central Arabia special agents to acquire Eastern stallions and mares. Also, the Ministry of Agriculture in the face of the demand made by the advisory board with respect to the perfecting of the St. Cloud stud, is asking for special credits to create in an ordinary stud and, in accordance with legislative desire, a pure Arabian strain of the highest order.

"All these facts give to your work an especial importance and interest. If it should be published, it would introduce us to traditions, customs, and convictions which offer priceless counsel. Persuaded of the usefulness of such a publication, the Ministry of Agriculture has, at this very time, ordered the translation and printing of an old Arabic manuscript whose existence in the National Library was barely known. Your work on the horses of the Sahara will have a much greater general importance. Also, I greatly wish that the Ministry of

War, whose solicitude for the progress of equine matters is so lively, would choose to have it printed and distributed; thereby the Ministry would perform a great service to equine matters, to the whole of France, and in particular to the cavalry units we maintain in Algeria.

"Receive, my General, the renewed expressions of a great consideration and of my old sentiments of devotion.

> "Oudinot, Duke of Reggio.
> *General of Division*"

[Nicolas Charles Victor Oudinot was a French general who took Rome in 1849.]

> "Paris, 19 February, 1851.

"My dear General:

"I thank you for having sent me the work on the *Horses of the Sahara*. I do not doubt but that it will be read with interest by cavalry officers and all lovers of the horse.

"If some customs, seemingly, cannot be attributed to anything other than the superstitious beliefs of the natives, it should be recognized that in their picturesque phraseology the Arabs feel, more often than not, with regard to the training and appreciation of the horse, ideas of indisputable justness, which are for them the result of a traditional experience. It is from Nature that they portray the pure-bred horse— the drinker of the wind. The portrait they paint of him is that of a horse essentially suited to war and capable of making long and swift gallops. Now that such a horse exists in our possessions in Africa, it is necessary to find him, although one might have to go to seek him to the furthermost limits of the desert. That would be yet one more service which the African army will have performed. Brought under our skies, those priceless horses would become a model for a pure indigenous breed.

"As far as the opinion, which is expressed in the chapter dealing with mating, gestation, etc., that the mare is nothing but a sack from which gold will be taken out, if gold was put in, but only copper will be taken out if only copper was put in—I am far from being in agreement. But it would be a good thing to print it with reservations and investigate if it might not be so believed in the Algerian Sahara only, contrary to the convictions of other Eastern peoples. It is possible that

that is one of the causes for the relative inferiority of the Barb as compared with the Arabian proper.[1]

"I recommend to you therefore, General, that you do not delay in having published a work which could not have been written by anyone other than yourself and which has, at this moment, all the merit of timeliness, now that the Government is on the verge of making considerable expenditures to concern itself with [the acquisition of] specimens of Oriental origin for reproduction.

"Receive, my dear General, the assurances of sincere affection from your devotee.

> "P. Descarrières
> *Director General of Cavalry
> in the Secretariat of War*"

> "Paris, 11 April 1851.

"My dear General:

"I have read with the greatest of interest the work which you were kind enough to entrust to me and which gives, in such a complete and interesting way, the history of the training of the horse in the desert. This combination of facts, so little known and so worthy of being known, enables one to understand the true causes for the perfection which the horse has attained in the hands of the sons of Ishmael. It would be most desirable that, while you are in the Ministry of War, the government order the printing of this work in which our breeders will find such useful teachings.

"Receive, my General, the assurance of my affectionate sentiments.

> "de Lamoricière
> *General of Division*"

[Christophe León Louis Juchault de Lamoricière had a brilliant military career, climaxed by taking the Emir Abd-el-Kader prisoner. General de Lamoricière was active in the organization of the first Arabic bureau in France and was also instrumental in the organization of the first regiment of Zouaves.]

---

[1] This opinion of General Descarrières I believe I have refuted successfully in the chapters titled "The Barb Horse" and "The Subject of Stallions and Mares."

"Saumur, 18 January 1852.

"My Dear General:

"If I have delayed somewhat in thanking you for having sent me your work, *The Horses of the Sahara*, it is because after having read it, I wished to reread it with the interest it deserves. It is, therefore, with conviction that I go on to tell you today that its publication is a real service rendered to the progress of equine science. I studied your work, not only with the interest it arouses and animates upon revealing to us the customs of the desert which are unknown to us, but also with the idea of finding a true instruction.

"I did not err and I tell you with the frankness of camaraderie. I learned upon reading it, and I found some excellent material to be used for study in the school which I have the honor to direct; and moreover I found the confirmation of our best equestrian principles and those of horse training, a very powerful confirmation as it stems from the customs of an essentially equestrian people who have preferred to follow the indication of nature rather than that of books.

"Our professors will have to ask you for many loans, which you will grant, I hope; even more so because they will be for the progress of an army in which you serve and which is very glad to have you in its ranks. Our library has but one copy of your book. In my opinion that is not enough and we all wish that the Ministry of War would supply us with six copies so that our numerous students [military cadets], who would be your greatest readers, could derive benefit therefrom.

"Accept, my dear General, the assurance of my greatest consideration and affection.

"Count of Goyon
*Brigadier General, Aide to the Emperor
and Director of the Cavalry School*"

[Charles Marie Augustin de Goyon, later Duke of Feltre, was commandant of Saumur and aide-de-camp to Louis Napoleon. He served with great distinction in Spain.]

"Paris, 15 February 1852.

"My dear General:

"Many affairs leave me little leisure for the perusal of new works, but I could not resist the necessity of knowing your writings on the horses of the Sahara.

"You give, with respect to the breeding of Arabian horses, ideas which I was far from having and I have experienced true pleasure on learning the most interesting details which you have published on the way in which the indigenes understand the training of the horse and on the minute pains which they take with the priceless animals in their foalhood.

"I do not believe that our breeders will ever imitate the Arabs in that respect. The latter have for their horses an affection which we will always be far from having. It is true that the Arab does not have a more or less assured and honorable life, except by means of his horse; which well justifies his love for that generous servitor.

"Among the customs of the Arabs, one above all the rest has astonished me very much: it is that custom of cutting the mane and tail hair for five years in succession. I can understand their repugnance for docking the tail; in Africa they do not have to take precautions against mire and mud as we do, and their horses carry their tails much better than ours, which adds to their conformation.

"I was also struck by the essential differences which you point out among the horses in different districts in Africa. Such judicious indications on your part seem to me to be a sure guide for amateurs in Arabian horses and above all for the acquisitions of stallions, which the government may desire to make.

"I cannot thank you enough, my dear General, for the favor you did me by sending me your book, so interesting from all points of view and so pleasant by reason of the charming anecdotes which accompany it.

"Will you accept, with all my thanks, my dear General and Councillor of State, the assurance of my high regard.

"Marshal Exelmans"

[Count Remi Joseph Isidore Exelmans was a Marshal of France. He had a brilliant military career. He died at the age of seventy-seven, as the result of a fall from his horse when he was on the way to pay a call on the Princess Mathilde.]

"Paris, 1 April 1852.
"My dear General:
"I thank you for having sent me your work, *The Horses of the Sahara*. It has been a long time since I read a book in which I was so

avidly interested, not only because it deals with a matter that is the object of all my thoughts, but also because it has that freshness of sentiment and that perfume of poetry which, as is asserted by the devotees of positivism, is contained in the divine stamp of truth. Two pages of your book make the horse and the Arabic horseman of the desert better known than all that has so far been written on this brilliant subject. You fill in where others perform an autopsy. You give life to the bare bones. My history of the horse would have been enriched with one beautiful chapter had I been able to consult your work before having mine printed. Unfortunately, my stand had been taken. But on reading the excellent principles which you have gathered from the voice of a people, the oldest in equestrianism, I saw with pleasure confirmation of the idea which is so applicable to equestrian matters: to wit, that the truth, everywhere, is the same and in order to arrive at the same goal, it is necessary to follow an identical path. Reasoning thus, one teaches oneself with the example of the ancients and with that of peoples who follow a good road. Thinking along other lines, one invents a science or school of thought out of whole cloth, which frequently has no merit other than that of antiquity or the deceptive phraseology in which it is enveloped. In effect, the Arabs began the equestrian instruction of the world. It is logical, therefore to find among them precepts and teachings. That is what the English do—who have inherited their equestrian glory—and the many similarities which your work points out in the customs and usages of the two nations is the proof of the infallibility of their doctrines.

"Both nations consider the horse to be the most useful servant of man and they have done everything to develop the physical qualities with which nature endowed him. Gradual, although strenuous, exercise, strengthening and appropriate feed—these are the principal bases of the equestrian system of those two peoples. "Air, exercise, and food."

"I cannot understand, my General, and still less after having read your book, how there can be persons who argue about the Arabian horse and the English horse. Looking at the matter clearly, no differences can be found between the two nations other than those of customs and climate. But the chieftain of the tent, as you say, and the English "sportsman," do they not both have that unity of belief in pure descent, consecrated from one generation to another by means of tests and a recognized merit? Do they not both demand that work in the early years, so useful when it is not exaggerated? Do they not both employ that methodical preparation about which the unfortunate English have so often been attacked—preparation which the English, nevertheless, had taken from the tents of the Bedouin, and which is nothing more than the preparation of the athlete of olden times for the Olympic combat?

"What do some bizarre practices, some eccentric prejudices matter now, among one or the other?

"What does matter is practicality and truth which must be sought wherever they may be found, paying no attention to time or place. To my sorrow, that is what is not always done amongst us. We frequently mistake the leaves for the radish or the shadow for the substance. The devotees of the Arabian horse generally think in terms only relative to blood. They think that they can rival the product of the desert by taking a stallion and a mare from the banks of the Euphrates, giving the offspring ground barley, only regretting that they cannot add camel's milk, when what is really necessary is that the colt be subjected from early foalhood to that hard and even terrible work which you have described so well on various pages. The [French] devotees of the English horse frankly believe that they can enter into rivalry with England by placing on the back of a horse a little man dressed in a silk blouse whose cut and colors are slavishly copied from the jockeys at Newmarket, without bothering to imitate the sage and serious principles of the English regarding the selection of a place for breeding horses, the utility and practicality of work, training, and a thousand other matters.

"Speaking of places where horses may be bred, I remember, my dear General, a conversation I had with a famous English horseman, shortly after our conquest of Algeria. He felt it keenly that that promised land had not become one of the *fleurons* of the British Crown. It would have been, he told me in a philanthropic way that was a bit suspect, a blessing for the entire world and even for France.

" 'You do not possess as we do the science of colonization; for example, the first establishment we would have built on Berber soil would have been a great stud.

" 'There, gathering together the remnants of the purest of Oriental blood, training the product in accordance with that which Arabic and English teachings have of greatest rationality and perfection, we would have recreated the Godolphin Arabians and the Moroccan Barb, which created the English Thoroughbred and we would even have surpassed it. For it cannot be denied that on the soil which produced them, with the specimens which we would have procured from all the stables on earth, with the help of experience and science, we would have succeeded in breeding a horse which would have been the highest expression of blood, quality, and conformation.'

"If France finally comprehends her dearest interests, she will, one day, fulfill the wish of my Englishman. Your work, my General, will have strongly contributed [to the result], now that you have shed light on and brought life to the question.

"Before finishing this letter, already very long, permit me, my dear General, to congratulate you on the discovery you have made. You have revealed to the equestrian world one more authority on equine science. Until now the Emir Abd-el-Kader was not known as other than an illustrious warrior. Now the notes which he has added to your work place him in the front rank among men of science in the matter of horses, and your name in that respect is inseparable from his.

"Receive, my dear General, the homage of my sentiments,

"Ephrem Houel
Inspector of Studs"

[Ephrem Houel deserves to be remembered as the father of French trotting races (at their inception the horses were either mounted or harnessed). Houel was one of the most distinguished officers of the Administration of Studs and conceived the idea of trotting races in 1832 but was unable to succeed in having it accepted until the municipal council of Cherbourg lent him its beach for the first trotting meet ever held in France, in 1836. One can appreciate the perseverance which Ephrem Houel must have applied to the realization of his project by the account which he has left of his long struggle to have his idea accepted, to gain the necessary financial backing, to find a suitable location, and to interest amateurs and breeders in the project.

A strangely familiar ring is heard in his words as he describes the proceedings of a Commission especially appointed (in 1834) to hear him present his case for instituting trotting races: many important people, many cavalry officers, and others were present. There was a lot of talk, a lot of discussion and a lot of questions. However, the conclusion was reached that the project had not one particle of common sense!

Nevertheless, he did receive some encouragement from several influential men who, although not horsemen themselves, knew a good thing when they heard it. Due to that encouragement, Houel continued his efforts and was finally rescued, so to speak, by a young wine-merchant with an eye to the main chance. The wine-merchant was not a horseman either, but an excellent businessman who wanted to attract visitors to his town of Cherbourg. He offered Houel the use of the beach for a race-track, underwrote money for the purses, and guaranteed spectators.

Thus it came about that trotting races were instituted in France on the 25th of September, 1836, in Cherbourg, on the lovely beach which lies in front of the cannon embrasures of Cherbourg's forts.

The first meet was a great success and the following year, as the program included an International Cup for mounted trotting, the success was even livelier.

(The foregoing was taken from an article written by Louis Cauchois, founder of the Stud Book of French Trotters. The article, "The Trotter and his History: The Birth of French Trotting," was published in *Le Prestige du Cheval*, Paris: Durel Editeur, 1951.)]

"Saumur, 18 September 1852.

"General:

"In your very interesting work about the horses of the Sahara, you make the reader penetrate into the intimate life of the Arabs. You make known the system of that equestrian people for breeding, training, and judging horses. Your book, my General, contains priceless documents. If you are so modest as to say that you do not make the announcement that this is good or that is bad, [but simply say] that that is what the Arabs do, I take the liberty of answering you, without fear of being given the lie by truly experienced men, that, with a few exceptions, all is good, very good, and hits the nail of truth on the head. When one has commented upon these documents, conviction will be complete and one will remain persuaded that one should have had faith in the ideas, in the precepts, in the experience of a people who have known how to preserve the horse's nobility and original purity.

"In Europe the men who are the best trainers of their horses and who obtain the best results from them put into practice and follow in every way Arabic principles.

"Unfortunately in France these principles are today very sparse. For the majority, everything which concerns the breeding, training, and schooling of the horse is no longer known or is badly understood. The art of equestrianism, so noble an art, so useful, so indispensable for making equine production worthwhile, now is neither honored nor practiced in our country. Schools once charged with passing on the old and good traditions no longer exist. We no longer have those old schools, directed by skilful men, with experience, whose counsels and example profited not only the gentleman destined for the career of arms, but also the man of the people who, once instructed, was to take his knowledge to the regions of breeders and thus assure by a rational and gradual training a market for their product. Of all that past, nothing remains now. The equestrian art, from the point of view of its real practicality, no longer has interpreters. One can no longer give the title of *écuyer* to those men who do not demand anything of the horse except eccentricities [tricks and fancy frills], and who instead of looking out for the horse's conservation, work to ruin him.

"If on one hand the sage and well-thought-out principles of the equestrain art have been effaced in our country, on the other hand the breeding of horses has been displaced and has fallen, generally speaking, into the hands of the farmer who does not breed a saddle horse except against his will and when he is forced to do so by the nature of the soil which he exploits. Not understanding any of that type of schooling, no longer having the aid of those horsemen, of those experienced men, who, more than ever, will be indispensable to them the breeders will content themselves with feeding their horses, hit or miss, and allowing them to live without any care, without any training in an almost savage [feral] state.

"You can understand, my General, what such a system can produce. That lack of primary training always makes a horse difficult to break. From that stem the blemishes, respiratory diseases, and the great loss of time before the animals can go to the [military] service.

"Moreover, the buyer, be he dealer or owner, repudiates our production and goes to seek in Germany or England the horse that we do not know how to prepare.

"For reasons of patriotism, the Ministry of War is today in France the only buyer of the French saddle horse. This patriotism is paid for dearly, thanks to that gap in the horse's training, for the troop horse is usually forced to remain for at least two years in the remount depot before it is fit to enter the ranks. Moreover, how many are found that have to be "dropped" before having given any service at all? I do not venture to say how many, but their number is considerable.

"In spite of such enormous expenditures on the part of the State, the breeder derives little benefit. His production, fixed in price as well as in market, is today limited to the annual needs of the remount service. In effect—what to do with an excess of production that cannot find a market and never will as long as training is no better than it is? What results from this state of affairs? That horse breeding is in suspense, that we remain dependent on foreign countries, and that the army, notwithstanding the daily expenses, is obliged to have recourse to them the day that an extraordinary remount is deemed necessary. There are 1830, 1840, and 1848, to prove what I advance.

"The enforced neglect in which our breeders leave their horses is so widespread that this deplorable system has now progressed to the stage of having become a principle. Persons whose word can be relied upon say that one should not begin to work the saddle horse until he is from five to six years old, as if the animal were a being apart.

"With regard to the draft horse, the matter changes completely. He works from the age of eighteen months; he is used in the plough from that age until he is four years old, at which time he is sold for immediate use in drays, diligences, and mail coaches, for which work he is already prepared and which he performs immediately. There the Arabic system is followed—with less discernment, with less care, perhaps, but it is followed; and those horses enjoy in France and even in Europe a great reputation.

"With regard to the breeding of saddle horses, my General, your book will serve to shed light. It is necessary for those who wish to breed horses to learn that in order to attain a profitable goal it is not enough to cause the horse to be foaled, to feed him and fatten him; it is also necessary that they know how to give him timely training so that he can enter service on the day he is put up for sale.

"Your work, my General, will be discussed in the cavalry school. I have already asked you for your permission to make an extract so that everyone may derive benefit; so that our cadets can master those general principles of the Arabic horseman—principles which must become their own.

"There are, sometimes, happy revolutions; and that which your book will bring about will be one of them. The entire question of horses, so long in a rut, should, at last, emerge. Above all, it is experienced men that we lack; and, nevertheless, the government has in its hands all the material needed to fill that gap. We hope that a strong and stable government will permit us to rebuild an industry which has been in suspense for so long.

"Receive, my General, all my compliments, the assurances of my profound respect.

"d'Aure[2]

The Écuyer commanding the Cavalry School"

[Vicomte Antoine Henri Philippe d'Aure was an adversary of François Baucher as regards theories of equitation. Although nowadays the theories of the latter are in more general acceptance, d'Aure's reputation as an outstanding horseman of the nineteenth century has not diminished. D'Aure served under Louis XVIII and Charles X. His work, *Cours d'Equitation*, of 1853 was officially adopted by the Ministry of War.]

"Metz, 1 November, 1852.
"My dear General:

"I have received your work on the horses of the Sahara, as well as the cordial letter which accompanied it. I beg you to accept my congratulations and thanks.

"Your work is distinguished by these divers merits: it contains new, exact, varied, curious, and important documents; it is full of charm in many of its details, such as good poetical works and the most moving of romances; it is clear, well written; in fine, it presents propoundments of great interest concerning the equine question, as much for Algeria as for France.

"You ask me my opinions and observations; although that would be like carrying water to the sea, they follow herewith: [Translator's note: In parts of this letter the writer made comments on the second half of General Daumas' work, *Les Moeurs du Désert*, which I did not translate. Such comments, therefore, have been omitted.]

"1. The love of many Arabs for their horses is well illustrated in your work. Your words characterize it. Ben-Senoussi, a distinguished

_____

[2] Today Inspector General of Studs and of the Stables of the Emperor.

marabout of Dira, had rendered us some most useful services; the events of 1845 threw him into the uprising and led him to us. He had suffered losses and reclaimed from me with great insistence his horse, which someone had taken. To satisfy him I made investigations which bore no fruit. I offered him a prize [*i.e.*, one of the horses taken as booty], preferable to his.

" 'It is not,' said he, 'the value of the animal that I demand; it is my mare, daughter of my mare, who was the daughter of my father's mare.' "

"2. The Arabic saddle is much more suitable than ours for combat. It at first galls the European who is not at ease in it until after a year or two years of continual use. It does not have the drawback, like ours, of allowing the saddle blanket to slip backwards during long, hard gallops, if one does not tighten the girth apropos. At a gallop it tires less both the horse and the rider, who has his body bent forward. It is to be remarked that that forward inclination of the body at the gallop is used among all the peoples and all the professions that have the reputation of getting the best out of their horses, such as the Arabs, the Turks, the Persians, the Tartars, the Cossacks, and the jockeys riding race horses. Our French Spahis find themselves very much at home in the Arabic saddle as well as with the Arabic bit, which is simple, powerful, solid, and today in use by all the officers in Africa. They have not adopted the Arabic spur, which has an energetic but at the same time dangerous effect for the horse and which is impossible to wear while on foot. The Arabic saddle has an exaggeration of height in the pommel and cantle, which is not true of the Turkish saddle. Generally, one can pass one's hand between the girth and the horse's body with the Arabic saddle. The horse, therefore, has his chest free, but a loose girth creates a difficulty upon mounting; Arabic politeness now includes holding the left stirrup to prevent the saddle from turning turtle. As the saddle is not kept in place by anything but rubbing and balance, the riders sometimes incline practically horizontally while riding in the *fantasias*.

"In olden times the use of the buckler on the left arm might have led to the horse being mounted from the off-side, especially before the recent advent of stirrups. The free right arm thus permitted the great effort necessary to spring into the saddle. When the buckler ceased to be in usage, when one carried on the left side, be it a long dangling saber, be it pistols, it was preferable to mount on the near side as we do. In the Orient, as well as in Algeria, one always mounts on the off-side; therefore the mane is trained to the right. Among us the mane hangs on the left except in the case of the pure-breds where, in spite of the inconvenience of mounting, it hangs to the right to preserve the stamp of the remarkable stallions brought from the Orient to regenerate the breeds. It is a fashion analogous to that of the docked tail. That mutilation had been performed on the first Arabian stallions brought from the Orient to prevent the renewal of thefts during the journey across the desert, upon making the horses scarcely recognizable and less seductive; the docked tail took on favor as a characteristic then of the very beautiful stallions come from the Orient.

"3. It has been noticed during cavalry marches that the chasseurs are generally better mounted than the *goums*. However, at the walk they are always overtaken by the *goums*. That is undoubtedly due to the saddle which places the spurs and legs of the European far from the horse's flanks whereas the Arabic saddle brings the legs closer to the flanks and animates the animal.

"4. The Arabs can, without dismounting, unbridle to allow their horses to drink, and rebridle. On one such occasion I saw a horseman run away with by his horse. I was most uneasy about the outcome of that gallop and sought a solution but did not find one. I was then astounded to see the Arab immediately master his horse, stop him short, and then rebridle him. It had been enough for that rider to throw over the animal's eyes the wide folds of his burnoose and thus prevent the horse from seeing.

"5. Arabic veterinarians are infinitely less knowledgeable than ours, but they have in many respects excellent practices. I can cite two personal experiences.

"I had a very beautiful horse that had a sprain of the thigh. Many able military veterinarians had treated him, but at the end of a year he was lame and it was declared that thus he would remain. I had an Arabic veterinarian look at him who said that he could cure the horse by firing him on the thigh. That operation gave results and the horse rendered long and good service.

"On another occasion my horses, during my absence, were replaced in their stable which had been inundated, just as soon as the water had disappeared. They fell ill of the fetlocks, pasterns, and hoofs. One died and three recovered. Another, who was an excellent horse, after eight months of treatment was declared incurable. I decided with regret to sell him. No Frenchman would have bought him. An Arab offered me one thousand francs and affirmed that he would cure him. I demanded that he consult the Arabic veterinarian. Both men agreed that it would be easy to effect a cure. I again sought the advice of officers and skilful veterinarians who found the lameness incurable. I refused to accept more than a nominal price, persuaded that the buyer was making a mistake. That horse, perfectly and promptly healed, three months later was sold for eighteen hundred francs and he is worth them.

"It is very desirable that a French veterinarian can study and make known the procedures of the Arabic maestros. Among the Spahis of Algeria I have appointed for that work M. Richard, our veterinarian who became, in 1849, the representative of Cantal. He is a young, intelligent, well-taught, and studious young man who speaks Arabic.

"6. The whorls and the colors of horses give, according to the Arabs, most useful indications. The Arabs attach great importance to the whorl on the haunch; according to whether it is situated high or low, the horse, they say, is a good or bad runner.

"We have seen, some years ago, a farmer recognized and recompensed by the government for having found a method of judging with almost complete certainty if a cow will be a good milker or not, according to the whorls on her thigh. It is possible that the indications of the whorls on the thigh of the horse might have more worth than we suppose.

"You indicate that the forearms of the legs should be long in good horses, according to the opinion of the Arabs. I have always heard it said among them that they consider the length of the cannon to be the indication of a fast horse. When the Arab buys a horse, he always lifts a forefoot and bends it back to the forearm to find out if it overlaps the olecranon, which would appear to be a good sign. Sage Arabs have pointed out to me that the gazelle and the bubalis which run very swiftly have excessively long cannons; this is also true of the stag and the hart. It seems to me that swift Algerian horses have long cannons; in Europe the opposite opinion prevails.

"7. The thickness which the Arabic horsemen who ride all the time have on their insteps is not an exostosis; it is a thickening of the skin which sometimes presents a boss of some two centimeters in height.

"8. The horses encounter in the bivouacs of the nomadic tribes the following advantages: they enjoy the fortifying effect of fresh air; they breathe unstale air; every three or four days they are moved onto a soil free of all dirt; when they are tethered they have a wide space in which to move about; they possess the faculty of playing when at liberty; their interest is maintained by the spectacle of external things; they are given lively, strong exercises, varied by current service; the *fantasias,* the chase, war; they participate in the interest, the feelings of domestic life, the horse being like the dog, under the eyes of and in the intimacy of the family; their feed is very varied, according to the season, the circumstances, and the countryside; in fine, they enjoy a fortifying, varied, agreeable, and interesting existence. If the tribe is situated on a good terrain with respect to the earth, water, air, and grazing grounds, the advantages are that much increased.

"In our stables, the heat is frequently excessive; the air is seldom renewed; miasmas, insects—owing to a long tenure—and crowding are unhealthy. Contagion is thus more powerful; cures are more difficult; never-changing feed is not favorable to either the taste or the health; the owners or the men in charge, rarely see the horses. The riders caring for the animals change frequently and do not have any feeling of attachment for them; no one knows the past of his horse and none ever bothers about his future. The men shout more than they caress. Horses to them are like a steam engine to the engineer, the object of duties the onerous side of which has no reward. The horse does some exercises, almost always the same, without any animation; he is in a condition analogous to that of men condemned to hard labor, except that he is less often in the fresh air. Everything tends as a whole to approximate him as closely as possible to a machine.

"Our cavalry has had detachments which have made many winter campaigns. In the insurrection of 1845–1846, they were almost completely outdoors all winter, which was a very severe one; we supposed that the horses—kept in bivouac despite the snow, the ice, the slush, the rain, and the wind—would all be lost. With great astonishment these are the results we saw: the horses that had not been overworked, that had their barley assured, and that were provided with blankets, were better off than if they had been bedded down in stables every night.

"Anyone who has seen expeditionary forces that have been out for three, six, or twelve months, upon their return has been struck by the air of good health of the men.

"The best horses known are those of Araby and they are always in the bivouac; the ardor of the sun does not wither them. In the north of Asia, there are some renowned breeds that are always in bivouac, in spite of very rigorous cold. In Europe and even in France itself, there are horses that are always or very frequently in bivouac, even in winter; one notes that they have great qualities.

"The wild boar is a strong, energetic, swift, fierce, intelligent animal. The pig is weak, heavy, unintelligent, and unenergetic. Both of them are initially descended from the same breed, which has been perpetuated during the centuries, one in fresh air and the other in sties.

"If a family of wild boars were to be installed like our pigs, after some generations it would become like the latter. If a family of pigs were set at liberty in the woods, after a few generations it would reacquire the characteristics which distinguish the boar.

"The consequences of life in the open air, animated, varied, after living in houses, are well characterized by those two states of being of one initial breed.

"The horse living in the bivouac of the nomads is, in comparison with our horses living in the stable, like the wild boar to the pig, with respect to hygiene, habits, strength, vitality, swiftness. The horse of the nomad has himself a hygiene superior to that of the wild boar, because to the advantages of fresh air, animation, and the variety of feed, he joins that of feed and care more wholly appropriate to the goal of achieving the greatest vigor possible.

"In breeding pigs, one proposes to arrive at the result of lard and flesh. *One does not aim at digestive vigor but as a means*: the goal is achieved. For the horse, it is the contrary. One does not aim at flesh, but at vigor, be it to pull heavy loads, be it to make long, hard gallops; one desires an animal that resembles in these qualities the wild boar more than the pig. Therefore, the hygenic life of a horse should more closely approximate that of the wild boar than that of the pig. Therefore, a life in the open air, animated, varied, is necessary—not a shut-up life, monotonous, uniform, melancholy. The first is found in the bivouacs of the nomads, the second in our stables.

"The Arabs believe that the open air is very favorable to the health and vigor of horses, as well as that of men; the tent shelters one from the sun, from the rain, and from public view; but the Arab does not close it as we do. On purpose he leaves a space between the bottom of the tent and the ground; the air always has a free passage through there.

"We hold to grooming our horses well and sheltering them from the weather by putting them in stables. What is certain, what still holds good, in spite of the great and justly appreciated talents of our horsemen, in spite of the great expenditures which they have made, is that in order to have the best stallions one still addresses oneself to the Arabs of Nedj, who, like all nomads, never groom their horses and always keep them in bivouac.

"The distinguished blood lines are those which, originally good, have been kept during centuries in the best of hygienic conditions. If a population had always been in a prison, of itself healthy, for two or three hundred years, it would most certainly have lost a great many of its primary physical and moral qualities. We see that in France the working population which lives forever shut up and crowded in workshops becomes altered very notably and very promptly. Our best soldiers are those that come from farming districts where one is, more than in other occupations, in the open air. All those who have seen in our camps Arabs of tribes employed as riders or muleteers have been struck by their resistance to fatigue, in spite of a very mediocre diet.

"The law has set a limit to the work of children in industry. That is wise, but the withering effect combatted by that law is caused less by the work than by the bad air of the workshops, where the workers are too crowded. The children of farmers work more than those of the manufacturers and yet they are better off.

"Highly recommended instructions exact in our cavalry that young horses before the age of five years, at least, should not be trained, because otherwise one would be using them prematurely. As regards children, one does not "operate" thus about their scholastic education. From the age of seven they are shut up in great numbers in school rooms, they work ten hours a day there, they do not take air or exercise for more than about an hour, of which they are deprived if they are punished by having to do lines. That abnormal state is prolonged until they are twenty. One thus profoundly upsets the health and vigor of youth. If a colt worked only six hours a day, from one year old to five years old, he would be at that latter age perfectly trained, but used. The lack of fresh air and exercise is what really withers the pupils of our schools.

"The force of circumstances wills that in Europe horses generally be stabled. Because of that they are like the population that lives in prison for centuries. It is true that under the circumstances it has been possible to better their feed and hygiene. Had the same talents and expenses been applied to the horses kept in bivouac, it is probable that the results would have been extraordinary.

"Open air frequently gives good results with nasal gleet. I have been authorized to send from Médéah to the desert horses and mules duly diagnosed as having it. The Arabs cured a great number.

"All the foregoing can be admitted as granting that fresh and open air has a very powerful fortifying virtue for health and vigor; that the inclemencies of the bivouac wither less than the bad air of the stable; that in man and horse, the strongest breeds are those of the open air, while the breeds which have been deprived of fresh air are generally weaker the longer they live under the influence of bad air.

"Should one pose this question: in order to succeed in obtaining from a horse all the development of which he is capable, or in order to build up in fifty years the best possible breed, should the stables or the bivouac be employed for the purpose, either in the case of the horse or in the case of the progenitors of the proposed new breed? The Arabs would reply that the bivouac, all other things being equal, would give the best results; their opinion would appear to be well founded.

"In order to form good studs in France, it would be impracticable to constitute them with a nomadic nature; but in Algeria, where there are many nomadic peoples, probably one might succeed in using them as an especially valuable resource to rebuild the equine race on binding oneself especially to the tribes who are particularly well situated with regard to air, water, and grazing grounds, and that distinguish themselves by the best of hippic practices. There are many Arabic chieftains already renowned for their studs. They would probably accept with enthusiasm any measure tending toward the betterment of their equine strains.

"Probably beautiful stallions would be better kept in nomadic studs than in our stables; the young horses would certainly be better developed there. Great expense could be avoided by choosing suitable Arabic chieftains helping them to obtain lovely stallions, and by assisting the chieftains to procure such animals which would be used by them and by the public; in fine, to form many private, nomadic studs instead of the great studs of the State which are almost inevitably placed in the least good of conditions. In the selection of a site, the very important requirement of a healthful location most often must give way to the indispensable requirements of security.

"There would be an advantage, even if only for purposes of comparison, to employing the two methods simultaneously. It could be worth while to go to great expense to obtain many private nomadic studs situated in excellent conditions, and to less expense for isolated and smaller studs fixed by the State and established in localities as salubrious as security permits.

"Receive, my dear General, the expression of my most affectionate consideration.

"Marey-Monge, Count of Péluze
General of Division, commanding the fifth military
division, former interim governor general of Algeria."

[Guillaume Stanislas Marey-Monge, Count of Péluze, fought in the French campaigns in Africa. He translated the poetry written by the Emir Abd-el-Kader. Marey-Monge organised the first regiment of Spahis. He was made a Senator of France.]

"Algiers, 7 April 1854.
"My dear General:
"I have learned with great pleasure that you are going to have published a third edition of your *Horses of the Sahara*. The marked favor with which the book has been received by the public bears witness to the extreme interest given to a question over which you have shed the brightest of light which you have "popularized" so to speak. No one has your talent for saying good things in a seductive form, and in your writing the brightness of color adds a greater charm to the truth of history.

"I have read and reread your book. I will be frank with you. I tried to find some error, to discover you in flagrant contradiction of what I know of the Arabs, of their character, of their customs, of their habits; and I must admit that your portrayal is always replete with resemblance and exactitude.

"The history of the training of the horse in the desert not only has an incontestable historical merit, the documents which it encompasses are not only curious and interesting, but our breeders will know how to borrow from its useful teachings priceless lessons for breeding horses and for the regeneration of the breed.

"Will you permit me to add a modest brick to an edifice already sufficiently complete? If so, I send you a prescription for the curing of blood-spavin.[3] It is in great repute among the Arabs. It differs slightly from that which you set forth. Many of such cures have been practiced in front of my eyes; they have been completely successful. I hold the cure to be infallible and, should you wish to benefit your readers, I give it to you; you may have confidence in it.

"Receive, my dear General, the assurance of my affectionate and devoted sentiments.

"Yusuf[4]

*Brigadier General Commanding the Native
Cavalry of the Army of Africa*"

[Yusuf or Joussouf was born Joseph Vantini or Vanini, it is said, on the island of Elba in 1810. He embarked on a ship to go to study in Florence, Italy. The ship was captured by Tunisian pirates and Yusuf was bought as a slave by the Bey of Tunis. The Bey took a liking to the boy and had him carefully educated. Later Yusuf entered the Bey's armed forces. Due to an amorous intrigue with the Bey's daughter he had to flee to Algeria where he had a very brilliant military career. He fought on the side of the French against the Emir Abd-el-Kader[5] and later commanded Turkish Irregulars in the Crimea. He

---

[3] This prescription has been given on pages 159–160 of this volume.

[4] Today General of Division, Commandant of the province of Algiers.

[5] The 2nd Regiment of Spahis was formed in Oran, by Royal command, on the 12th of August, 1836. Called to the honor of serving France, the native Algerian troops were not long in covering themselves with glory and the numerous campaigns in which they took part are eloquent witnesses thereof. In 1841 they took part in the battle of Sidi-Lakdar in which 250 regulars of the Emir Abd-el-Kader were killed and the fortress of Taguedempt was taken and destroyed. The 2nd Spahis also took part in the battles of Sidi-Yahia and Oued-Mdoussa in which 1,600 horsemen put 6,000 horse of the Emir to flight. In 1844, the Emir,

went to Paris, which was captivated by him, embraced the Roman Catholic faith and married a niece of one of France's great military figures. He died in 1866.]

"Paris, 1 June 1856.

"General:

"When I returned from the Crimea you appeared to be anxious to learn, within the framework of facts which took place in my sight, how the horses of Algeria endured the campaign and what comparison could be established between them and the French and English horses, from the point of view of war. I am happy to have been able to note an indisputable superiority in favor of the horses of Africa.

"The horses of the Eastern army, so frequently embarked and disembarked, were subjected to some harsh tests which should have made patent their qualities and defects. In all these maritime problems I never saw the African horse putting up the least opposition to being embarked; he was always easy [to handle] upon disembarking, enduring admirably well the long crossings without being incommoded, and never showing other than a mild astonishment in the face of cannon fire close to him on the deck of the same vessel which was transporting him. However, his English and French companions, sometimes mad with fear, would not allow themselves to be hoisted [aboard ship] except after a long struggle and the sailors did not triumph without having to go to a great deal of work. I was a witness to some serious accidents which endangered the lives of many of these horses and caused their owners the greatest of alarm.

"Once disembarked and in camp, the Barb always had the advantage. Life under the open sky, hobbles, pickets, or a tether were no novelty or difficulty for him. He was easier to feed with less ex-

---

having been beaten at the battle of El-Melah, took refuge in Morocco. Marshal Bugeaud marched toward the Moroccan border at the head of a column comprising all branches—cavalry, artillery and infantry. On that occasion the Spahis were under the direct command of General Yusuf. During the ensuing battle, that of Isly, the Spahis, distinguished themselves notably, capturing six banners and part of the enemy artillery. Soon after the battle of Isly the battle of Chotts took place during which engagement the Spahis were in the saddle for twenty-seven hours and captured a large booty of horses and slaughter animals (Condensed from 2e. Spahis, Historique du Régiment, Tlemcen, Algeria, Petit Tlemcénien, 1920). [Translator's note]

pense. Any feed seemed to agree with him and do him good. The English and French horses, on the contrary, were very affected by the change from barley to oats and by the changes in temperature. Toward the end of the stay of the allied armies in Varna, the English cavalry, our cuirassiers, and our dragoons had lost many of their remounts, whereas the Chasseurs of Africa and the Spahis were complete [in strength].

"I would have been very much interested to see English squadrons executing, in conjunction with our Chasseurs of Africa, war games at fast paces: a long reconnaissance, a fast march, a demonstration; I had no opportunity to be a witness. But, how can I help but recall those enormous distances traversed in a few days by the African squadrons on their way to make contact with the enemy, even to the center of the desert? Those continuous forays, on the double, for days on end; those charges to which you were a witness on the plain of Eghris, which were launched in the morning and continued without halting until night? Those three squadrons which left Constantine one day, succeeding in arriving the following day to strike the tribes four leagues beyond Batna, and which returned immediately to Constantine after having traversed more than fifty leagues in two days, without losing a horse? All these facts are so well known and plead so well the cause of our African cavalry that in the hypothetical event of a combined Anglo-French operation, well might it be thought that our allies would have expressed for it the most open and loyal enthusiasm.

"I frequently observed, when the English and French general staffs were mixed, traversing together a broken country or one covered with scrub, that our African horses—easy to manage, clever, and intelligent—got over all the obstacles with much less work than the English animals, which, although they would have beaten our horses on a race track, turned out, in those circumstances, to be really inferior to them.

"Finally, my General, the raw winter which he has just spent in the Crimea seems to me to be the most conclusive argument which can be advanced in favor of the Barb. He underwent so victoriously that terrible test, in which his companions died, that it is necessary, unless one wishes to be considered blind, to accept this truth: the African horse is, today, the model for war horses.

"I honor you, my General, for having defended the former and for having propagated this truth which is destined to lend a great service to our country.

"Accept, my General, the expression of my respectful affection.

"G. de Place[6]
Lieutenant Colonel of the General Staff"

"Paris, 1 March 1861.

"My dear General:

"Before having known you or your works, I had published the first volume of a considerable work on the complete study of the horse.

"The day on which I had the honor of being introduced, I had already read attentively the *Horses of the Sahara* and I said to you: 'General, had I known your work before writing mine, there are many things which I would not have written.'

"I wished to pay you a compliment, no doubt; but, apart from your viewing that in a kindly light, I wanted your esteem and a banal compliment or a sterile disavowal were not what I needed for that object. I have now said what I wished to say and today I shall explain it.

"Yes, there are many things which I would not have written; some because they were already to be found in the *Horses of the Sahara*, as well and better said than I have said them; others because I find, among the Arabs, practices which I have seen and approve of among the English; whether they came from Arabia or England, Birmingham or Mascara, matters little, if they are the same and good. But there is more. I cannot see why these analogies of opinions and practices among the Arabs and the English cannot be attributed to borrowings made by the latter.

"In effect, it is by Arabian blood that the English have begun and continued the perfecting of their breeds, the creation of their racing breed [race horse]. Why could they not have borrowed from the first masters of the Arabian horse the primary principles of the art of care, training, and breeding in which they are today so superior to us?

"True patriotism consists, not in vaunting one's fellow citizens, but in being useful to them if one can; not in advocating in their favor but

---

[6] Today Colonel, Chief of the General Staff of the Sixteenth Military Division.

in fighting together with them or in making clear to them whatever knowledge one has. Well then, according to me, General Daumas has made the same reproach to Frenchmen as I. I say: 'Why do you do badly that which is done well in England?' The General says: 'Why do you do badly that which is done well among the Arabs?' And as we are basically saying the same thing, it seems to me that I am right.

"In speaking of the Arabic people, of whom Mohammed is really the creator or regenerator, I have said that that great genius did not neglect any means of inspiring in his followers a taste for horses whose importance he fully realized; that is one of the things which I would not have said if I had had knowledge of the first thirty pages of the *Horses of the Sahara*. The idea is there developed and supported by a thousand proofs as incontestable as they are interesting and curious.

"On the other hand, the chapter on blood lines would have been of great help to me in giving an idea of the African varieties; for, not being a traveller, I was forced to reduce my studies of foreign breeds to documents which bore in themselves the stamp of truth and authenticity.

"The part which deals with breeding is not only a curious and interesting narration; it is a treatise for the use of our breeders, on the sole condition of knowing how to read it; unfortunately, it is not given to all to know how to do so. Those who know how to read will see that the same importance must be attached to both the sire and dam; that the essential point is not to mate perfect animals, of which there are not very many, but suitably matched individuals, which is always possible with a little intelligence. They will find the proper precautions to take to ensure conception, precautions so useful, so efficacious, that in my thirty years of experience, I have seen this happen:

"Mares sent by me to strange stallions, out of four, one in foal.

"Strange mares brought to me for my stallions, out of three, one in foal.

"Mares belonging to me or entrusted to me to be bred to my stallions under my supervision: five out of six. I having—let it be well understood—the prerogative of refusing such mares which I knew in advance to be unfit for breeding.

"I cannot state that with respect to the care given to foals everything is in agreement with my ideas; but one thing is certain and that is, that if everyone in France followed those practices, breeding would be incomparably better.

"'The Training of the Colt' forms a chapter which has, to my eyes, at least, the most singular nature. When in school I read a small book of Tacitus titled *Germania*. It occurred to me, as to everyone, that it was a satire; that to each eulogy made of the Germans for whatever virtue or for some respectable custom, it was necessary to add mentally, in the manner of a litany: 'It is not like that among the Romans.'

"This meaning perhaps I lent too freely to Tacitus. It would not please God if I were to permit myself to make General Daumas say that which he has not said. I shall bear the responsibility and I say:

"'All the training of the Arabian colt differs essentially from the education of our Norman colt; I cite the Norman because Normandy is still the district where the most and best [horses] are bred. All the Bedouin horses which I have ridden were docile, went freely, had long been made, and were fit for any service in proportion to their individual capacities. The French colt is, at five years old, soft, heavy, clumsy, and restive. Either he or his rider must fall. Without deciding if, in this world, there might not be a superior method to that of the Arabs, I say with regret on reading this chapter: "It is not like that among us."'

"The principles of the Arabic horseman did not teach me much, because I have forty years of experience and also I taught myself all that; but thirty years ago I would have been astounded to hear my professors say such very good things.

"The chapter on feed and hygiene, well read, will not lead the European reader into giving his horse camel's milk, but to judiciously giving him oats, because *the barley of the morning goes to the dung-heap and the barley of the evening to the rump.*

"I have heard so many people say: 'I am going to go fast and far; I am only waiting until my horse has finished eating! ! !'

"Colors have always been a mania with me; I have laughed at Thiroux who only sees in color a thing as indifferent as the paper of an antichamber. I have laughed at those who will not have anything but a solid color. I have laughed at those for whom *the eye is all.* I have read with curiosity the coats and elements of Grison, the coats and temperaments of Solleysel; I myself have corrected the nomenclature of the coats of Bourgelat, of Saumur, and of Alfort, which I find misleading and, on reading General Daumas, I have re-encountered all that which pleased me in the ancients, all that which I have recognized as being true.

"Yes, the chestnut flies through the air;
Yes, the bay can fall over a precipice without injuring himself;
Yes, the black is like the negress of the Sudan;
Yes, the white melts in the sun;
Yes, the roan is a sea of blood;
Yes, the Jew's yellow [yellow dun] is unworthy of a gentleman;
Yes, the pie is the brother of the cow.

"And yet, I have had pied horses which I preferred to certain brown bays.

"White socks on the hindlegs are an indication of good fortune. The bald-face carries his shroud with him. Should you laugh, I beg you to postpone your hilarity to thirty years from now and study by waiting as I have done.

"Cold shoeing is done in Algeria as in England; are the Arabs slavish imitators of the English like me, or have the English taken up Arabic customs? What does that make me?

"Someone has been good enough to tell me that the hoof is a poor conductor of heat, a most agreeable axiom in chemistry; when I see a hot shoe applied to the foot of a living horse I say with the Arabs: 'Look at the Christians adding fuel to the flames.'

"And then the Arab shoes by himself; and then he never shoes more than two feet at a time; and, should one shoe be cast, he removes the shoe from the other foot.

"With respect to the art of veterinary medicine, to diseases known and unknown in Europe, I leave such things to be examined by men whose competence is official.

"With regard to the use to be derived from the indigenous horse, I recall that axiom of agriculture that a skilful farmer who changes land has need to experiment for many years on his new establishment, and I refrain from all eulogy and all criticism. If the native horse is useful and valuable as he is now, much care must be taken to save him from changes and alleged betterments, which someone will not fail to try.

"I shall not speak of the chase, or salukis, or wars in the desert, or of anything which is not my specialty.

"It is absolutely impossible for me not to point out certain curious observations which an attentive reader should note. For example, the illness which affects the horse *stricken by barley* was known to the Greeks and pointed out by Xenophon in his treatise on equitation. That illness is reproduced among us, although with less intensity perhaps, when the oats are badly administered.

"The remedy used for the dislocation of the hip joint, consisting of tying a horse by the pastern and forcing him by means of the whip to make violent efforts, was known at the time of Louis XIV, and Solley-sel speaks of it in his *Parfait Maréchal.* He calls it "causing the spine to be stretched"—a practice borrowed to all appearances from the Spanish blacksmiths who got it from the Moors.

"Lastly, the chase of the ostrich and the gazelle make evident to what point the Arabs appreciate the advantage and necessity of gradually preparing horses for violent exercise.

"That preparation, in a broad sense, constitutes training.

"There will come a time when the monomania and the pedantry of specialties will reach a result of general usefulness which everything should have for the wise man who derives benefit from all.

"To get a horse to gallop one league in less than five minutes, on a given day, is assuredly not a science whose application is of general and habitual usage. But to laugh at the result in itself, to deny the usefulness of races and the talent of those who win them, is not only ridiculous, but a great error.

"To put a numerous body of cavalry in a fit condition to enter effectively on a battlefield far from the point of departure, is also an important and beautiful task, for victory and the fate of nations could be the prize. What other thing is that but the science of training applied to a special object? Whether one learns that at Epsom, on the running of the Derby, or in Africa, on chasing the ostrich, what does it matter to a sensible man?

"I am not a passionate lover of Arabian horses; I would be more inclined to disparage them in view of the circumstances in which I have always lived, finding myself in France, where their qualities are of secondary use and where I find other breeds which fulfill better my tastes and needs.

"There is more: I am led to believe that the horses of Africa have undergone a degeneration and dire changes which make them far removed from the true Arabian type. Will one find in Africa stallions capable of bettering our French horses as can be done with the true type of Upper Asia, as I myself have done? Undoubtedly, yes. But in what quantities? That is a very important question, on which a man, a stranger to Algeria like me, should not voice any opinion.

"There is another question just as important, which may be divided into two distinct parts. Algeria being ours with its breeds just as they are, can one without bothering to import into France the Algerian type to preserve it or to cross it, can one, I say, think of making Algeria into a perpetual remount depot for our cavalry, make it the military stud for France, as Sicily was at one time the granary of Rome? First part of the question.

"Is the African horse really the best mount for light cavalry or even cavalry of the line?—Why not?—General Lawoestine has told me of having seen in 1810 dragoons superiorly mounted on the little Spanish horses from the mountains of La Ronda. Meanwhile, trials should be made and I shall be silent to allow the soldiers themselves to choose their mounts like their arms.

"Here is the second part of the question: the principal condition for raising a horse is to do it economically; in other words, the best soil is always that which produces the most vigorous animal. Create studs in Beauce, in Brie, and from them of necessity must come the best horses. Why does not someone do it? It is because the soil used to feed a horse could produce, with some other type of cultivation, much more than the worth of that horse, excellent though he might be.

"That formulated, it is evident that Africa, by reason of its very remoteness, is apt—and should continue to be so for a long time—to give products more difficult to sell than lands lying in the vicinity of large European towns in the center of civilization. Therefore, Algeria could raise [horses] for export, always with the condition that the animals produced please the consumer to whom one offers them.

"Why then does not Algeria furnish, apart from her native breed as it is, other breeds capable of replacing among us the animals whose production is the most costly because of the increased value of the lands and forage? What might these types be? I do not know; I have not seen any; but there must be something that can be done along those lines.

"I do not know the country. I have no ties with it, either of [pecuniary] interest, or those souvenirs of military glory or of services rendered, noble enthusiasms which make of Africa, for certain Frenchmen, a second homeland.

"I sympathize with these sentiments, when they are no more than illusions; but it is impossible, in the coldest and most skeptical spirit, to seek to justify those aspirations whose goal is, after all, that of seeing our national interests profit from the glory and blood of our compatriots.

"Therein, it seems to me, lies the best spirit for conquest.

"Receive, my dear general, the assurance of my high and affectionate consideration.

"Baron de Curnieu"

[Charles Louis Adelaide Henri Mathevon, Baron de Curnieu (1811–1871), true horseman and man of letters, was an outspoken critic of the system of horse-breeding and training as it was practiced in France in his day. He was a supporter of François Baucher, the appearance of whose *Méthode d'Équitation* touched off a great uproar in France among the leading exponents of the art of horsemanship, both military and civilian. Today, the Baron de Curnieu is best remembered, perhaps, for his excellent translation of Xenophon's treatise on the *Art of Equestrianism,* the best (into French) until that of Delebecque in 1950. (For the foregoing information I am indebted to an article written on the Baron de Curnieu by M. André Monteilhet, published in *L'Information Hippique,* No. 113, October, 1966, France. The material is used with the kind permission of the author.)]

"Bordeaux, 1 November 1861.

"My dear General:

"I have read and frequently reread, always with renewed interest, your work on the horses of the Sahara. A long sojourn in Upper Asia, during which I received hospitality under the tents of a great number of tribes, has permitted me to appreciate the true worth of your book. All that which you say with regard to the customs of the Arabs, as well as what you say about the horse, that inseparable companion of their existence, is true—strictly true. Permit me, nonetheless, to give you again some details: they can do not less than corroborate that which you have written on a subject which can exercise a very great influence on the breeding and training of the horse in our country.

"Yes, you are right, a hundred times right, when you say that the Arabian horse *can endure thirst, can endure hunger,* that he can carry very heavy loads without suffering, and that no horse is better able than he to withstand fatigue, miseries, and inclemencies of weather. Do you want a new proof? Here it is:

"When I was in Nineveh my tent was pitched on the banks of the Tigris and I had at my side the Makhzen (Bachi-Bouzouf) tribe of Haïtas. Well then, the horses of those people were kept in the camp by hobbles and, under the horrible sun of Asia, they were constantly under saddle. I can say constantly, because they were never unsaddled except once a day to rub them down. After being rubbed down, they were watered, an enormous nose bag full of chopped straw covered with an abundant ration of barley was hung on their heads and then the saddles were replaced on their backs.

"But that is not all: after many months of inactivity, an unexpected order to depart suddenly arrived; *voilá,* the horses of the Haïtas, animals from a locality of atrocious heat, entering the campaign, went without any transition whatever to the icy mountains of Kurdistan or Armenia, the usual goal of expeditions. There the horses encountered cold, hunger, thirst, snow, insomnia, terrifying roads, great distances, and very difficult terrain. On their return, in what condition might they be? When they returned, I examined them all, in detail and with care; their absence had been long, they had carried huge loads, they had endured unheard-of fatigues, and their condition was exactly the same as it was at the moment of their departure.

"The foregoing, my dear General, no one told me. I myself saw it repeated many times during four years of travel among the Arabs of Upper Asia, from which I concluded that if the English horse is first for luxury and on the race course, the Arabian horse is without any doubt first among the war horses of the whole world.

"The most beautiful horses of the places through which I travelled in Upper Asia are those of the Nedj, where only five strains are recognized as being truly pure-bred:

1. The Kohilet-Adjouz (this line, reputed to be the first, is numerous);

2. The Heudeban Ez-zaï;

3. The Saklaoui-ben-Djedrane (This line is almost extinct. In 1853 there were no more than two mares; one was to be found close to Damascus with the cadi Berri-Sakeur and the other among the Anézés. Her master was named Ben-Soudam Tersabéhha.);

4. The Ouadina-Korassana;

5. The Hamdania-Samery.

"The Arabs of the Nedj are, to other Arabs, what the English are to other Europeans. For the past forty or fifty years only they esteemed and used pure blood. That, of course, means that they are of an unbelievable severity on mating, and they would rather lose a mare than dishonor her by a misalliance.

"In Upper Asia what was not my astonishment when I heard all the Arabic grooms hissing while they groomed the horses, never using the currycomb on them, and putting into practice all the methods we know to make the coat sleek and shining.

"If one could suddenly transplant a French sportsman to the banks of the Tigris he would be very surprised to see passing by, on either bank of that watercourse, good Arabic riders having in their hands little canes with curved handles, mounted on horses well enveloped in excellent coverings, with hoods, preparing them for the track with the best of training methods. They do not use the trot except for going into a gallop from a walk or into a walk from a gallop, and—an even more curious thing—when they trot they trot English fashion; which simply means that the English trot Arabic fashion.

"In summation, my dear General, in dealing with horses and their breeding, during my long sojourn in Asia, I have acquired the conviction that the Arabs, with their ancient hippology have not had any need to take anything from anyone, whereas the English have borrowed everything from the Arabs.

"Receive, I beg you, my dear General, the assurance of my high consideration and my whole-hearted devotion.

"Pétiniaud
Inspector General of Studs"

APPENDIX

A Note on the Influence of the Barb
in the Formation of the Thoroughbred

"And it is well known that Horace's observation of Hereditary
Valour in the Families of the Great is by that author himself applied to that generous Breed of those noble Animals, which is
only to be expected from generous Progenitors."

> "Tis from the Noble and the Good,
> A gallant Race proceeds:
> So the strong Herds, a gen'rous Brood,
> The Barb a Barb succeeds."

(Reginald Heber, preface to
An Historical List, &c. [London: 1751], Vol. I)

Barb blood is predominant in the English Thoroughbred as the following
excerpts and quotations will show. Most are taken from a quaint publication with a formidable title, *An Historical List of Horse-Matches Run. And
of Plates and Prizes Run for in Great Britain and Ireland, in 1751. Containing the Names of the Owners of the Horses that have run as above, and
the Names and Colours of the Horses also, with the Winner distinguish'd
of every Match, Plate, Prize or Stakes: The Conditions of Running, as to
Weight, Age &c. and the Places in which the losing Horses have come in,
with a List also of the principal Cock-matches of the Year above, and who
were the Winners and Losers of them &c.,* by Reginald Heber, London,
Printed in the Year M DCC LI.

The worthy Mr. Heber states in a somewhat anxious preface to Volume
I (in all, he published eighteen volumes of his *Historical Lists* from 1751 to
1768) that: "On the Death of the late Mr. John Cheney, and before any
Person had signified his Intention to the Public, I first undertook to carry
on the Work he had with so much Approbation set on foot. The Truth of
which will easily appear by consulting the Papers published the last Sporting Season." The Mr. Cheney to whom he refers is the Cheney who, in
1727, issued the first *Match Book,* which, after his death turned into Mr.
Heber's *Historical Lists.* This work, in turn, after the latter's death in 1768
or 1769, turned into *The Sporting Calendar, containing An Account of the*

Plates, Matches, and Sweepstakes, that have been Run for in Great-Britain and Ireland, in the Year, 1769 by William Tuting and Thomas Fawconer [William Tuting was Keeper of the *Match Book* at Newmarket and Thomas Fawconer was Secretary to the Jockey Club]. The three publications referred to were some of the forerunners of the *General Stud Book,* more generally known as "Weatherby's" and colloquially as the "Book." The *General Stud Book* was founded by the Weatherby family in 1791, a member of that family being at the time a Keeper of the *Match Book.*

I have, in the following quotations, retained most of the spelling, punctuation, and capitalization of the original. In addition, the reader might be helped by consulting the table explaining the relative monetary equivalents, which appears at the end of this appendix. It is interesting to note the differences in the stud fees of Eclipse, King Herod, and Match'em who are considered to have been, after, of course, the Byerley Turk, the Darley Arabian, and the Godolphin Barb, the leading sires of the English Thoroughbred. Of Oronooko or Chrysolite blood little is said nowadays, but in their day those two animals were highly rated, in so far as stud fees were concerned.

Thus we read in an advertisement for a stallion standing at stud, in Volume I (for the year of 1751), of Mr. Heber's *Historical List* the following:

"A true Copy of an English translation of the Arabick Records, of the Genealogical History of Mr. Brown's Arabian Horse, given out by the Order of the Emperor of Morocco, and attested by the British Consul at Tanger [Tangiers]. This Horse is fifteen hands high; Strong, Beautiful and Nimble. He is to be let to Mares at Mr. John Green's, in Bedal, Yorkshire, from the Middle of February next, to the End of the Season, at Five Guineas a Mare and a Crown the Groom; Good Grass for Mares at 2s. 6d. per Week.

" 'Praise be unto One God, there is but one God and Mahomet is his Prophet.

" 'We the underwritten Publick and authorized Scribes give Witness and proclaim that the Most Excellent Bashaw [Pasha] Ganim Ben Hadgee, Great Master of Horse to our Sacred Majesty, Muly Ismael Ben Aly, Sheriff, Emperor of the Faithful, whom God preserve, has Declared unto us, and required this Testimony, that his Imperial Majesty, Willing to favour the Most Excellent Bashaw, Hamet Ben Aly, Ben Abdala, with Marks of his Esteem, did order him to Deliver unto the said Bashaw Hamet, a Horse of the best and most beloved Breed in the Royal Stables, and that he did accordingly Deliver unto him the Horse named Azees, Son of Sherrar, of Six Years old, and Chestnut Colour, begot on the Mare named Hamala, which was presented to his Majesty by the most Excellent Bashaw Gazee Buhassara, Governor General of the Kingdom of Sus, the said Horse Azees, being named so by the Emperor himself from his regard to his Sire, Sherrar, who saved his Majesty's Life at Guyea; and at the Desire of his Excellency, the said Bashaw Ganim, we give this Publick Witness at Mequineze [Mequinez], the Sacred Residence of our Great Master, which God Preserve from Ruin, this 6th Day of the Moon Ramadan, Year of our Prophet, 1127.

Aly el Gander,

Not. Pub.

Hamet Ben Omar Azagam'

" 'Praise be unto One God, there is but One God, and Mahomet is his Prophet.

" 'We the underwritten Publick and authorized Scribes give Witness and proclaim that the most Honourable Alcaid Milood al Elgee, Great Master of Horse to our Sacred Master, Muly Abdala Ben Muly Ismael, Emperor of the true Musselman, whom God preserve, has Declared unto us, and required this Testimony, that his Imperial Majesty having commanded the most Excellent Bashaw Hamet Ben Aly Ben Abdala, to return unto the Royal Stables, if alive, the Horse Azees, Son of Sherrar, which our late Master Muly Ismael of Glorious Memory, had given him in the Year 1127, with Every and Each of his Breed, Male and Female now Existing; the said Bashaw Hamet has accordingly returned a Horse of twelve Years old, his Colour Grey, and name Mirezigg, which he declares to be the only one left of said Azees Breed, begot on the Mare, named Embarca, who had been presented and sent unto his Excellency from Sus, by his late Majesty, Muly Abdelmelick, Ben Muly Ismael, of Glorious Memory, when Governor General of those Provinces, and the said Horse Mirezigg now remains in the Royal Stables of this Capital Mequineze, the 10th Day of the Moon, Milood, Year of our Prophet, 1145.

El Hazan Ben Negun,

Not. Pub.

Larby Ben Taxar'

" 'Praise be unto One God, there is but one God, and Mahomet is his Prophet.

" 'We the underwritten Publick and authorized Scribes give Witness, and make known, that the High and Mighty Sheriff, Muly Tamy Ben Larby, the Son of Blessing, and Prince of Wazan, has Declared unto us, and required this Publick Testimony, that he has Presented unto the Excellent Alcaid Azus Ben Mahomet, Governor of Tanger, and Nephew to the late most Excellent Bashaw Hamet Ben Aly, a Grey Horse of five Years old, whose Name is Jerry, and that the said Horse was begot by the Royal

Mirezigg, ben Azees, ben Sherrar, belonging to our Sacred Master, Muly Abdala, Emperor of the Faithful, &c. On the Mare Dabama, which was formerly sent his Majesty (whose Reign we pray Heaven to prolong and prosper) by the Arabs of Zaara; thus Declared by his Highness, and Witness by us in Wazan the Holy, On the 10th Day of the Moon, Hedgja and Year of the Prophet, 1160.

El mequi Ben Aly el Wazany,

Not. Pub.

Mesod el Hetib, &c.'

" 'Izaac Diaz Carvalho, Esq; his Britannick Majesty's Consul for this Port of Tanger, &c.

" 'Certifies to whom it may Concern, that the foregoing is a true Translation of the Arabick Manuscript, Counter-signed by me, that the same is an Authentick Transcript of the Three Original Certificates preserved in the Register of this Regency, and to all which full Credit may be given, that the Explanatory Notes at the Foot hereof are true Explanations, and finally that the Last mentioned Horse Jerry, was purchased by me from Alcaid Azus Ben Mahomet, Governor of this Place, for the Use of their Excellencies F ---, and L --- B ---, and shipped from this Coast for G --- [Gibraltar?], by the Special Favour (to them granted) and Permission of his Imperial Majesty Muly Abdala, Emperor of Morocco, &c. Witness my Hand and Seal in Tanger, May the 3d, 1750. N.S.

Izaac Diaz Carvalho,
British Consul'

"Sherrar   signifies Warrior
 Azees   " Beloved
 Hamala " A shaft for a Scimiter
 Embarca " Blessing
 Jerry   " Swift
 Dabama " Black Beauty
 Guyea   " The Frontier of Algier, where Muly Ismael was discomfited
 Sus   " The Southernmost Province of Morocco.
 Zaara [Sahara?] signifies A Province Bordering on the Arabian Deserts.
 1160 of the Arabian Stile (or Hegera) Answers to 1747.
"The Arabick Records are to be seen at Mr. Brown's House in Dublin."

The horse whose pedigree is given above was advertised in 1753 as follows: "Mr. Brown's Horse, is to serve Mares the ensuing Season, at Breafy, in the County of Mayo, at ten Guineas a Mare, and a Crown to the Groom."

His stud fee had gone up five guineas in two years of standing at stud; and, claims that he was an Arabian notwithstanding, his pedigree indicates that he was a well-bred Barb.

Another advertisement appears in Volume III of Mr. Heber's work for the year 1753: ". . . likewise, at the same Place [two other stallions, Sloe and Bolton Starling were included in the same advertisement], the famous Bay Horse, called Second. Second is very healthful, and in good Order. He was bred by the Duke of Devonshire, and got by the said Duke's Childers; his Dam by Basto, and was the Dam of Old Crab, Puff, Black-Legs, Snip, Bay Motte, &c. his Grand Dam by the Curwen bay *Barb* [italics mine], and was the dam of Mr. Croft's Stallion, Partner; his Great Grand Dam by the Curwen Spot, his Great, Great Grand Dam by the White-Legged Lowther *Barb,* out of the Vintner Mare. Second is very near fourteen Hands three Inches high, and a fine, strong, well proportioned horse, Master of twelve Stone [one stone is fourteen pounds], clear of all natural Blemishes, goes well upon his Legs, was thought by most Men, to be the best Horse of his Year." Second's stud fee in 1755 was five guineas and went up to ten in 1758.

Yet another advertisement states: "The Brown Bay Arabian, that covered last Year at North Allerton, Yorkshire, will Cover this Season at Bedding-ton in Surry, 1 mile from Croyden, at 5 guineas, and five Shillings the Groom. He is allowed by the best Judges to be the finest and most likely to get Racers of any ever brought into this Kingdom. He is at Mr. Gibson's Stables in May-Fair where he will remain until the Beginning of the Season.

"This is to Certify to whom it may concern, that the Brown bay Stone [entire] Horse, which I sent from Algeirs [*Algiers*] to Paris to the late Lord Albemarle, in the Year 1752, and was then about 5 years old, and about 15 hands high, was of the very best and truest of the Arabian Breed that was in the hands of the late Hassan Bey of Constantine, (or Viceroy of the Eastern Province of the Kingdom of *Algiers*) and who was the only Bey in all that Country, that kept up that Breed, this I had full Experience of through the Course of my Residence in Algiers near 30 Years, and that I never could come at a Horse of that Breed but from that very Bey, by his being my very particular Acquaintance, and he never gave nor parted with one of that Breed to any but myself; I have sufficient Reason to believe, and am fully persuaded that the above mentioned Brown Bay Arabian Horse is now actually in the Possession of Palmes Robinson, Esq; in London, and to the Truth of which I have here unto set my Hand and Seal, in Biddeford, the 24th of February, 1757, Devon: John Ford, signed and sealed in the Presence of us in Biddeford, Devon, Richard Blinch, Deputy Mayor, Richard Blinch, Jun." From the foregoing, it would appear that although the animal is referred to as an Arabian, in reality he was a Barb.

After Heber's *Historical Lists* had turned into *The Sporting Calendar*, in Volume II of that publication for the year 1770 an advertisement reads that: "Sappho was got by old Regulus, out of Lodge's roan mare, got by Partner, out of a sister to old Mixbury, got by Jigg, her grand dam by Dale's Horse, bred by Lord Cardigan, out of a full sister to Leeds, and got by the Richmond Turk, her great grand dam by Why Not, got by Fearnought *Barb* [italics mine], her great great grand dam by Wilkinson's bay Arabian, out of a natural *Barb* mare, bought of Lord Arlington.—As witness my hand, Francis Salt." The foregoing was only part of the advertisement, as Sappho was the dam of the stallion, Young Regulus, being advertised.

Zahara was advertised as follows: "The bay Arabian horse Zahara, in May next, will cover at Guilford, in Surry, at three guineas, and 5 shillings the servant, till then, where he now is, near Portsmouth, Hants.

"He is 15 hands 3 inches [very tall for an *Arabian* in those days], and in high health, having got the better of all ails, occasioned by two long Sea voyages, first from *Algiers* to Gibraltar, and from thence home, as proper certificates will be left with the servant, the gentlemen of the Turf, are referred to as fine a made horse, and as likely a figure to get running cattle, as any ever brought to this country, which his colts of this year evidently show.

"There will be good grass and proper care."

Now might be a good time to examine the somewhat contemptuous manner in which Barbs are defined by three modern authorities on the horse. In *The Horseman's Dictionary*, compiled by Lida Fleitmann Bloodgood and Piero Santini, the entry on the Barb is as follows: "Barb: Light breed of riding horse of the Barbary states; possibly a mixture of Arab and Moroccan or Algerian blood. Resembling, but inferior to, the Arab in conformation, with a coarser head, low-set tail, and goose rump. Slightly more knee action at the trot. Usually grey, bay or brown in colour. Average height: 14 to 14.3 hands. Weight: approximately 800 to 1,000 pounds. Etymology: The word 'Barb' originally signifying any horse of foreign— 'barbaric' origin." Mr. R. S. Summerhays in his *Encyclopaedia for Horsemen* is even more unkind. His entry on the Barb is the following: "Barb. Originated in Morocco and Algeria. Stood 14–15 h.h. and had flat shoulders, rounded chest, relatively long head, and tail set lower than an Arab, with hair of mane and tail very profuse. The breed was hardy in constitution and docile in temperament, though less spirited than the Arab and of far less refinement and quality. Owing to cross-breeding, the pure-bred Barb is hard to find."

Nevertheless, in pedigree after pedigree of some of the most noted Thoroughbreds in England in the 1700's appear such names as Layton Barb mare; old bay Moonah Barb mare; the Fearnought Barb; King William's white Barb, called Chelleby; Sir John Harper's Barb; Chestnut White-Legged Lowther Barb; Curwen bay Barb; St. Victor's Barb, which latter was the sire of the Bald Galloway. The Bald Galloway [a pony] figures in the pedigrees of such animals as Babram, Bald Partner, Bosphorus. Brittanicus, Camilla, Careless, Genius, Harlequin, Redstreak, Regulus, Sappho, Shakespeare, Snail, Snap, Sportsman, Young Blossom, and the immortal Eclipse.

The foregoing does not mean to imply, of course, that no pure-bred Arabians were introduced into Great Britain at the same time that the Barbs were making their contribution toward the formation of the English Thoroughbred. Certainly, Arabians were imported, but the Barbs played a part which is generally glossed over and many so-called Arabians were, in fact, Barbs. The following advertisements would appear to be for genuine pure-bred Arabians, if their claims can be believed.

"To cover, the fine bay Arabian Horse Dowla at Mr. Oxlade's at Bisham Park near Maidenhead in Berkshire, at ten guineas a mare, and five shillings the groom;—Dowla was bred in the mountains of Moses, in Arabia, by the Imaum [Iman], or King of Senna [Sinai], whose medal he was chose to wear, at three years old, on account of his being the finest high bred horse in Arabia Felix. He was brought down the Red Sea to, Mocha, and from thence to England, in the *Royal Charlotte*, East-Indiaman, commanded by Captain John Clements and was landed at Erith, near Dartford, in Kent, in the year 1767.

"N.B. The above horse is remarkably strong and boney, all over sound, and free from blemish, now 7 years old, and has the merit of being allowed by all who have seen him, to be superior in shape, size, and strength, to any Arabian ever brought to this kingdom—Colts of his get may be seen at Mr. Oxlade's, which are remarkable for bone and fine shape.

"Note, There are exceeding good conveniences for mares, at Bisham-Park, where the greatest care will be taken of them.

"Maidenhead is twenty-seven miles from London. The money to be paid before the mares are taken away."

The claims made for Dowla were modest in comparison with those made in an advertisement for another imported Arabian in 1766:

"Notice is hereby given, that the fine GREY ARABIAN Horse, late the Lord Viscount Barrinton's, and which has been lately seen at the Riding House in May-Fair, being now purchased of his Lordship by Mr. Gibson, will cover at 10 Gs. a Mare, at Brands, near Kilburn, Middlesex. This Horse, which is near 15 Hands high, extremely beautiful, remarkably strong, and in perfect Health, was purchased at Yemine [Yemen], in Arabia Felix, of the Imaum, or King of Senna, for four hundred pounds sterling; was brought from Yemine down the Red Sea to Bombay, and from thence to

England, on board the *Earl of Elgin*, Indiaman, as upon Inquiry will most undoubtedly appear; so that considering how very few, (if any Horses) that are called Arabians, have such authentic Proofs of their being really so; the Distance of the Place from whence he came, famous in Arabia for the best Breed of Horses; and the Length and Hazard of the Voyage; it may be presumed no Man could undertake to bring a Horse of equal Merit from thence, for less than 2,000 pounds sterling.

"Note, There are exceeding good Conveniencies for Mares and Colts, at Mr. Gibson's, at Brands, where the greatest Care will be taken of them."

However, the following advertisement tops them all—horsemen in 1766 being just as inclined to embroider then as they are now:

"Mr. Bell's Grey Arabian, so much esteemed by all who have seen him, will Cover this Season, at 10 Guineas and five shillings to the Groom, at Mr. Carber's Farm, at Goulder's Green, near Barnet, Hapstead and Hendon, in Middlesex; where the greatest Care will be taken of all Mares sent to be covered; the best Corn [Oats], Hay, and Grass, will be provided at a reasonable Rate, with great Convenience for Mares foaling.

"N.B. This most beautiful and valuable Horse, is one of the purest and most esteemed Breed amongst the Arabs, that has ever yet been brought to the western Parts of Europe; having been purchased at the Distance of thirty Days Journey from St. John d'Acre [Acre, Israel], the nearest Sea Port to the Deserts of Arabia, by Philip John, an Armenian, sent by Mr. Bell about four years ago, on Purpose, and with an unlimited Commission, to buy the best and most genuine bred Horse he could find in all Arabia, at any Price; and who, as well from his great Skill in Horses (as is now well known to many Noblemen of the highest Rank here) as from his perfect Acquaintance with the Language and Manners of the Arabs, was enabled to execute the Commission Mr. Bell had given him in a Manner no European could have done: In Consequence whereof, by his Address, and by means of the valuable Presents he made to Beny Suckr [Beni Sudr?], the principal Chief, and Commander of all the different Tribes of Arabs of those Deserts, and to the Skeks [Sheiks], other great Men there, he not only got Permission to travel into any Part of the Deserts, and to take his Choice of all the most esteemed Horses there, but even obtained the Favour of purchasing the Horse, now Mr. Bell's, out of Beny Suckr's own Stud, with an undoubted Assurance and Testimonial, (now in Mr. Bell's hands) signed by all the principal Officers and chief Men of the Country, of this Horse being of the right Jelfy [Jilfan] Blood, the most valued Breed in all Arabia, and in every respect a true and perfect Arab Horse. Mr. Bell hopes he may therefore, without Presumption, repeat, that this is the most perfect, if not the first and only Horse of the genuine and most valuable Arab Breed, that has ever before been brought to England; and at the same

Time, from the great original Price paid for him, the Value of the Presents made to the Arabs, the great Expence incurred by having a Guard of ten Men, that Beny Suckr sent to attend him during a Journey of 30 Days, through the Deserts to St. John d'Acre, his being carried from thence, by Land, to Aleppo [Syria], from Aleppo to England by Sea, with the Charges of the Person who purchased him during his Journies and Voyages, for upwards of three Years, that he is also the most costly Arabian Horse that has yet been seen here. Mr. Bell, therefore, flatters himself that his having procured this inestimable Horse, at so very great an Expence, of Trouble and Money, for the Service of the Noblemen and Gentlemen Breeders, will intitle him to their Favour, and to the Continuance of that Encouragement they were pleased to give him the last Season and for which he begs Leave to return them his most grateful Acknowledgements of Thanks."

In conclusion here is what James Reynolds in his *A World of Horses* has to say about the Arabian/Barb controversy with respect to the origin of the Thoroughbred:

"In the recent acute controversy, carried back and forth across the loose-boxes, so to speak, concerning just how much the Barb breed has influenced English Thoroughbred bloodlines, Lady Wentworth, as keen and sound an authority as lives today [1947], calls out that the Barb is no longer a pure breed. Only the Arabian blood has significance in the Thoroughbred horse. However, we assume that in the days of Moulay Ismaïl and his progenitors the Barbs raised at the Royal Studs in Morocco were purebred.

"If we take the word of Sir Alfred Pease, another outstanding authority on Arabian breeding, we find him upholding the Barb as the more important contributor to the characteristics, conformation and endurance of the English race horse. Sir Alfred contends that the Barb may be found in greater numbers in foundation stock than the Arabian . . .

"Differences of opinion about the prominence of the Barb in Thoroughbred breeding are still to be heard after many years. The arguments will continue as long as devotees of either Arab or Barb are alive and have their strength."

POUNDS STERLING

	Contemporary Prices 1766			1965 Equivalents	
Arabian Stallion (Purchase price)	£ 400: −: −			£ 2,433: 4: −	
Name of Horse	Stud Fee	Groom		Stud Fee	Groom
1752 Oronooko	£ 21: −: −	£ −: 5: −		£ 158:15: 6	£ 1:18: −
1768 Match'em & King Herod	£ 10:10: −	£ −: 5: −		£ 61: 2: −	£ 1: 9: −
1769–1770 Match'em & Chrysolite	£ 21: −: −	£ −: 5: −		£ 133: 7: 6	£ 1:12: −
1770 King Herod	£ 10:10: −	£ −: 5: −		£ 66:16: 6	£ 1:12: −
1771 Eclipse	£ 52:10: −	£ 1: 1: −		£ 307:16: 6	£ 6: 3: −

For those readers interested in converting the 1965 equivalents given above into United States dollars, the par value of the pound in 1965 was $2.80. The guinea, which appears in some of the advertisements quoted earlier was equal to £ 1: 1: −, or $2.94.

SELECTED BIBLIOGRAPHY

Batchelor, Denzil. *Horses, Horses, Horses, Horses*. London: Paul Hamlyn, 1964. Third edition.

Blanch, Lesley. *The Wilder Shores of Love*. London: John Murray, 1956.

Bloodgood, Lida Fleitmann, and Piero Santini. *The Horseman's Dictionary*. London: Pelham Books, Ltd., 1963.

Brown, William Robinson. *The Horse of the Desert*. New York: The Derrydale Press, 1929.

Cauchois, Louis. *Le Prestige du Cheval*. Paris: Durel Editeur, 1951.

Columbia Encyclopedia. New York: Columbia University Press, 1950. Second edition.

Disston, Harry. *Know about Horses*. New York: The Devin-Adair Company, 1961.

Dodge, Theodore Ayrault. *Riders of Many Lands*. New York: Harper & Brothers, 1894.

Dwyer, Francis. *On Seats and Saddles*. New York: International Book Company, [*circa* 1879].

Gordon, Helen C. *A Woman in the Sahara*. New York: Frederick A. Stokes Company, 1914.

Goubaux, Armand, and Gustave Barrier. *The Exterior of the Horse*. Philadelphia: J. B. Lippincott Company, 1892.

Hayes, M. Horace, F.R.C.V.S. *Points of the Horse*. London: Hurst and Blackett, Ltd., 1904. Third edition.

Heber, Reginald. *An Historical List of Horse-Matches Run. And of Plates and Prizes Run for in Great Britain and Ireland, in 1751* . . . London: n.p., 1751.

Moore, Veranus Alva. *The Pathology and Differential Diagnosis of Infectious Diseases of Animals*. Ithaca, New York: Taylor and Carpenter, 1908.

Murch, Alma Elizabeth (translator). *Adventures in Algeria*, by Alexandre Dumas. New York: Chilton Company, Book Division, 1959. First American edition.

Odriozola, Miguel. *A los Colores del Caballo*. Madrid: Publicaciones del Sindicato Nacional de Ganaderia, 1951.

Premiani, Bruno and Beatriz. *El Caballo*. Buenos Aires: Ediciones Centauro, [*circa* 1957].

Reynolds, James. *A World of Horses*. New York: Creative Age Press, Inc., 1947.

Ridgeway, William. *The Origin and Influence of the Thoroughbred Horse*. Cambridge: Cambridge University Press, 1905.

Shantz, H. L., and C. F. Marbut. *The Vegetation and Soils of Africa*. New York: American Geographical Society, 1923.

Sidney, S. *The Book of the Horse*. London: Cassell, Petter & Galpin, [*circa* 1874].

Solanet, Emilio. *Pelajes Criollos*. Buenos Aires: Guillermo Kraft, Ltda., 1955.

Summerhays, R. S. *Encyclopedia for Horsemen*. London: Frederick Warne and Co., Ltd., 1962. Revised edition.

———. *The Observer's Book of Horses and Ponies*. London: Frederick Warne & Co., Ltd., 1961. Revised edition.

Walsh, J. H., F.R.C.S. (Stonehenge) *The Horse in the Stable and the Field*. London: George Routledge and Sons, Ltd., 1899. Fifteenth edition.

White, James, and W. H. Rosser. *The Improved Art of Farriery*. London: Henry G. Bohn, 1851.

INDEX

aâcheub, el (plant): 102
aâder, el (ailment): 58, 167
Aadjaz: 98
Aaïn Mady, marabout of: 45
Aaïn-Toukria (place): 182
Aâmoure (Sahara tribe): 43
Aâmrou-el-Kaïs: quoted, 22; as Arabic
  king, 23; on Berber horses, 24
aâraya (the despoiler—implement):
  141
Aâtifa (horse's name): 90
Aatik (horse's name): 90
Aâtika: 189
Abd-el-Kader: 3, 91, 159, 181, 187,
  211; as emir, xix; bodyguards of,
  xix; as authority on horses, xx, 6, 21,
  198; observations by, 5, 38–40, 51–
  54, 71–73, 97–100, 106–107, 113–
  114, 120–121, 130–131, 148–152,
  170, 173; letters by, 7–13, 20 n., 22–
  24; 181–187; full name of, 13, 24; in
  war against French, 31, 45 n., 92, 93,
  193, 211 n.; poetry of, 210
— on horses: on origin and history, 7,
  18; on colors, 16, 18, 120; on the
  pure-bred, 20; on breeding, 55 n.,
  71; on value of mares, 56; on training, 81, 97
abdomen, horse's: 157 n., 167; condition of, 41, 42, 107; horse raked on,
  79
Abou-Obeida: 5
*About the Arabian Horse of Asia and
  Africa:* 87
Abou-Zeid (Hilal tribe): 60, 61
Abraham: 18; as father of Ishmael, 9
absinthe (plant): 65 n.
Abyssinians: 24
Acre, Israel: 230, 231
Adam: 10; created from clay, 7; descendants of, 8, 49; as first rider, 9;

era of, 18; horse created before, 49;
  son of, 128
âdem (thorn bush): 104
Adventures in Algeria, by Alexandre
  Dumas: 39 n., 84
Africa: 10 n., 22, 87, 88, 132, 172, 177,
  185, 195, 203, 210, 218, 219, 220;
  author's life in, 3, 142; horses in, 10,
  22, 174, 175, 192, 195; named for
  Afrikes, 10; conquerors of, 17, 41;
  wars in, 93; domination of, 174;
  cavalry in, 176, 213; studs in, 177;
  poetry of, 188; French Army of, 211
African horse sickness: 168 n.
Afrikes: 10
age, horse's: determining of, 62
Agriculture, Ministry of: 191
Aghrazelias (tribe): 44, 132
Ahmian (Sahara tribe): 53
Aïad (tribe): 185
aids: confusion of, 141
Aissa-ben-Meryem (Jesus, Son of
  Mary): 39
Albemarle, Lord: 227
Alélik: stud at, 177 n., 178
Alexandria, Egypt: 24; horseraces in,
  24
alfa (plant): 182, 183; *bouse* as, 104,
  106; use of, 104
Alfort: 217
Algeria: 76, 92, 99, 122 n., 168 n.,
  175, 176, 177, 178, 184, 185, 188,
  192, 197, 202, 204, 210, 211, 212,
  217, 219, 228; conquest of, 3, 22, 93,
  109; author's residence in, 4; horses
  of, 4, 176, 179, 219; Arabs of, 10,
  88, 154; customs in, 13; *alfa* in, 104
  n.; studs in, 209. SEE ALSO Algiers
Algerian Bureau, Ministry of War: xix
Algerian Sahara, by Daumas: 44 n.;
  45 n.